From
Roman Britain
to
Norman England

To Mary

P. H. SAWYER

From
Roman Britain
to
Norman England

METHUEN & CO LTD

First published in 1978
by Methuen & Co Ltd
11 *New Fetter Lane, London* EC4P 4EE
© 1978 *P. H. Sawyer*
Printed in Great Britain
by Richard Clay (The Chaucer Press) Ltd
Bungay, Suffolk

ISBN 0 416 71610 5 (hardbound)
ISBN 0 416 71620 2 (paperback)

CONTENTS

LIST OF FIGURES

Cover illustration

The Alfred Jewel (actual size). The inscription 'Alfred ordered me to
be made' suggests it was made for King Alfred. It may have been
the handle of one of the costly pointers Alfred sent to each of his
bishops with his translation of Gregory's *Pastoral Care*.

NOTE ON REFERENCES AND CHRONOLOGY

Quotations are identified and references are also given for some particular points, but for most general topics and more details further literature may be found with the help of the bibliography, which also serves as the key to the abbreviations. Plummer's index to Bede's *Historia Ecclesiastica* has made it possible to reduce the number of references to that work. Where possible sources are identified by reference to *EHD* where further details may be found. Charters are cited by their number in Sawyer (1968) which gives details of manuscripts, editions, translations and discussions.

For the period covered by *HE*, Plummer's chronology is followed, with the few correction made by Harrison (1976). For the *Chronicle* the chronology of Whitelock *et al.* (1961) is followed here.

ABBREVIATIONS

Abt   Laws of Æthelberht
Alf   Laws of Alfred
As   Laws of Athelstan
ASE   *Anglo-Saxon England*
Atr   Laws of Æthelred
B   W. de G. Birch, *Cartularium Saxonicum*
BBCS   *Bulletin of the Board of Celtic Studies*
CLA   E. A. Lowe, *Codices Latini Antiquiores*
Cn   Laws of Cnut
DB   Domesday Book
Edg   Laws of Edgar
Edm   Laws of Edmund
Edw   Laws of Edward
EHD   D. Whitelock, *English Historical Documents c. 500–1042* (texts here referred to by number)
EHR   *English Historical Review*
Episc.   *Episcopus*
GR   William of Malmesbury, *Gesta Regum Anglorum*
HE   Bede, *Historia Ecclesiastica Gentis Anglorum*
HSC   *Historia de Sancto Cuthberto*
Ine   Laws of Ine
Med. Arch.   *Medieval Archaeology*
MGH AA   *Monumenta Germaniae Historica, Auctores Antiquissimi*
PBA   *Proceedings of the British Academy*
PP   *Past and Present*
S   P. H. Sawyer, *Anglo-Saxon Charters: An annotated list and bibliography* (references by number)
TRHS   *Transactions of the Royal Historical Society*
Wi   Laws of Wihtred

PREFACE

This book is an attempt to interpret early English history in the light of recent research. Like all work done on this period in the past three decades, it is based on the foundations laid by Sir Frank Stenton whose great book *Anglo-Saxon England* is, and will long remain, the indispensable guide for all serious students. There are, however, a number of topics on which it may be helpful to offer an alternative view, determined in part by the discoveries made since 1943 by numismatists, archaeologists, linguists and others, and in part by the insights of earlier scholars, notably H. M. Chadwick, F. W. Maitland, E. W. Robertson and by the founder of the modern study of the subject, J. M. Kemble. The present book is not a comprehensive treatment of all topics; attention is rather concentrated on those that appear to be in particular need of some revision; for others reference may be made to publications noted in the bibliography.

Many people have helped in the preparation of this book. I should like to thank Sheona Ferguson for typing it, and John Dixon and Geoffrey Hodgson for drawing the maps. I should also like to acknowledge my debt to students and colleagues in the University of Leeds and elsewhere, and to my own teachers from E. A. Greening Lamborn to Christopher Cheney. I have also gained much from the advice and criticism of Dorothy Whitelock, who has generously allowed me to use her translations of many texts. Many scholars have helped on particular points; Christopher Arnold, Pierre Chaplais, William Ford, Margaret Gelling, John Hind, Harold Mattingly, Richard Morris, William Nicolaisen, and Eric Stanley. Martin Biddle, Wendy Davies, Molly Miller, David Rollason, David Wilson and Susan Youngs have all generously allowed me to see work in advance of publication. Gillian Fellows Jensen and Janet Nelson have read parts of the book, David Dumville, Ian Wood and Patrick Wormald have read it all. They have saved me from many mistakes, and suggested many improvements. To all I should like to express my thanks.

P. H. SAWYER

I

The seventh century
and before

The first recognizable Germanic settlements in Britain were apparently organized in the late fourth century by the Romans who then governed the greater part of the island. Distinctive Germanic cemeteries that were already in use at that early date have been discovered near several Roman towns and forts, including York, Ancaster, Leicester, Cambridge and Caistor-by-Norwich, and similar early cemeteries have also been found close to Roman roads, for example at Sancton on the road from the fort at Malton to the port of *Petuaria*, now Brough-on-Humber (pp. 80–1). These, and other similar, cemeteries have most reasonably been interpreted as the burial-places for groups of Germans who were recruited by the later Roman government to help strengthen the defences of Britain. In the fifth century, when the Roman government had neither the will nor the resources to maintain its authority in Britain, power passed into the hands of native chieftains and aristocrats, some of whom continued the Roman policy of recruiting German warriors. Before long some of these barbarians rejected British rule, asserted their independence and, reinforced by a large number of new immigrants, began to enlarge their territory by conquest, a process that continued for centuries and culminated, but did not end, in Edward I's conquest of Wales and his attempt to conquer Scotland.

The German immigrants came from many parts of the North Sea coastal plain beyond the Roman frontier, from the Frisian islands north of the Rhine estuary to the peninsula of Jutland, but most appear to have been Saxons and Angles from the area between the river Ems and the Baltic. The Romans called them all Saxons and the Britons naturally tended to do the same, but the descendants of the immigrants themselves recognized that while some had Saxon ancestry, especially in the kingdoms of the West, South and East Saxons, others in the Midlands and the North were Angles, descendants of emigrants from the area north of the Elbe, a small part of which is still called Angeln. By the eighth century the names Angle and Saxon were used inter-changeably by the Germanic inhabitants of Britain to describe them-selves, but there was already a tendency to prefer the former (*EHD*, p. 8), possibly because of the dominance, at that time, of rulers who claimed to be of Anglian descent. This preference led in time to their language being called *Englisc*, even by the West Saxon king Alfred (the term *Saxonisc* is not recorded), and by the eleventh century the united kingdom was called *Englaland*, the land of the English. The term Anglo-Saxon, often used by modern scholars for the period before the Norman Conquest of England, was apparently coined on the continent to distinguish the Saxons (or Angles) of Britain from the Old Saxons who had remained in their continental homeland. It was used by the English in some early tenth-century charters issued by West Saxon kings, who probably attempted in this way to express their newly won authority over all the English kingdoms, Anglian and Saxon alike (Asser, pp. 148–52; Levison, 1946, pp. 92–3). The early preference for Angle as a general term is best shown by the title given to the first history of the new inhabitants of Britain, the *Ecclesiastical History of the English People* (*Historia Ecclesiastica Gentis Anglorum*), completed in 731. The author, a Northumbrian called Bede, was well aware of the diverse origins of the invaders, he was indeed the first writer to attempt to identify their continental homelands, but he chose to call them all the *gens Anglorum*, the English people, and his example will be followed in this study of their early history and of their achievement in making the united kingdom of England.

1 *The sources for early English History*

The history of the English begins with their conversion to Christianity in the seventh century. Missionaries came from Rome in 597, from Iona in 635, as well as from Gaul, and by the end of the century Christianity was firmly established in all the English kingdoms, each of which had at least one bishopric and several religious communities, for women as well as for men. Christianity is a literate religion and the missionaries certainly brought books with them, in particular the Gospels. There is no reason to doubt the tradition that the copy of the Gospels that was written in Italy during the sixth century and belonged to Christ Church, Canterbury until the Reformation, was brought by Augustine, the leader of the Roman mission (*CLA*, ii, no. 126). By the second half of the century the libraries of some English churches were being greatly enlarged by the efforts of such men as Benedict Biscop, the founder of the joint monasteries of Wearmouth and Jarrow. He made several journeys to Gaul and Italy and returned with many treasures for his churches, including a large number of books (*Life of Ceolfrith*, cc. 9, 15, 20). There were also gifts from visitors; to give only one example, an abbot of Iona called Adomnán gave Aldfrith, king of Northumbria (685–705), a copy of a book he had written on the Holy Places of Christendom (*HE*, v. 15).

Once the English had mastered the art of writing they were able to make their own books; King Aldfrith had copies made of Adomnán's book, as Bede says 'for lesser folk to read', and Bede himself made a shortened version of it. One of the books acquired by Benedict Biscop was a copy of the Bible in one volume, an unusual thing in the western church at that time, and his friend Abbot Ceolfrith had three copies made of it, one for each of the joint houses of Wearmouth and Jarrow and, according to the *Life of Ceolfrith* written soon after his death in 716, 'the third he resolved to offer as a gift to Peter, Prince of the Apostles'. This last copy has survived intact and is now in Florence, although it is called the *Codex Amiatinus* because it was formerly in the monastery of Monte Amiate, about seventy miles north-west of Rome. This magnificent book is very large, consisting of 1030 leaves each measuring over 50 × 30 cm, and is so closely modelled on its Italian prototype that its English origin has only been demonstrated by a very careful and detailed study of its script (*Life of Ceolfrith*, c. 20; *CLA*, iii. 299). Other lavish copies of the Gospels were made in Northumbria at about that time. In the last years of the seventh century no fewer than three copies were made at Lindisfarne including the most ornate and beautiful to survive, the so-called Lindisfarne Gospels (*CLA*, ii. 149, 187; v. 578; Brown, 1972). Some time earlier another Northumbrian churchman, Wilfrid, had a copy of the four Gospels made for his monastery at Ripon 'written out in letters of purest gold on purpled parchment and illuminated. He also ordered jewellers to construct for the books a case all made of purest gold and set with most precious gems.' His biographer reports that it was preserved in the church 'as a witness to his blessed memory' and Wilfrid's epitaph at Ripon commemorated the gift:

> Golden the Gospels four he made for it
> Lodged in a shrine of gold as is their due.
>
> (Eddius, c. 17; *HE*, v. 19)

Not all books were so extravagant; but they all, from the simplest and most utilitarian to the most luxurious, display in their scripts as well as in their contents and ornament, the combination of influences, Celtic and continental, that shaped the English church.

Apart from the Bibles, commentaries, calendars and liturgical books needed for teaching and worship, English churchmen also produced a great variety of texts that make historical study possible: charters, lawcodes, records of church councils, letters, saints' *Lives*, royal genealogies, lists of kings and annals as well as poetry, secular and spiritual. Much of this material was produced in and preserved by religious communities whose members were, naturally, most interested in their own affairs. The charters in their archives granted and protected their own endowments and privileges; in their annals or chronicles they tended to pay particular attention to events that affected the life of their own community, the death of an abbot or the consecration of a bishop was recorded along with such natural phenomena as eclipses and comets that might well portend great events, and they also noted the triumphs or failures of the rulers on whom they depended for protection and support. The interests of most communities, like their membership, were largely aristocratic, and many of these religious men and women maintained close links with their relatives in the secular world. Founders and benefactors were, of course, remembered, that was why gifts were made, and that remembrance was sometimes given permanent expression in the form of a *Liber Vitae* kept on, or near, the altar. A *Liber Vitae* consisted of lists of the names not only of abbots, bishops and members of the community but also of other communities with whom they had special relations, including kings and queens and other powerful people. A ninth-century *Liber Vitae* from Lindisfarne has survived and some of its entries must have been copied from earlier lists of the same kind; it includes some names that are unlikely to have been commemorated for the first time in the ninth century (p. 34). It was not a large step from such commemorative lists to the copying of royal genealogies and lists of kings. These had certainly been kept in pagan times by word of mouth, possibly by people who had that particular responsibility, but there was certainly great interest in such records in some religious communities of the seventh and later centuries.

Saints' *Lives* were one of the most important forms of Christian literature, often coupled with accounts of miracles performed by their mortal remains or even by objects that had been associated with them. Religious communities were careful to record and proclaim the power of saints whose relics they claimed to possess. Thus the community of Lindisfarne treasured the memory and relics of its saintly founder Aidán and his royal patron, St Oswald, but its greatest treasure was the memory, and relics, of St Cuthbert who had been their prior and, for a short while, bishop, but who had spent most of his last years as a hermit on the Farne Islands. In his life he was revered as a holy man and after his death in 687 his remains proved a source of great power. His *Life* was written soon after his body was found to be incorrupt and transferred to a new shrine in 698, and a few years later the community asked Bede to rewrite this *Life*, and he did so in both verse and prose. St Cuthbert's fame spread rapidly and far, partly helped by Bede's reputation, and many copies of his *Lives of St Cuthbert* were made for churches on the continent as well as in England. Other saints had a more limited appeal; Eddius Stephanus was invited by the bishop and abbot of Hexham to write the *Life* of the founder of Hexham, Wilfrid, but that survives only in two manuscripts, as does the anonymous *Life of Ceolfrith*, abbot of Jarrow.

Through the cults of their saints and their connections with the local aristocracy religious communities served a variety of religious needs in their localities, but even in the seventh century some English churchmen had wider interests and larger purposes, and their writings consequently have a more general significance. Some churches became famous as schools and attracted scholars from far afield. Archbishop Theodore and his companion Hadrian, who became abbot of St Augustine's Abbey at Canterbury, established a notable school at Canterbury soon after their arrival there in 669. One of its most distinguished and influential pupils was Aldhelm. In 671 he wrote a letter that vividly conveys the excitement of discovery as he describes his studies at Canterbury which included musical theory, metre and

Roman Law (Aldhelm, pp. 475–8). There were schools in England before Theodore and Hadrian arrived but many young men had been attracted by the prospect of studying in Ireland. Bede explains how in the 650s many Englishmen, including nobles,

> had left their own country and retired to Ireland either for the sake of religious studies or to live a more ascetic life. In course of time some of these devoted themselves faithfully to the monastic life, while others preferred to travel round to the cells of various teachers and apply themselves to study. The Irish welcomed them all gladly, gave them their daily food, and also provided them with books to read and with instruction, without asking for any payment. (*HE*, iii. 27)

Ireland continued to have an appeal, although Aldhelm later expressed surprise (pp. 488–94) that so many should want to go there when there were learned Greek and Roman teachers in Britain itself. The rich library resources of Canterbury , and the high quality of the teaching there, made it a very influential school. Irish scholars attended it and Aldhelm (p. 493) describes them surrounding Theodore 'like a pack of grinning hounds round a truculent boar'. It was also responsible for training many of the leaders in the next generation of English church-men including Aldhelm himself and Albinus, who succeeded Hadrian as abbot of St Augustine's. Others probably went abroad as mission-aries among the Germans. The letters written in the eighth century, especially between English missionaries on the continent and their friends at home, show a generally high standard of literacy, scholarship and intellectual curiosity that owed much to the English schools at Canterbury and elsewhere.

The most influential scholar of the period, Bede, was trained at Wearmouth and Jarrow, abbeys that, thanks to the efforts of their founder, had fine libraries. Bede was born in Northumbria in about 672. He entered the monastery at the age of seven, and died there in 735. Towards the end of his life he made a list of his writings (*HE*, v. 24). It includes collections of hymns and epigrams, books on ortho-graphy and metre, many homilies and voluminous commentaries on the scriptures which he described as 'extracted from the works of the venerable fathers to which I have added my own notes to clarify the sense and interpretation'. He also wrote a book on 'the festivals of the Holy Martyrs', and also several saints' *Lives* apart from his works on Cuthbert. He compiled two chronicles, wrote two treatises on chronology, and in 731 completed what is now his most famous book, the *Ecclesiastical History of the English People*, the indispensable basis for all later study of the subject. The very popularity and importance of the *Ecclesiastical History* (it survives in over 150 medieval manuscripts) has naturally tended to emphasize Bede's role as a historian, but he was primarily a teacher, a Christian teacher whose passion and urgent concern was with the preaching of Christ's message. His remarkable abilities and wide intellectual interests all served his main purpose, the better understanding of the divine scriptures and the literature of the church. He was not alone in this. Aldhelm regarded the study of grammar as the necessary basis for the study of the scriptures: 'for you will only understand easily the most profound and sacred meanings of divine eloquence in your reading in so far as you have fully learnt those rules beforehand' (p. 500). A century later another Northumbrian, Alcuin, who had been trained in the school at York, expressed this attitude very clearly in a letter he drafted for Charlemagne:

> For since there are figures of speech, metaphors and the like to be found on the sacred pages, there can be no doubt that each man who reads them will understand their spiritual meaning more quickly if he is first of all given full instruction in the study of literature.
>
> (Wallach, 1951)

It is easy to forget Bede's pastoral purpose although, as he explained in the preface to the *Ecclesiastical History*, he wrote it for 'the instruction of posterity' in the belief that:

> if history relates good things of good men, the attentive hearer is excited to imitate that which is good; or if it mentions evil things of wicked persons, nevertheless the religious and pious hearer or reader, shunning that which is hurtful and perverse, is the more earnestly excited to perform those things which he knows to be good and worthy of God.

The *Ecclesiastical History* begins with a brief description of Britain, an outline of the period of Roman rule, and the coming of the English; Bede then moves to his main theme, the conversion of the English not just to Christianity but to the authentic tradition preserved and authorized by Rome. His sources of information included papal correspondence, copied for him at Rome by Nothhelm, a priest from London who later became archbishop of Canterbury, and he incorporates many of these letters in the *History*, together with other correspondence, such as Abbot Ceolfrith's letter to Naitan, king of the Picts. He also had some information from the *Liber Pontificalis*, the official biographies of the popes. He used, and quoted from, a wide variety of texts, such as saints' *Lives*, including some that have otherwise disappeared, and works of Aldhelm, Adomnán and Gregory the Great. For many details Bede had to rely on what he was told by informants, such as Daniel, bishop of the West Saxons, who was his main source for information about Wessex. Outside his own Northumbria he knew most about Kent, thanks to Albinus, the abbot of St Augustine's, Canterbury, who first encouraged him to write the *History*. For Kent he had not only detailed knowledge of the Roman mission but also a royal genealogy and some information about Kentish traditions, for which he provides our earliest evidence. For Northumbria he could rely on his own knowledge and on the 'faithful testimony of innumerable witnesses, who either knew or remembered these things', among whom were several of the leading figures in the Northumbrian church. The limitations of his knowledge about other areas in his own day are well shown by the absence of any mention of his contemporary, St Guthlac of Crowland, who was the subject of a very important, and popular, *Life* written in the first half of the eighth century. St Guthlac's connections were with other royal courts than Northumbria or Kent and Bede does not mention him.

Bede recognized that many of the stories he related were not literally true. In the Preface of the *Ecclesiastical History* he emphasizes the trustworthiness of his witnesses, but asks the reader who

> finds anything other than the truth set down in what I have written not to impute it to me. For, in accordance with the principles of true history, I have simply sought to commit to writing what I have collected from common report, for the instruction of posterity.

Elsewhere he explains even more clearly that it is the beliefs of common people that are the true law of history (Hunter Blair, 1970a, pp. 201–2). In reporting such common beliefs Bede is often careful to use such cautionary words as 'It is said', or 'They say', or even 'The story goes'. This caution is well illustrated in what is perhaps the most famous of all the stories in the *Ecclesiastical History*, the account of Gregory's meeting with English slaves in Rome. Bede introduces this tale with the words, 'We must not fail to relate the story about St Gregory which has

come down to us as a tradition from our forefathers', a cautionary note
that he reinforces not only with the words, 'It is said that one day', but
also with a concluding sentence: 'I have thought it proper to insert this
story into this Church History based as it is on the tradition which we
have received from our ancestors.'

Bede saw great value in what people believed. Miracles, or miracle
stories, were an aid to faith, a guide for simple people to understand
deep mysteries. In the words he puts into Aidán's mouth:

> It seems to me brother that you have been unreasonably harsh upon
> your ignorant hearers: you did not offer them the milk of simpler
> teaching, as the Apostle recommends, until little by little, as they
> grew strong on the food of God's word, they were capable of
> receiving more elaborate instruction and of carrying out the more
> transcendent commands of God. (*HE*, iii. 5)

These words, Bede tells us, persuaded Aidán's audience that 'he was
indeed worthy to be made a bishop and that he was the man to send to
instruct ignorant unbelievers, since he had proved himself pre-
eminently endowed with the grace of discretion, which is the mother of
all virtues.' Bede's aim was, therefore, to edify, and to instruct posterity
about the good deeds of good men and the evil deeds of evil ones, but
to do so with discretion, the mother of all virtues. This may explain in
part why he says relatively little about his own disordered times; he
may well have found little that was edifying in them. There were other
considerations, ranging from the need to be especially discreet about
contemporaries to the more elevated thought that God's purpose was
not yet fully revealed in the contemporary world. This is the most
satisfactory explanation for the differences between Bede's account of
Wilfrid, and that presented by Wilfrid's biographer, Eddius. Bede
knew Eddius' work and quoted some passages from it, but he wanted
to draw from it what helped his theme, and there was much about
Wilfrid that did not appear to do so.

That theme was, simply, the triumph of the true religion, not just
through the conversion of pagans, fundamental though that was,
but also by correction of other errors or sins. He devotes much space
at the beginning of the *History* to the efforts of St Germanus to combat
heresy in fifth-century Britain, and throughout the work one of his
main concerns is with the dispute over the date of Easter, a dispute that
epitomized, for Bede, the conflict between Celtic tradition and the true,

Roman, one. At the heart of the *History* there is a long account of the Synod of Whitby at which the Roman cause triumphed. And the work ends, significantly, with the conversion of Iona itself to the Roman system of calculation. This preoccupation with the Easter controversy helps explain his lack of sympathy for the British, Christians though they were. His attitude was, indeed, one of hostility. Their refusal to conform powerfully reinforced attitudes that must have been deeply influenced by the British invasions of Northumbria. There is indeed a marked contrast between Bede's hostility towards the British and his more neutral, even approving, remarks about the Picts and the Scots.

The disputes about the correct liturgical calendar and in particular about the date of Easter stimulated a lively interest in chronology and Bede was a leading authority on the subject. One of his great, and novel, achievements was to use the new system of dating by years of the Incarnation invented early in the sixth century by Dionysius Exiguus and probably brought to England by Wilfrid (Harrison, 1976, pp. 72–5). The dating systems current in his day were varied; papal documents were dated by imperial years, by consulships, and indictions, and in his first attempt to compile a chronicle Bede used 'years of the World'. Many events were remembered by the year of a king's reign and many kings ruled at the same time. These different systems had to be synchronized, and what Bede did was to set them in a new chronological framework, of years *anno Domini*. Two, among many possible, illustrations will show something of the problems he faced, and the neatness of the solution. First, the dating clause of a letter of Pope Honorius I:

> Given on 11 June in the 24th year of the reign of our most religious emperor Heraclius and the 23rd year after his consulship, the 23rd year of his son Constantine and the 3rd year after his consulship; in the 3rd year of the most illustrious Caesar his son Heraclius, in the 7th indiction.

To which Bede (*HE*, ii. 18) adds, simply,

> That was in the year of our Lord, 634.

The second example concerns the death of a bishop, Paulinus, which was associated with the second year of the reign of Oswiu, king of Northumbria.

After Oswald had been translated to the heavenly kingdom, his brother Oswiu succeeded to his earthly kingdom in his place, as a young man of about thirty, and ruled for twenty-eight troubled years. . . . In his second year, that is in the year of our Lord 644, the most reverend father Paulinus, once bishop of York and then of Rochester, departed to be with the Lord on 10 October having held the office of bishop for nineteen years, two months, and twenty-one days. (*HE*, iii. 14)

To us this new system of dating is a great advance and convenience, but we may suspect that to Bede its significance was that these were the years of the Christian era.

As the account of Paulinus' death suggests, Bede may well have had some record of episcopal successions that indicated how long each bishop served; he certainly had lists of the kings of some kingdoms recording how long they each reigned. One of these is appended to a very early copy of the *History*, and it has been shown that Bede worked out his Northumbrian chronology on the basis of that list or one very like it, and was consequently able to deduce that Ida of Bernicia began to reign in 547 (Hunter Blair, 1950). There has recently been an attempt to question much of Bede's chronology partly on the basis of other king-lists and similar sources. But these other texts have certainly been much corrupted in transmission, or are later rationalizations of tradition, and can hardly be used to correct the lists that Bede had in the early eighth century. What is more, Bede was the author of two treatises of chronology and probably understood the complexities and problems of synchronizing different systems rather better than his critics (Kirby, 1963; but see Hunter Blair, 1970a and 1971; Harrison, 1976). He certainly made some mistakes, and it is a wonder that he did not make more, but in general he can, and here will, be trusted as a reliable guide to the chronology of the period for which he had texts (that is from the arrival of the Roman mission with its papal letters) to provide a system of reference into which he could fit events otherwise only datable by the years of kings.

For the period before the mission arrived Bede had to rely on information that can only have been transmitted by word of mouth in the form of king-lists, genealogies or as stories, possibly in poems. In the process of transmission, written as well as oral, many changes, deliberate or accidental, occurred. Recent studies have revealed, for example, the many different ways in which royal genealogies can be modified (Dumville, 1977b). It is now clear that these texts, which have often been treated as reliable statements of dynastic history, cannot automatically be accepted as biologically accurate; they may in fact have been intended to serve some ideological or political purpose and could consequently have been subject to various alterations. Bede himself describes how the name of King Eanfrith, who ruled for a year, was omitted from the list of Northumbrian kings after his apostasy. This form of *damnatio memoriae*, which has modern as well as ancient parallels, shows how unreliable such lists can be even when they are preserved in writing. As one scholar has remarked, there is no such thing as a non-defective king-list (Kelleher, 1968, p. 149).

English traditions, in whatever form they were kept, cannot have been written down before the seventh century and in most English kingdoms not before the second half of that century. By then the limit of living memory, trustworthy or not, cannot have extended earlier than the middle of the sixth century. There were, of course, traditions about a more distant past and later writers, including Bede and the compiler of the *Chronicle*, had some information about earlier events in English history, but they had been passed by word of mouth through many generations before they were committed to writing, and in such a process of oral transmission there were many opportunities for mis-understandings, inventions, conflations and reinterpretations. To give one example. Bede certainly knew of a genealogy of Æthelberht, king of Kent (*HE*, i. 15; ii. 5). In one passage he lists his ancestors back through three generations to Oisc, and explains that it was this man who gave the Kentish royal family their name, *Oiscingas*. He goes on to explain that Oisc was the son of Hengest and that they came to Britain together at the invitation of Vortigern. Earlier in the *History* Bede explains that the first leaders of the English invaders were said to have been two brothers, Hengest and Horsa, and he then gives their ancestors through four generations to the pagan god, Woden. He concludes this remarkable section with the information that it was from the stock of Woden that 'the royal families of many kingdoms claimed their descent'. A similar, but not identical, version of this Kentish royal genealogy is preserved in other, later, texts, and in the *Chronicle* the exploits of Hengest and his son, Æsc, are reported with some additional details. The pagan god Woden is obviously mythical and probably symbolized, even for Bede, the royal descent of Anglian kings (Miller, 1975a, p. 254 n. 1). The historian has to ask at what point mythology gives way in this genealogy to historical, or biological, reality. By Æthelberht's time the Kentish royal family were known as *Oiscingas*, and it is therefore possible, if not certain, that Oisc was a real leader, king even, who had played an important part in earlier English history, and that it was from him that the Kentish kings traced their descent, although that did not, of course, mean that they were in fact his descendants. Hengest, 'the first leader', was not integrated into the genealogical tradition in this way, the family were not *Hengestingas*. His association with Horsa strongly suggests that they were both as mythological as Woden, for the names meant, in Old English, 'Gelding' and 'Horse' respectively (Turville-Petre, 1957). In the origin legends of many peoples twins, or brothers, play an important role, the best known being Romulus and Remus, founders of Rome; and brothers with names meaning 'Gelding' and 'Horse' are more likely to be mythological figures drawn from pagan religion, in which horses played an important role, than from real life. This doubly divine ancestry, from Woden and from Hengest, of the Kentish royal family marked them out as very special. Their inclusion in the Kentish royal genealogy was a mythological statement that was certainly made before the end of the seventh century when it reached Bede, who reports it with the characteristic caution, 'It is said'. It probably dates from before the conversion of Kent and, although it tells us something about the ideology of seventh-century Kent, it has no value as a statement about the realities of the English conquest.

For modern historians these genealogical traditions, whatever their significance, suffer from a total absence of any chronological framework. If Oisc was a real leader, we have no firm information about the time he lived. The pagan English, like other illiterate peoples, certainly had a great interest in chronology and may well have had a mnemonic system for remembering important events, but we cannot know how well they worked or were understood in the seventh century or later. The existence of duplicate entries at intervals of nineteen years in the *Chronicle*'s account of the late fifth and early sixth centuries reveals a degree of confusion that undermines confidence in the reliability of any of the dates attached to these early traditions (Harrison, 1976, ch. 7).

The unreliability of oral tradition needs no emphasis, and the difficulty of testing it is obvious, but even the use of writing did not ensure the accurate transmission of information. There was, in the first place, the kind of deliberate manipulation that Bede describes when he reports the omission of Eanfrith's name from the list of kings. There is also the possibility that a text has been miscopied accidentally. If a text is only known in a late version that may have been copied from a copy, and so on, the opportunities for error are greatly increased, and if it survives only in one version there is no possibility of detecting errors by comparison. Mistakes can, of course, be detected when the text as preserved is nonsense, but some copyists were alert enough to restore some sense to whatever they were copying, although that sense may not have been the same as the original. It was even possible for mistakes to be made in the original versions, or in the first copies made for distribution, and these are especially difficult to detect, for they may well be repeated in all later copies. One instance of such an early mistake occurs in Bede's account of the crucial battle fought at *Winwæd* in 655, which in all surviving versions presents some difficulties that can be overcome by assuming that a small error in punctuation was made at an early stage (Prestwich, 1968). A common error was in the copying of roman numerals; xxi, for example, can easily be miscopied as xvi. There is, of course, a danger that editors may be over-enthusiastic in correcting texts to make them fit preconceived ideas, but the possibility of such mistakes in the copying of manuscripts can never be ignored.

Bede and his contemporaries were well aware that Britain had formerly been under the authority of Rome. There were many physical reminders of that period in fortifications and monumental structures, as well as in Roman sculptures that survived to impress, and to provide models for early English monuments. Bede also knew at least some of the writings of the imperial period. We are even better informed thanks to our knowledge of other texts of these authors, and we also have the advantage of some records such as the *Notitia Dignitatum*, a listing of military commands that was probably first compiled in the late fourth century. There are also many monumental inscriptions to help the dating of buildings, and to identify some of those who claimed responsibility. Coins, found either singly or in hoards, are not only valuable in their own right, they also make it possible to date with some precision many of the finds made by archaeologists investigating the rich material culture of the period. This relative abundance of evidence ends in the early years of the fifth century. The *Life of St Germanus*, bishop of Auxerre, who is said to have made two visits to Britain, the first in 429, is the last substantial continental text concerning

Britain for two centuries (pp. 76–7). It is not necessarily very reliable as a text for British history; in a *Life* of a bishop of Auxerre written by a priest from Lyons the details of his adventures in Britain are likely to be more hagiographical than historical, but whatever credence is given to this evidence, there is little else for two hundred years, apart from some interesting remarks of the sixth-century Byzantine historian Procopius who speaks of the role of the Frisians in the conquest of Britain, and of the claims of Frankish kings to authority across the Channel (p. 82).

The end of Roman imperial authority in Britain did not, however, mean the end of literacy. Many British aristocrats of the fifth century were sufficiently Romanized to be able not only to speak Latin but also to read and write it (Jackson, 1953, pp. 117–21). It is possible, probable even, that after the mid-fifth century secular literacy in Britain declined, although there is some evidence to suggest that at least one sixth-century British king, Maelgwn of Gwynedd, was educated. The church, however, certainly maintained high standards. It is unfortunate that hardly anything has survived before the middle of the sixth century, but one substantial work by a British cleric called Gildas entitled the *Ruin of Britain* (*De Excidio et Conquestu Britannie*), completed by about 550, is clearly the work of a man who was thoroughly acquainted with much church literature and had been trained not only to read, understand and interpret it, but also to write Latin (Kerlouégan, 1968). This work is a remarkable demonstration of the standards of literacy and learning that could be achieved in Britain over a century after the end of Roman rule. Gildas wrote vigorous and effective Latin, somewhat old-fashioned, but correct, even elegant. His main source was the Bible, which he knew well, but there are also echoes of other writings, including the fifth-century Spanish historian Orosius.

The *Ruin of Britain* is in the form of a letter addressed to a number of British princes and to the clergy of Britain, calling them to repent of sins that are the cause of the ruin. It has been interpreted as a work of denunciation with a 'historical' introduction that has been dismissed as irrelevant or even a later addition. There is certainly no good reason for the extreme view that the historical section is an addition, the language throughout is the same and the work is essentially a unity. Gildas himself insisted that he was not writing a denunciation. In the opening, as in the closing, passage of the work he emphasized that his purpose was to call sinners to repentance.

Whatever my attempt shall be in this epistle, made more in tears than in denunciation, in poor style, I allow, but with good intent, let no man regard me as if about to speak under the influence of contempt for men in general, or with an idea of superiority to all, because I weep the general decay of good, and the heaping up of evils, with tearful complaint. On the contrary, let him think of me as a man that will speak out of a feeling of condolence with my country's losses and its miseries, sharing in the joy of remedies.

The possibility of remedy, of repentance, is the note on which the work ends, and the final biblical quotation is of Christ's words: 'I will not the death of a sinner, but that he may be converted and live.' Gildas was, in short, writing a work of admonition, in the hope of waking the consciences of 'foolish apostates', cruel tyrants and 'imperfect pastors'.

Like other Christian polemicists of an earlier age, notably St Augustine and Salvian, Gildas saw in the events of his own, and earlier, days a demonstration of Man's apparently inexhaustible capacity to bring judgement on himself by attempting to frustrate God's purpose, a purpose that is continually manifested in history despite Man's impotent opposition. Gildas certainly placed more emphasis on penitence and less on divine grace than his fifth-century predecessors, but he, like them, was concerned with the sins of his own people.

I pondered – if the Lord did not spare a people, peculiar out of all the nations, the royal seed and holy nation, to whom he had said: Israel is my first born – if he spared not its priests, prophets, kings for so many centuries, if he spared not the apostle his minister, and the members of that primitive church, when they swerved from the right path, what will he do to such blackness as we have in this age? (Gildas, c. 1)

From this an interest in the history of his own people was a natural consequence. Gildas was not, however, a historian in any modern sense. Bede describes him as *historicus* but he clearly used that word in the special sense that he had so carefully defined (p. 8). Gildas would probably have accepted that the true law of history was the opinion of the common people, for to him history was the equivalent of morality (Gildas, c. 93). History, that is Man's belief about his past, was important as a revelation of both the nature and the cause of God's judgement and it was therefore natural for him to begin with a description of his country and of the sufferings of his countrymen from enemies and plagues, of their defeats and victories, and of the crimes which included the election of tyrannous kings who

> were anointed not in the name of God, but such as surpassed others in cruelty, and shortly afterwards were put to death by the men who anointed them, without any enquiry as to truth, because others more cruel had been elected. (Gildas, c. 21)

His concern was with Christian history and he therefore omitted those ancient errors, common to all nations, by which before the coming of Christ in the flesh the whole human race was held in bondage (Gildas, c. 4), and began with the Roman emperors who subjugated the world and under whom the bright sun, Christ, spread everywhere. It was, indeed, one of the sins of the Britons that they had kept the Roman name, 'though it was no more than the echo of a word', but had abandoned Roman morals and law, and chosen tyrants instead. Gildas was writing in a time of relative security that had been assured under the leadership of Ambrosius Aurelianus, a 'Roman' to whom 'by the Lord's favour, there came victory' followed later by a more decisive triumph over the English invaders at Mount *Badon* that was 'the gift granted by the will of God in our own times' (Gildas, cc. 2; 25).

For his knowledge of British history Gildas depended on Roman authors, whether he knew them directly or through extracts, and he possibly knew of some correspondence that had passed between Britain and the imperial government in the first half of the fifth century. He knew that there were two Roman walls in the north, and that one was made of turf, although he misunderstood or inferred wrongly when they were built. He also knew about forts that had been constructed along the coast towards the south (Gildas, cc. 14; 18). He explains that he could not use

> native writings or records of authors inasmuch as these (if they ever existed) have been burnt by the fires of enemies, or carried far away in the ships which exiled my countrymen, and so are not at hand. (Gildas, c. 4)

There may, of course, have been annals or historical writings of which he was unaware but no trace of these survives. Gildas himself gives no dates, although he attempts to give his historical section some narrative sequence and indicates the passage of time by such words as 'after this', 'at that time' or, most confusingly of all, 'meanwhile'.

Aldhelm studied Gildas's work at Canterbury, Bede did so in

Northumbria and Alcuin also read and quoted it. It was also known in Brittany. Of the later British writers who knew of, and used, Gildas, one of the most important was the compiler of the *Historia Brittonum*, completed in 829-30, apparently at the court of Merfyn, king of Gwynedd. Like Bede a century earlier, this anonymous scholar used a variety of other sources, many of which depended in part on orally transmitted traditions. These British sources were like the English ones in many ways, not least in having a historical horizon in the middle of the sixth century. Welsh genealogies, for example, appear in some cases to be reliable back to that period, but not earlier (Miller, 1975b). This horizon was not, like the English one, due to earlier illiteracy. Gildas shows how literate the British could be. A major cause for the absence of earlier records is probably the devastating plague that swept through the British Isles in the late 540s. This must have caused a hiatus that was made worse by the expansion of the illiterate and pagan English in the second part of the century. Many libraries were probably destroyed and the disruption and deaths must have made it necessary for later generations of Britons to reshape their own history.

The art of poetry was highly valued in both British and English society and many of the surviving poems are about the people and events of the fifth and sixth centuries. Some were composed so much later that they have no value as evidence for that period although they have some interest in showing what people then thought about their past. A few British poems have been claimed as authentic compositions of the sixth century, including twelve poems of Taliesin and a longer work, by Aneirin, called the *Gododdin*. These Welsh poems are generally elegies on particular heroes, and they now survive only in copies made in the thirteenth century or later. Some have archaic features that have been taken to prove their antiquity, but even if they are genuine, their historical value is general rather than particular; they are evidence for the attitudes and ideals of the sixth century, not for the details about either events or individuals, and they have certainly been greatly modified in transmission. It is, for example, significant that there is disagreement among scholars about which twelve poems can be regarded as the authentic work of Taliesin (Dumville, 1977a, p. 178).

English poetry differs from the British in that much of it is narrative, notably the long poem *Beowulf*, but such narratives have little or no historical value; for the historian this poetry is important for the light it casts on the ideals and assumptions of contemporary aristocratic society. The surviving poems were composed after the conversion, they were indeed probably written in, as they were certainly preserved by, religious communities. The fact that the subject-matter of some of the most important of these poems was the pagan past is perhaps a surprising aspect of monastic culture but it should be remembered that the leading Christians of the seventh century were mostly converts from a secular life which, to judge by Bede and other writings, was not much altered by the new religion. More important, some of the most influential saints, including Cuthbert and Guthlac, were not only converts themselves, but were especially admired for the heroic quality of their spiritual life. There was indeed a close affinity between the world of Beowulf and of St Guthlac (Whitelock, 1951, pp. 80–1).

The many and close contacts between Ireland and the peoples of Britain in the seventh and later centuries give Irish sources a particular value for early English history (Hughes, 1972). Most of the lives of Irish saints are relatively late but one, Adomnán's *Life of Columba*, was written between 688 and 704 and is fortunately preserved in a manuscript copied in or before 713. Some of the details of Columba's activity as reported by Adomnán may well reflect reinterpretations and misunderstandings that developed in the century after Columba's death in 597, but Adomnán's information is of the greatest value in providing an insight into the secular and religious ideals of the seventh-century Irish church, and as a source, independent of Bede, of information about both Pictish and Scottish society. Most Irish texts are preserved in later copies but such was the conservatism of the Irish, especially Irish scholars, both the *filidh*, poets and keepers of native traditions, and *brithemhain*, keepers of the law, that the law tracts and the poetry composed in the sixth, seventh and eighth centuries have not only been faithfully, if sometimes uncomprehendingly, preserved by later copyists and commentators, but they themselves incorporate some elements from the pagan past. These Irish texts are of the greatest value not so much for the little information they give about Britain, but rather for what can be learned from them about a Celtic society that escaped the direct influence of Rome. They are, therefore, invaluable as a guide and control in any study of the influence of the Romans and the English on British society.

The historical darkness of the fifth and sixth centuries is lightened a little by other types of evidence. Unfortunately inscriptions and coins, which have contributed so much to our understanding of the

Roman period in Britain, are of less help for the post-Roman period. The custom of erecting monumental inscriptions died out long before the fifth century and the inscriptions, generally in Latin, that were made in and after the fifth century were of a very different character, being mainly funerary and with one exception undated. They are, however, found throughout the northern and western parts of Britain and provide precious clues for the study of early British society (Macalister, 1949). Few coins were imported into Britain after the year 400, twenty years later the supply apparently ceased completely and by 430 coins were no longer used in Britain as currency (Kent, 1961). During that century the material culture of Britain became progressively more British than Roman and its remains are consequently more elusive; settlements have certainly been discovered but they are difficult to date and the graves of the Britons in that period cannot easily be recognized, let alone dated. We are far better informed archaeologically about the English settlers whose graves, both cremations and inhumations, are distinctive, and which contain pottery and other equipment that can yield valuable clues to the progress of the English colonization. In recent years there have also been important discoveries of early English settlements, one very early example being at Mucking in the Essex marshes of the Thames estuary. This meagre material can be supplemented by the study of place-names, but scholars are now far less confident than they once were about the interpretation of these names and there is some uncertainty about their value for early English history (pp. 150–63).

The inadequacy of our sources for the fifth and sixth centuries means that we can never hope to trace in any detail the first stages in the creation of the English kingdoms. There are not many certainties, we know the names of a few individuals but have little or no knowledge of what most of them did, and the chronology of those centuries is a matter of dispute. We cannot, however, ignore the period in which the foundations of English and British history were laid, but it may be more helpful to begin this account of early English history by attempting first to describe the situation revealed by our seventh-century sources, and only then to consider how that situation came about. By approaching the fifth and sixth centuries from the seventh it may be possible to recognize, and perhaps make some allowance for, the influence later events may have had on successive attempts, from Bede onwards, to interpret that obscure period.

2 *Seventh-century Britain*

By the end of the seventh century the English controlled most of
Britain south of the Firth of Forth. Some natives preserved their
independence in the west; the most extensive territory under British
rule being Wales where there were several kingdoms, but there was
also a British kingdom, Dumnonia, in the south-west, now Cornwall
and western Devon, and the English territory around the Solway
Firth was bounded on the north by the kingdom of Strathclyde with
its main stronghold at Dumbarton, 'the fort of the Britons'. There were
several English kingdoms; the number at any one time in the seventh
century cannot be determined for certain, our sources are not sufficiently comprehensive or systematic, but as there appear to have been
seven main kingdoms at the end of the century, they are sometimes
collectively called the Heptarchy: Kent, the East Saxons, the South and
West Saxons, the East Angles, the Mercians and the Northumbrians.
Some, perhaps all, of these had been created by the fusion of smaller
kingdoms which preserved traces of their former independent status in
still being described as kingdoms or subkingdoms, under the rule of
reges, reguli or *subreguli*. Northumbria, for example, comprised several
kingdoms including Deira and Bernicia, which were often described as
separate kingdoms even though the ruler of one of them appears to have
had some form of superiority over the other for most of the seventh
century. Similarly, there is a significant distinction between the original
kingdom of the Mercians and the greatly enlarged territory over which
the seventh-century Mercian kings ruled. One of the most important
considerations in any study of seventh-century Britain is, indeed, the
degree of independence, or subordination, of these components of the
main kingdoms but it will be helpful to simplify this preliminary survey
by describing the situation initially in terms of the seven familiar
kingdoms of the Heptarchy. Northumbria and Mercia, separated by
the river Humber, were by far the largest. The northern kingdom
extended to the Firth of Forth and included the north shore of the
Solway Firth, while the southern boundary of Mercian territory was
the river Thames, and London, which had formerly been an East Saxon
city, was by 700 firmly under Mercian control. The modern counties of
Kent, Essex, Sussex and the two counties of East Anglia correspond
quite closely to the four kingdoms whose names are thus preserved,

and the West Saxons controlled the remaining area south of the Thames as far west as Exeter.

There was a vigorous, often violent, competition for superiority between these seventh-century kings in which the eastern kings were relatively unsuccessful. By the end of the century the East Saxons had, in fact, been reduced to subordinate status by the Mercians and the independence of the South Saxons was threatened by both the Mercians and the West Saxons. It is true that in the early years of the century Æthelberht, king of Kent, and Rædwald, king of the East Angles, were successively overlords of the southern English, but later rulers of these kingdoms could not claim so much. The Northumbrians, Mercians and West Saxons were more fortunate because they had the opportunity to dominate British as well as English neighbours, and the rapid growth of these three kingdoms was largely at the expense of the British. The rulers of these expanding kingdoms did not, however, find it so easy to extend their authority permanently over English kingdoms. Northumbria never gained more than temporary overlordship south of the Humber and even the Mercians, the most successful English rulers in the late seventh and eighth centuries, were unable to destroy East Anglian or Kentish independence.

The competition for lordship and resources in the seventh century can best be studied in the north, thanks to Bede and Eddius. Sometime before 600 an English kingdom called Deira, a British name, had been created north of the river Humber. Archaeological evidence shows that the main early English settlements in that area were in the Wolds and around Malton and York, but by the beginning of the seventh century Deira probably extended as far north as the river Tees (Faull, 1974). Across that river there was another English kingdom with a British name, Bernicia, based on the coastal stronghold of Bamburgh. To judge by the few known English graves far fewer invaders settled north of the Tees than in Deira (p. 90). Bernicia and Deira were bounded on the west and north by British kingdoms; we know the names of three of these, Elmet, Rheged and Gododdin. Elmet lay in the foothills of the Pennines south-west of York. Its full extent is not known but it certainly included the area between the rivers Aire and Wharfe, later described as the region of *Loidis*, now Leeds (Jones, 1975). Rheged lay somewhere round the Solway Firth; its name is preserved in Dunragit, in Wigtownshire, on the northern shore of the Firth (Watson, 1926, p. 156). The kingdom of Gododdin was the successor of the Uotadini, a British tribe that occupied the lands around the head of the Firth of Forth as well as the coastal plain as far south as Hadrian's Wall (*Gododdin*). The establishment of Bernicia meant that by the beginning of the seventh century the British had lost control of the coast south of the Tweed, but they may well have retained some inland areas rather longer.

By the middle of the seventh century two of these British kingdoms, Elmet and Gododdin, had been conquered by their English neighbours and, although our sources are silent about the fate of Rheged, English expansion into the north-west had reached Carlisle by 685 (Bede, *VC*, c. 27) and the Whithorn peninsula in Galloway soon after (*HE*, iii. 4). These conquests greatly enlarged the resources of the northern English kings and after their conversion to Christianity in the first half of the seventh century they used some of these new lands to endow religious communities. When the church of Ripon was consecrated in about 678, it was given some land west of the Pennines, including an estate on the Ribble, together with 'consecrated places in various parts which the British clergy had deserted when fleeing from the hostile sword wielded by the warriors' of the English (Eddius, c. 17). This extension of their territory brought the northern English into direct contact with new neighbours: Strathclyde and, north of the Forth, the Picts, divided into northern and southern groups by the high mountains known as the Mounth. The southern Picts and the Britons of Strathclyde were not only threatened by the English, but also had to face a challenge in the west by Irish settlers known as Dál Riata who were by then occupying the area that later became Argyll (Duncan, 1975, pp. 41–6).

The first seventh-century king of Bernicia was Æthelfrith who, according to Bede, died in 616 after a reign of twenty-four years. For much if not all of that time he also ruled Deira. By marrying the daughter of Ælle, the previous king of Deira, he doubtless hoped to give his heirs the best possible claim to rule both kingdoms, a claim that would have been greatly strengthened by the death of Ælle's male descendants of whom there were apparently only two: his son Edwin and Hereric, Edwin's nephew. They both fled into exile, Hereric to Elmet and Edwin 'wandered secretly as a fugitive for many years through many places and kingdoms until at last he came to Rædwald and asked him for protection against the plots of his powerful persecutor' (*HE*, ii. 12). Æthelfrith unsuccessfully attempted to persuade Rædwald to kill his guest, but Hereric was less fortunate and died by

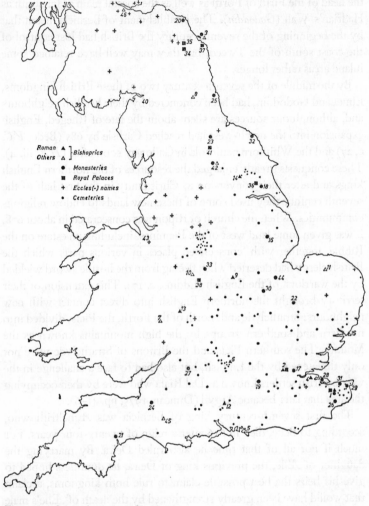

Figure 1   Seventh-century England

All seventh-century bishoprics but only a few of the known monasteries and palaces are shown. The Eccles (+) names are taken from Cameron (1968, p. 89) and Barrow (1973, p. 62). The cemeteries are of the seventh and eighth centuries, excluding churchyards. I am indebted to Christopher Arnold for supplying the list of cemeteries.

poisoning in Elmet. Bede asserts that Æthelfrith 'ravaged the Britons more successfully than any other English ruler'. We have no details of his achievement but it was probably his successes in the north that provoked Aedán, king of Dál Riata, to oppose him in a battle fought in 603 at *Degsastan*. Aedán's defeat must have greatly enhanced the reputation of the Bernician king, but it also appears to have led, sooner or later, to the establishment of friendly relations between his family and the rulers of Dál Riata, for after Æthelfrith's death his son Oswald was exiled in Dál Riata. Bede remarks that after *Degsastan* 'no Irish king in Britain has dared to make war on the English race to this day'. Some ten years after defeating Aedán, Æthelfrith won another memorable victory against the Britons at Chester. There is no suggestion that either battle was fought primarily for territorial gain and their locations cannot be taken to indicate the extent of Æthelfrith's dominion; they were, rather, incidents in campaigns whose main purpose was either the acquisition of plunder and prestige, or the pursuit of old enmities.

Æthelfrith was, at last, defeated and killed in 616 by Rædwald, Edwin's protector, in a battle fought by the river Idle where it was crossed by the Roman road from Lincoln to Doncaster, about twenty miles from Lincoln. As a result Edwin took Æthelfrith's place as ruler of both Deira and Bernicia, and in their turn Æthelfrith's sons fled into exile. Eanfrith, the eldest, went to the Picts where he married a Pictish

---

Key to figure 1.

1 Canterbury	17 Barking	33 Repton
2 London	18 Beverley	34 Yeavering
3 Lindisfarne	19 Chertsey	35 Milfield
4 Rochester	20 Coldingham	36 Goodmanham
5 Selsey	21 Exeter	37 Bamburgh
6 Dorchester on Thames	22 Ely	38 Tamworth
7 Hereford	23 Gilling	39 Whithorn
8 Hexham	24 Glastonbury	40 Carlisle
9 Leicester	25 Jarrow	41 Catterick
10 Lichfield	26 Lyminge	42 Ripon
11 North Elmham	27 Malmesbury	43 Chester
12 Winchester	28 Minster in Sheppey	44 Crowland
13 Worcester	29 Minster in Thanet	45 Sherborne
14 York	30 Oundle	46 Abercorn
15 Dunwich	31 Reculver	
16 Bardney	32 Whitby	

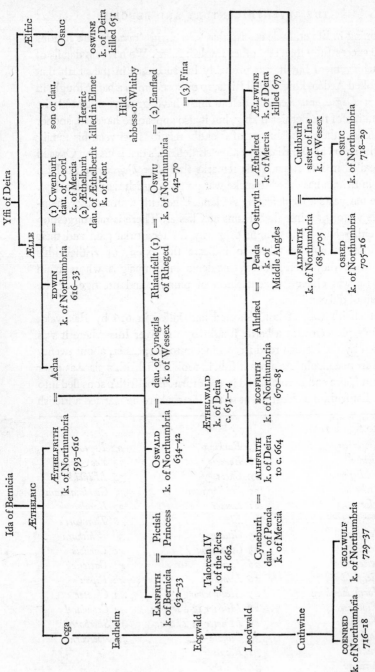

Figure 2 Northumbrian kings in the seventh century

Many known relations are omitted, for the sake of clarity. Names of Northumbrian rulers are given in capital and small capital type.

Abbreviations: d. died; dau. daughter; k. king.

princess, his young brother Oswald, then aged about twelve, possibly accompanied by Oswiu, aged only four, went to Dál Riata. One of Edwin's early actions was to seize Elmet, probably because of the fate of his nephew Hereric, but he soon extended his authority much farther afield for, as Bede reports, 'he even brought the islands of Anglesey and Man under his power' (*HE*, ii. 5). We do not know how quickly he established this overlordship, which also extended over all southern English kingdoms except Kent, or what opposition he had to overcome in the early years of his reign. When, after 625, our evidence becomes more detailed, thanks to the missionaries who converted him, his power in the south was enough to provoke a West Saxon conspiracy to assassinate him. According to Bede, he was saved from death, but not injury, by the self-sacrificing loyalty of one of his companions, and when the king recovered from his wound, he took revenge on those responsible, a good example of what overlordship could mean (*HE*, ii. 9). Edwin's first wife was Cwenburh, daughter of a Mercian king, a marriage that may mean he spent part of his exile in Mercia, but in or before 625 he married Æthelburh, daughter of Æthelberht, the king of Kent who was converted to Christianity by the Roman missionary Augustine. Æthelburh was therefore a Christian and one of the consequences of the marriage was the arrival in Northumbria of one of Augustine's companions, Bishop Paulinus. After Edwin's death Paulinus fled back to Kent where some memory of his Northumbrian activity was preserved and later reported to Bede by his Kentish friends, and he also had the opportunity to learn about it at first-hand from the deacon James (*HE*, ii. 16, 20). Bede's account of Paulinus' mission is consequently relatively full and it is from Edwin's reign that we first have details of the activity of a Northumbrian king within his own kingdom. We hear, for example, of royal halls or palaces. One of these, the *villa regia* of Yeavering, near Wooler, has been discovered and shown by excavation to be a most elaborate complex of buildings, including a great hall over 80 feet long (Rahtz, 1976). Paulinus spent thirty-six days there.

> from morning till evening he did nothing else but instruct the crowds who flocked to him from every village and district in the teaching of Christ. When they had received instruction he washed them in the waters of regeneration in the river Glen, which was close at hand. (*HE*, ii. 15)

The *villa regia* in which the West Saxon assassination attempt occurred was by the river Derwent, probably not far from the pagan temple of Goodmanham. A third was at *Campodonum*, an unidentified place, probably near the river Don, and apparently in Elmet. The distribution of these *villae* suggests that Edwin had at least one in each of the kingdoms over which he ruled; Yeavering in Bernicia, *Campodonum* in Elmet, and another by the Derwent in Deira. He is also said to have stayed frequently at the *vicus* of Catterick, and York must also have been an important centre of royal activity for it was there that Edwin chose to be baptized. Bede's account of Paulinus' activity at Yeavering shows that he made at least one major missionary journey to Bernicia but he also reports a tradition that 'so far as we know, no symbol of the Christian faith, no church, and no altar had been erected in the whole of Bernicia' in Edwin's reign and that the first to do so was Oswald (*HE*, iii. 2). The apparent concentration of missionary effort in southern Northumbria, where Bede reports the construction of two churches, at York and at *Campodonum*, is not surprising for Deira was, according to Bede, 'the cradle of Edwin's family and the foundation of his power' (*HE*, iii. 1).

Bede eloquently describes that power:

It is related that there was so great a peace in Britain, wherever the dominion of King Edwin reached, that, as the proverb still runs, a woman with a new-born child could walk throughout the island from sea to sea and take no harm. The king cared so much for the good of the people that, in various places where he had noticed clear springs near the highway, he caused stakes to be set up and bronze drinking cups to be hung on them for the refreshment of travellers. No one dared to lay hands on them except for their proper purpose because they feared the king greatly nor did they wish to because they loved him dearly. So great was his majesty in his realm that not only were banners (*vexilla*) carried before him in battle, but even in times of peace as he rode about among his cities, estates and kingdoms with his thegns (*inter civitates sive villas aut provincias suas cum ministris*) he always used to be preceded by a standard bearer. Further, when he walked anywhere along the roads there used to be carried before him the type of standard which the Romans call a *tufa* and the English a *thuf*. (*HE*, ii. 16)

Edwin's reputation as an effective ruler who behaved in some respects like a Roman no doubt owes much to the disruption that followed his overthrow when Cadwallon 'tore the Northumbrian kingdoms to pieces with fearful bloodshed' and it probably lost nothing in being kept alive in Kent. There is, however, no reason to doubt that if a seventh-century king could keep his kingdom free of invaders it could be both peaceful and prosperous.

Whatever love and respect Edwin may have enjoyed in his own kingdoms, there were those elsewhere who wished him ill. The West Saxon attempt to destroy him failed but in 633 Cadwallon, the British king of Gwynedd, was more successful. According to Bede, Cadwallon rebelled; the word is carefully chosen and is consistent with his earlier statement that Edwin had brought Anglesey, then part of Gwynedd, under his power. The British king, in alliance with Penda, king of the Mercians, defeated and killed Edwin in a battle fought in the district known as *Hæthfeld*, now Hatfield Chase, not far from the site of Æthelfrith's defeat sixteen years earlier.

The unity of Northumbria was broken. Deira passed to Edwin's cousin Osric and Bernicia to Æthelfrith's eldest son Eanfrith, who returned from exile among the Picts. Both had been converted to Christianity, Osric by Paulinus and Eanfrith while in exile, but reverted to what Bede called 'the filth of their former idolatry' (*HE*, iii. 1). Within a year they had both been killed by Cadwallon who then 'occupied the Northumbrian kingdoms for a whole year, not ruling them like a victorious king but ravaging them like a savage tyrant'. Cadwallon's triumph was, however, short-lived and in 634 he was killed by another of Æthelfrith's sons, Oswald, near Hexham.

After Edwin's death one of his loyal thegns organized the escape of his queen, two of his children and a grandson who, with Bishop Paulinus, were taken by boat to Kent where they were given shelter by the queen's brother, King Eadbald. The queen later feared that Oswald might attempt to have the boys killed, much as Æthelfrith had tried to kill Edwin, and sent them for safety to the Frankish king Dagobert, but they nevertheless died in infancy.

The Roman mission had collapsed, but Oswald was also a Christian, having been converted while in exile in Dál Riata, and he clearly regarded his victory over Cadwallon as a sign of divine support. In response to a request from Oswald, Bishop Aidán was sent from Iona, the religious centre of Dál Riata, and he chose Lindisfarne as the site of his new bishopric, probably because it was, like Iona, an island; it was also conveniently close to both Bamburgh and Yeavering.

Oswald not only reunited Northumbria, he also quickly re-established Edwin's overlordship throughout Britain. Within two years of his victory over Cadwallon he attended, as god-father, the baptism of the West Saxon king Cynegils, whose daughter he later married. He also had some part in the establishment of the first West Saxon bishopric at Dorchester-on-Thames, close to the boundary between West Saxon and Mercian territory. The West Saxons may well have welcomed an alliance with Oswald for fear of Penda, the Mercian king. Oswald was, in fact, killed by Penda, in 642, in battle at *Maserfelth*, which has been identified as Old Oswestry, a name that means 'Oswald's tree', possibly in the sense of cross, for the Welsh form of the name is *Croesoswald*, 'Oswald's Cross'. Bede clearly knew very little about Oswald's brief overlordship; most of the pages devoted to him in the *Ecclesiastical History* describe miracles connected with either his victory over Cadwallon or his defeat by the pagan Penda. A miracle that was said to have been wrought by Oswald's intercession among the South Saxons can be cited as evidence of overlordship in that kingdom (*HE*, iv. 14), but a more revealing episode is the hostility with which his remains were treated at Bardney, a monastery a few miles east of Lincoln. Some of Oswald's dismembered remains had been recovered by his brother Oswiu and buried, the head on Lindisfarne, the hands and arms at Bamburgh. The other remains may have been first buried at Oswestry but they were later removed by Oswiu's daughter, then queen of Mercia, who wished to place them in the monastery of Bardney which she and her husband greatly favoured. That community did not, according to Bede (*HE*, iii. 11), welcome them: 'They knew that Oswald was a saint but, nevertheless, because he belonged to another kingdom and had once conquered them, they pursued him when dead with their former hatred.' Their opposition was miraculously overcome, but the incident shows the attitude of at least one group over whom Oswald extended his overlordship.

After Oswald's death Northumbria again broke up into its constituent kingdoms. His brother Oswiu retained Bernicia while Deira passed to Oswine, son of Edwin's cousin Osric who had ruled Deira for a short while after Edwin's death. After a few years the rivalry between Deira and Bernicia led to a conflict that was resolved not by battle but by assassination. Oswine was betrayed by a friend and, in Bede's words, 'Oswiu caused him to be most foully murdered'. The crime occurred at Gilling, a few miles north-west of Catterick, where Oswiu later built a monastery in expiation. Deira survived but its next kings were kinsmen of Oswiu's, first his nephew Æthelwald and then his own son Alhfrith. Kinship did not, however, ensure that friendly relations would be maintained. Bede mentions that Oswiu suffered from the hostility of these two kings of Deira; Æthelwald may well have thought that he should have succeeded his father Oswald as king of Bernicia as well as Deira. He was certainly believed to have been implicated in Penda's last invasion of Northumbria. Deiran opposition to Bernicia appears to have been encouraged by the Mercians; Alhfrith married Penda's daughter and had friendly relations with Penda's son, Peada. It was indeed the Mercians who posed the main threat to Oswiu and we know of two invasions of Bernicia by Penda. The first must have occurred sometime before Aidán's death in 651 for, as Bede reports, it was his prayerful intervention that changed the direction of the wind and so frustrated Penda's attempt to burn the royal stronghold of Bamburgh. That episode need not have been in Oswiu's reign, but the second certainly was, for Bede specifically reports that Oswiu was forced to 'promise Penda an incalculable and incredible store of royal treasures and gifts as the price of peace, on condition that Penda would return home and cease to devastate, or rather utterly destroy, the kingdoms under his rule' (*HE*, iii. 24). The offer was, according to Bede, refused. This episode is probably the same as that reported in the *Historia Brittonum* where Penda is said to have gone on an expedition as far as *Iudeu*, which has been identified as Stirling but is more likely to be the Roman fort of Cramond on the south of the Firth of Forth (Rutherford, 1976). One manuscript of the *Historia* continues: 'Then Oswiu rendered into Penda's hand all the riches that were with him in the city; and Penda distributed them to the kings of the Britons. That is, the *atbret Iudeu*, meaning the restoration or ransom of *Iudeu*' (*EHD* 2). The British and Northumbrian traditions agree that Oswiu was forced to offer a huge treasure to Penda, but whether it was accepted or not Penda must have been able to reward his allies richly. They were, however, finally defeated. Both Bede and the *Historia Brittonum* imply that it was during the same campaign that Penda was killed in a battle fought at *Winwæd*, an unidentified river in the district of Leeds, on 15 November 655. Oswiu became overlord of Mercia but after three years Penda's son Wulfhere came out of hiding and quickly re-established his father's dominant position south of the Humber. Some years after Oswiu's death in 670, Wulfhere invaded Northumbria but was defeated and as a result Lindsey again became a Northumbrian province, but not for long. In 679 Wulfhere's brother and successor as king of Mercia, Æthelred, defeated the Northumbrians in the Battle of the Trent, a battle that marked the end of Northumbrian attempts to exercise overlordship south of the Humber. It was more than two centuries before another Northumbrian king, a Scandinavian called Olaf Guthfrithsson, attempted to extend his authority beyond that river, and with as little success as his seventh-century predecessors (p. 127). Thus it was the Mercians who confined the Bernicians and Deirans north of the Humber, making them, in effect, Northumbrians.

This Mercian opposition must have encouraged the North-umbrians to concentrate on the opportunities for expansion in the north. The friendly relations that Æthelfrith appears to have had with the Picts, who sheltered his eldest son, Eanfrith, as an exile and even arranged Eanfrith's marriage to a Pictish princess, appear to have been sustained by Æthelfrith's other sons despite Eanfrith's apostasy. The Picts do not seem to have taken advantage of Oswiu's plight at *Iudeu* and it is possible that relations became even closer after Eanfrith's son Talorcan succeeded to the kingship of the Picts in 658 (Miller, 1978a). This alliance between the Picts and the Northumbrians did not, however, survive Oswiu's death in 670. His son and heir, Ecgfrith, was soon at war with them. According to Eddius it was the Picts who seized this opportunity to 'throw off the yoke of slavery', but the initiative was quickly seized by Ecgfrith who, with his subking Beorn-hæth, led a force of cavalry to victory against the Picts, and reduced at least some to slavery, who remained subject to him until his death in 685 in the battle of *Nechtansmere*. This battle, which was, according to Bede (*HE*, iv. 26), fought against the advice of his friends, marked a decisive turn in the fortunes of the English. The Picts then recovered their land, which the English had formerly held, while the Irish who lived in Britain and some part of the British nation recovered their independence. There were later incidents of unexplained significance: in 698 Berhtred, a *dux* of the Northumbrian king, was killed by the Picts and in 711 a *prefectus* or reeve called Berhtfrith is said to have fought against the Picts, but by 731 when Bede wrote, a treaty of peace had been established between the Picts and the English.

Relations between the Northumbrians and their northern neighbours were probably affected by the death of Eanfrith's son Talorcan, king of the Picts, in 662, and broke down altogether after the death of Oswiu, the last of Æthelfrith's sons. Ecgfrith appears to have behaved in a very highhanded manner towards his father's friends, but his death at *Nechtansmere* led to the restoration of peace on the northern frontier, at the price of some cession of territory. The Northumbrians still controlled the lands around the Solway Firth and in Lothian, probably as far as the Pentland Hills, but they had lost much.

Ecgfrith left no son and the Northumbrians chose another son of Oswiu, Aldfrith, whose mother is said by late Irish sources to have been Fína, a princess of the Irish royal family, the Uí Néill. Aldfrith was then an exile in Iona, possibly sheltering from Ecgfrith himself. On his death in 705, his eldest son Osred was only eight years old but despite that and in the face of a determined and briefly successful challenge by one Eadwulf, whose family connections are unknown, Osred became king. Twelve years later he was assassinated and Æthelfrith's family lost the monopoly of the Northumbrian kingship that they had enjoyed for almost a century. His place was taken by Coenred; in late eighth-century documents Ida, the sixth-century founder of the Bernician dynasty, is claimed as his ancestor (Dumville, 1976). After a reign of two years he was succeeded by Osric, whose family connections are also unknown, but he in his turn chose Ceolwulf, Coenred's brother, as his successor and it was to this king that Bede dedicated his *Ecclesiastical History*.

A number of generalizations can be based on the dynastic history of seventh-century Northumbria and it may be helpful to summarize these before considering contemporary developments elsewhere in Britain; this should at least make points of similarity and difference more readily apparent. It is, in the first place, important to emphasize that our knowledge is far from complete. For example, according to Bede, Aldfrith was succeeded by his young son Osred, but Eddius in his *Life of Wilfrid* reports that the succession went first to Eadwulf, who was deprived of the kingship after two months. The details are obscure, but Eddius implies not only that Eadwulf lost his throne because of his opposition to Wilfrid, but also that there was a violent dispute in which Osred's supporters, led by Berhtfrith, a man 'second only to the king', were besieged in Bamburgh. Without Eddius we would know nothing of Eadwulf or his brief reign, and the later references to the death in 740 of Earnwine, Eadwulf's son, would be even more mysterious (*EHD*, 3).

Eddius also reveals the existence of Northumbrian subkings about whom other sources are silent. They are mentioned in his account (c. 17) of the consecration of Ripon, a ceremony that was attended by King Ecgfrith and his brother Ælfwine, who ruled Deira, together with abbots, reeves (*prefecti*) and subkings (*subreguli*). Eddius elsewhere names one *subregulus*, Beornhæth, who was Ecgfrith's companion in a campaign against the Picts. Northumbria had grown by absorbing several kingdoms; we know the names of three and there may well have been others. Our knowledge of Elmet, Rheged and Gododdin is very slight and depends on a handful of references, most of which are of doubtful reliability. Rulers of formerly independent kingdoms, whether they were of British or English descent, who accepted Northumbrian overlordship, may have been allowed to continue as subkings over what had become, in effect, Northumbrian provinces. Other provinces were ruled by royal agents called *prefecti*, whose high rank is sometimes concealed by the translation of *prefectus* as 'reeve'. Some *prefecti* were alternatively called *duces*, 'dukes or leaders', a description that underlines their military role, a responsibility that must have been particularly important in frontier areas. In the commemorative lists preserved in the Durham *Liber Vitae* these men are grouped with kings in a section headed *Nomina Regum vel Ducum*, which includes Beornhæth, probably the man Eddius described as a *subregulus*. Other members of his family played a very important role in Bernician history both in campaigns against the Picts and also in dynastic politics; the Berhtfrith who was responsible for securing the succession of Aldfrith's young son may have been a member of the same family as Beornhæth.

In the first half of the seventh century Northumbrian kings were chosen from two families, the kinsmen of Æthelfrith and Edwin. The violent conflict between them appears to have ended with the murder of Oswine in 651. Deira continued as a separate kingdom, but was ruled by members of the Bernician royal family, an arrangement that did not, however, ensure friendly relations between them. There was, for example, the conflict between Oswiu and Oswald's son Æthelwald and relations between father and son were no better, for Oswiu is said to have suffered much from the opposition of Alhfrith. After the death of Ælfwine at the Battle of the Trent in 679, the two kingdoms were apparently united under one Bernician ruler, although it must be admitted that our sources are predominantly Bernician and there are some later episodes which may reflect continuing Deiran separatism.

For over seventy years after Edwin's death in 633 the kings of Bernicia were either sons or grandsons of Æthelfrith, but early in the eighth century some kings came from other branches of the same family. Coenred, who succeeded Osred after his assassination in 716, and his brother Ceolwulf (729–37) traced their descent from Ida, as did Æthelfrith's family. Descent from Ida seems to have become normal for Northumbrian kings and those whose pedigrees are known all claimed him as an ancestor. The family connections of Eadwulf, who contested the succession after Aldfrith, are unknown, probably because he was unsuccessful. Had he lasted more than two months his ancestry, real or claimed, would more likely have been recorded.

It was natural for kings to try to secure the succession for a member of their own immediate family, and to this end they attempted to kill potential rivals. Æthelfrith did his best to remove the main Deiran claimants, and Edwin's heirs had good cause to fear that Oswald, whose sanctity was less obvious to contemporaries than to later generations, would be as ruthless in pursuit of dynastic security as his father had been. No wonder unsuccessful contenders or members of ousted branches of royal families sought safety in exile.

The reception of a royal guest as an exile implied a significant political decision – it meant taking sides – and the places in which Northumbrian exiles found refuge are therefore significant. Hereric went to the British kingdom of Elmet, and Edwin 'wandered secretly as a fugitive through many places and kingdoms'. According to twelfth-century evidence he spent part of his exile at the court of Cadfan, Cadwallon's father (Bromwich, 1961, pp. xcvii–xcviii). Æthelfrith's sons went to the Picts and to Dál Riata, and in 685 Aldfrith was called from exile in Iona.

Another way in which alliances were expressed, and formed, was by marriage. Some marriages were contracted during exiles: Eanfrith married a Pictish princess and Edwin's first wife was the daughter of a Mercian king. Others were arranged as acts of policy by reigning kings. Both Æthelfrith and his son Oswiu attempted to strengthen their hold on Deira by marrying members of the Deiran royal family. Edwin's second wife was Æthelburh of Kent. Both Oswald and Aldfrith married West Saxon princesses. The most fascinating of these marriage alliances were those contracted by Oswiu. His first wife appears to have been Rhiainfellt of Rheged and it is a pity that we do not know whether this marriage occurred before or after Edwin's death, when Oswiu was aged twenty (Jackson, 1964, pp. 41–2). Soon after his accession to the throne in 642 he married Edwin's daughter Eanflæd who survived him to become abbess of Whitby, an office she still held in 685. Oswiu had another son, Aldfrith, by an Irish princess. Bede considered that marriage illegitimate and Aldfrith a bastard, but such considerations did not prevent his being chosen by the Northumbrians as their king in 685, a decision that St Cuthbert apparently encouraged. Aldfrith had by then gained an impressive reputation as a scholar, and it is likely that he was born before Oswiu became king, and that Oswiu's Irish liaison occurred during his brother's reign. There were also marriages between Northumbrians and Mercians. Three of Oswiu's children married children of Penda; his son Alhfrith married Cyneburh, Alhflæd married Peada two years before his father's death at *Winwæd*, and Osthryth's husband was Æthelred, who became king of Mercia in 675. Marriages were therefore a means of expressing and confirming alliances whether they were formed voluntarily on the basis of common interest or were enforced by superior power. They were also a means of patching up quarrels. Whatever the basis of an alliance, a dynastic marriage could contribute to its permanence, for any son would have a claim to rule both kingdoms. Oswald and Oswiu were, through their mother, members of the Deiran royal family and the connection was further strengthened when Oswiu married Edwin's daughter.

The power of a king, and his ability to dictate the terms of alliances, depended in large measure on his success as a warrior, both in defending his kingdom against external attack and in offensive campaigns. It was by fighting that a king could gain not only prestige but also the land, booty and prisoners that he needed to reward his followers and so retain their loyalty. Æthelfrith's power as king of Bernicia was greatly increased by his acquisition of the richer resources of Deira, and he went on to win more wealth by successful campaigns against the Britons and the Dál Riata. Edwin not only recovered his own inheritance, Deira, but took all Æthelfrith's territories, and more besides. Oswald re-established the dominance of Bernicia, and it was in his reign that the Bernicians reached the Firth of Forth; Edinburgh fell to them in 638. This enlargement of territory under their direct control provided the early seventh-century Northumbrian kings with a secure and expanding base for their assertions of superiority over other, sometimes very distant, kingdoms. Their vulnerability to the ambitions of others, driven by similar motives, was demonstrated by Cadwallon and Penda. It is true that neither of these conquerors of Northumbria enjoyed his triumph for long, but the Northumbrian overlordships over the southern English, the Britons and the Picts were similarly short-lived. Even after his defeat of Penda, Oswiu was unable to restore for long the position his brother had briefly won south of the Humber. He gained some compensating superiority in the north, but that was lost by his son Ecgfrith, after whose death, in words of Bede that echo Virgil, the 'hopes and strength of the Anglian kingdom began to ebb and fall away' (*HE*, ii. 26). When Bede wrote, the Bernician domination of Northumbria seemed secure, but their apparently vast territory, stretching from the Humber to the Forth, included large areas of barren hill and moorland, and to make matters worse, much of the best land had been given to religious communities. In the middle of the eighth century the Northumbrians were briefly successful in extending their territory in south-west Scotland – they are reported to have taken the Kyles in 756 – but in general the eighth-century Northumbrian kings had to rely on the limited internal resources of their kingdom. This relative poverty was politically disruptive, for no king, or claimant, was rich enough to dominate his rivals as successive members of Æthelfrith's family had done in the seventh century and dynastic disputes were consequently a recurrent theme of later Northumbrian history.

In the *Ecclesiastical History*, Bede normally describes the Bernicians and Deirans collectively as Northumbrians, *Nordanhymbri*, a term that appears to have been relatively new (Myres, 1935). In earlier eighth-century texts they were called *Transhumbrana gens*, *Ultrahumbrenses*, or simply northerners, *Aquilonales*. In the late seventh century there are references to the *Humbrenses*, 'people of the Humber', a word that serves as a reminder that the system of rivers that flow into the Humber was as much a routeway as a barrier. When Edwin's family fled in 633 they went by boat, and Edwin's daughter returned in the same way when she came to marry Oswiu. In the later middle ages a normal route from southern England to York was by boat from Torksey on the Trent. It was politics as much as geography that made the Humber a frontier, and turned the *Humbrenses* into the *Nordanhymbri*.

On the south bank of the Humber lay the kingdom of Lindsey, treated throughout the seventh century as a province of either Northumbria or Mercia. The Mercians were probably regarded as originally belonging to the *Humbrenses*, for their territory included the middle Trent valley, which was as much an extension of the Humber as the rivers of Yorkshire. The heart of the Mercian kingdom is best indicated by its principal *villa regia*, Tamworth, its bishopric, Lichfield, and the monastery in which some Mercian kings were buried, Repton. The fact that Bede states that the site of the battle of 616, which was fought on the east bank of the river Idle, less than seven miles west of the Trent, was close to the boundary of the Mercians suggests that the modern, and medieval, boundary of Lindsey, which here follows the Trent, was already determined in the seventh century. The name of the Mercians, in Old English *Mierce*, means 'boundary folk' and possibly reflects their origin as a frontier group of the *Humbrenses*; and the ninth-century *Historia Brittonum* could well be right in asserting that it was Penda who first separated the kingdom of the Mercians from the kingdom of the northerners.

Penda is first mentioned in the *Chronicle* in 628 when he is said to have come to terms with the West Saxons after fighting at Cirencester. The terms are not stated but as the area round Cirencester thereafter remained under Mercian control they must have involved some West Saxon withdrawal from an area that they had conquered from the Britons some fifty years earlier (p. 43). Later in the seventh century this area formed part of the kingdom, or subkingdom, of the Hwicce, for which a bishopric was established at Worcester in about 680. The bounds of the medieval diocese of Worcester probably give a good indication of the extent of the kingdom of the Hwicce and include Cirencester. Penda's status in 628 is unclear. Little is known about earlier kings of Mercia (see Davies, 1977). Ceorl, whose daughter married Edwin, does not figure in later Mercian royal pedigrees, possibly because he belonged to a collateral branch of the royal family that was later excluded from the succession by Penda and his successors. Penda was king of the Mercians in 633 when he appears as Cadwallon's ally against Edwin, and by the time he died in 655 he had established his authority over a very large part of southern England. With the exception of Bede's reference to its eastern boundary, the limits of Mercia in the seventh century are not known for certain. Bede elsewhere indicates that the northern and southern parts of the kingdom were divided by the Trent and that the northern division was more heavily assessed for purposes of tribute collection. It is therefore likely that the medieval diocese of Lichfield, before the tenth-century transfer of Nottinghamshire to the diocese of York, gives a good general indication of the extent of the kingdom. Penda's acquisition of the kingdom of the Hwicce has already been mentioned. He later also extended his authority over the *Magonsæte* whose territory is probably indicated by the diocese of Hereford established in the late seventh century. It was ruled by kings or subkings, one of whom, Merewalh, was later said to be Penda's son, a claim that gains some support from a charter (S, 91) in which Æthelbald of Mercia describes Merewalh's daughter as a relative (Stenton, 1970, pp. 194–5). South-east of Mercia was the territory of the Middle Angles over whom Penda placed his son Peada as king, and the extent of his kingdom is probably indicated by the bishopric of the Middle Angles with its see at Leicester. Superiority over Lindsey was vigorously contested by Mercia and Northumbria for much of the seventh century but under Penda it was certainly Mercian. The kingdom of the East Angles was separated from Lindsey and the Middle Angles by the Wash and its associated fenland, but these barriers did not save it from Penda, who killed at least two East Anglian kings, Ecgric and Anna, while a third fought alongside Penda at *Winwæd*. Penda's influence also extended among the West Saxons; their king Cenwealh was married to Penda's sister and, when he repudiated her in favour of another, Penda 'deprived him of his kingdom'.

Penda's reputation and success enabled him to recruit a large army and in his final battle he is said to have had thirty legions, each commanded by a royal *dux*. Only one of these is named, Æthelhere, king of the East Angles, but the others doubtless included most if not all the rulers of the kingdoms that he had brought under his authority and, according to the *Historia Brittonum*, one of them was Cadafael, king of Gwynedd. Thanks to his victory in that battle, Oswiu took Penda's place not only as ruler of Mercia but also as overlord of the southern English. Under him Peada was made king of the southern Mercians but he was murdered in the following spring, 'by the treachery, or so it is said, of his wife' (*HE*, iii. 24), that is, Oswiu's daughter. Three years after *Winwæd* the Mercians rebelled in favour of another son of Penda, Wulfhere, who had been kept in hiding. He re-established Mercian supremacy over the southern English. London was certainly under his control for he sold its bishopric to Wine, and he was acknowledged as overlord of the East Saxons. He is the first overlord for whom there is charter evidence and we are fortunate to have a copy of an authentic charter of Frithuwold 'of the kingdom of the men of Surrey, subking of Wulfhere' which is witnessed by four subkings including Osric of the Hwicce (S, 1165; *EHD*, 54). Wulfhere's overlordship had a religious aspect and it was in Mercia that Æthelwealh, king of the South Saxons, was baptized 'at the suggestion and in the presence of Wulfhere who, when Æthelwealh came forth from the font, received him as a son' and gave him, as a token of his adoption, 'two kingdoms namely the Isle of Wight and the kingdom of the *Meonware*', that is the men of the Meon valley (*HE*, iv. 13). Almost nothing is known of Wulfhere's activity in the north apart from the fact that sometime before his death in 675 he was defeated by the Northumbrian king Ecgfrith, who consequently gained control of Lindsey.

Wulfhere's defeat may have undermined his authority in some areas, and one of the first actions of his brother and successor Æthelred, in 676, was to devastate Kent. Bede offers no explanation but it was most probably a response to Kentish rebellion against the Mercians. Three years later Æthelred regained control of Lindsey thanks to his victory at the Battle of the Trent. The increasingly abundant charter evidence suggests that after 690 Æthelred failed to maintain what overlordship he had achieved over the southern English kingdoms of Kent, and the South and West Saxons, and in 704 he designated his nephew Coenred as his successor and retired to the monastery of Bardney, where he later became abbot. Five years later Coenred also abdicated and the next Mercian king was Ceolred, Æthelred's son, who with his contemporary Osred in Northumbria was criticized by Boniface (p. 192). He died in 716 and was succeeded by Æthelbald, a grandson of Penda's brother. Æthelbald figures prominently in Felix's *Life of Guthlac* as an exile 'driven hither and thither by King Ceolred and tossed about among diverse peoples' (c. 49). He made several visits to the saint who prophesied that he would succeed to the Mercian kingship 'not as booty nor as spoil' but from the hand of God. When that prophecy was fulfilled Æthelbald set about re-establishing the Mercian supremacy (p. 100).

To the east of the Mercians lay the East Angles who, despite the astonishing richness of the royal ship-burial at Sutton Hoo (Bruce-Mitford, 1976), remain one of the most obscure of all early English

kingdoms. After their conversion a bishopric was established with its
see at Dunwich, but in 673 a second see was created at Elmham, an
arrangement that reflects the fundamental division of the East Angles
as the North and South Folk. As already mentioned, one East Anglian
king, Rædwald, was numbered among the overlords of the southern
English; his power was dramatically demonstrated when he defeated
Æthelfrith and so enabled Edwin to recover his inheritance. After
Edwin was overthrown, East Anglia tended to be dominated by the
Mercians, but the East Angles were nevertheless ruled by their own
kings, some of whom successfully defied the Mercians.

Our knowledge of early Mercian history is limited because Penda
died a pagan. In contrast Kent was the first kingdom to be converted,
and there is consequently a relative abundance of information from the
early years of the seventh century. When the Roman mission, led by
Augustine, reached Kent in 597 they found a well-established kingdom
ruled by Æthelberht, who was soon converted. He gave land in
Canterbury, where he had a palace, for the construction of a cathedral
church, and in 604 a second Kentish bishopric was established in
Rochester. The boundaries of the two bishoprics, traceable in later
medieval evidence, suggest that Æthelberht's kingdom had much the
same extent as the modern county. Æthelberht was remembered as an
overlord who, according to Bede, 'had extended the frontiers of his
kingdom as far as the boundary of the river Humber'. It was this overlordship that enabled him to sponsor a meeting between Augustine
and British bishops on the borders of the West Saxons, possibly in
modern Gloucestershire. He was also responsible for the creation of a
bishopric in London which then lay in East Saxon territory. Æthelberht's
son and successor, Eadbald, did not at first accept Christianity and
caused great offence by marrying his father's widow. He was, however,
soon converted and, although he appears to have maintained his
independence during the Northumbrian overlordship, his sister,
Edwin's widow, feared that her children were not safe from Oswald
even in Kent. The extent of Northumbrian influence in Kent cannot, in
the absence of authentic charters before 675, be assessed, but there are
several indications that Wulfhere, who was married to a Kentish
princess, had some authority there. As already suggested, the Mercian
devastation of Kent in 676 may have been provoked by a Kentish
rebellion, and in his account of this Bede refers specifically to the
destruction of Rochester, whose bishop abandoned his see to pursue

musical interests in Mercia. The first Kentish, indeed English, charter to survive in its original form, issued by Hlothhere as king of Kent in 679, makes no reference to Æthelred's overlordship and it is therefore possible that eastern Kent preserved its independence. Hlothhere was the first king of Kent since Æthelberht to have succeeded as the brother, not the son, of the preceding king; his nephew Eadric had to be content with a subordinate role and occurs in the charter of 679 as one of those consenting to the grant. Like Oswald's son Æthelwald in Northumbria, Eadric in the end opposed his uncle and encouraged the South Saxons to attack Kent. Hlothhere died of wounds he received during this conflict and Eadric succeeded him. Bede summarizes the sequel:

> Eadric ruled for a year and a half after Hlothhere and, when Eadric died, various usurpers or foreign kings (*reges dubii vel externi*) plundered the kingdom for a certain space of time until the rightful king, Wihtred, son of Egbert, established himself on the throne and freed the nation from foreign invasion by his devotion and zeal. (*HE*, iv. 26)

We know the names of two of these *reges dubii vel externi*, Oswine, who issued three charters in 689–90 concerning land in east Kent, and Swæfheard, whose charter of 690 shows that he was the son of the East Saxon king Sebbi and that Æthelred was his overlord. Although none of Æthelberht's successors could claim his extensive overlordship, some exercised authority outside Kent. Hlothhere's father, Egbert, founded the monastery of Chertsey in Surrey, but before his death its endowment was greatly enlarged by a subking of Surrey who acknowledged the overlordship of Wulfhere. It is possible that the Kentish king briefly recovered control of London after the collapse of Wulfhere's power; that at least is the implication of the reference in the Laws of Hlothhere and Eadric, who ruled Kent between 673 and 686, to the hall and reeve of the king of Kent in London.

South-west of Kent, and separated from it by the broad belt of woodland known as the Weald, lay the kingdom of the South Saxons. The first seventh-century South Saxon king whose name is known was Æthelwealh, whose baptism was sponsored by Wulfhere, but the Mercian overlordship in Sussex was soon challenged by the West Saxons. Before he became king of Wessex in 685 Cædwalla killed Æthelwealh, but he was then driven out by two South Saxon *duces*. After becoming king he returned, killed one of these *duces* and reduced the South Saxon kingdom to 'a worse state of slavery' (*HE*, iv. 15). It was presumably shortly before this that the South Saxons helped Eadric in his conflict with Hlothhere of Kent. According to Bede, 'Ine, who ruled after Cædwalla, also oppressed the province [of the South Saxons] in the same harsh way for many years' (*HE*, iv. 15). By the end of the century there was a new South Saxon king, called Nunna or Nothhelm, who issued a few charters, and was, according to the *Chronicle*, a kinsman of Ine's. The South Saxons nevertheless continued to be a potential source of trouble to the West Saxons as they had earlier been to Kent and towards the end of his reign Ine had to deal with an exiled prince called Ealdberht, who appears to have attempted to find support in Sussex. In 722 and again in 725 Ine fought against the South Saxons and on the latter occasion Ealdberht was killed.

The original name of the West Saxons was the *Gewisse*. Bede describes Cædwalla as a member of the royal family of the *Gewisse* and the first bishops of Dorchester were called bishops of the *Gewisse*. It is in connection with their conversion that Bede carefully explains that 'about this time the West Saxons, who in early days were called the *Gewisse*, received the faith' (*HE*, iii. 7). The new name, which also occurs as a title in one reliable charter of Ine, probably reflects the growing importance of the western expansion and will be used here even for the early period (Walker, 1956). When Cædwalla had control of Surrey he issued a charter as *rex Saxonum* (S, 235; *EHD*, 58), an appropriate title for a man who ruled the South Saxons as well as his own people. Had his successors been able to maintain permanent control of their eastern neighbours the name West Saxon might never have been invented. In the early seventh century the West Saxons controlled the lands south of the lower Severn as well as the middle Thames valley. These were apparently won in campaigns reported in the *Chronicle*; in 571 they are said to have taken Limbury, north of London; Aylesbury; and, in the Thames valley, Benson and Eynsham. Six years later they 'fought against the Britons and killed three kings, Conmail, Condidan and Farinmail, at the place which is called Dyrham, and they captured three of their cities, Gloucester, Cirencester and Bath.' Their control of this large area was soon challenged by the Mercians and after a battle with Penda in 628 they lost the last three places. They still had control of the middle Thames valley when the first bishopric was established at Dorchester-on-Thames in 634, but within thirty years they had abandoned Dorchester and the West

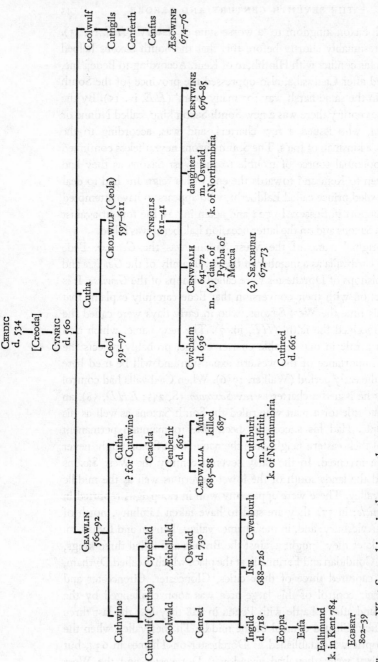

Figure 3 West Saxon kings in the seventh century

The relationships shown are those claimed in various entries in the *Chronicle*, e.g. Preface, 597, 611, 648, 685.
The names of those said to have been kings are given in capital and small capital type.
Cutha may be a short form of Cuthwine. In some versions Cynric is said to be Cerdic's son, not grandson.

Saxon see had, in effect, been transferred to Winchester. By the end of his reign Wulfhere had occupied the lands north of the Thames, and his confirmation of Frithuwold's charter to Chertsey was made in his *villa* at Thame. Under his brother, Æthelred, Dorchester was revived as a Mercian bishopric.

In the early seventh century West Saxon territory extended as far as Selwood Forest and in the south-west was probably defined by Bokerly Dyke on the modern boundary between Wiltshire and Dorset. In the middle of the seventh century they drove the Britons back to the river Parret and perhaps beyond, and also began their occupation of Dorset where, in 705, the bishopric of Sherborne was established. By then the English had already been in control of Exeter for over twenty years, as is shown by the early career of the great English missionary Wynfrith, who took the name Boniface. He was born west of Selwood in about 675 and sent as a child to a monastery near Exeter.

In the second half of the seventh century the *Chronicle*, in describing the succession of West Saxon kings, implies that they ruled over a united kingdom. There is, however, one entry earlier in the century that suggests that this had not always been the case. It occurs in the Peterborough version of the *Chronicle* under the year 626. Edwin is said to have taken revenge after the attempt to assassinate him by going to Wessex with an army and destroying five kings. This copy of the *Chronicle* ultimately derives from a northern version that included much detailed information drawn from early northern sources, and the reference to the five kings of Wessex merits respect. It would indeed be an extraordinary embellishment in an entry confected long after the event. According to Bede a similar situation existed fifty years later.

> When Cenwealh was dead (that is 672) during whose reign Leuthere had been made bishop, subkings took upon themselves the government of the kingdom (*regnum*), dividing it up and ruling for about ten years. While they were reigning Leuthere died and was succeeded by Hædde, who had been consecrated in London by Theodore. During his episcopate the subkings were conquered and removed and Cædwalla assumed the overlordship (*devictis atque amotis subregulis Caedualla suscepit imperium*). (*HE*, iv. 12)

This passage, including as it does detailed information about the episcopal succession in Wessex, deserves careful consideration because it was probably based on the information supplied by Bishop Daniel.

It has been rejected on the grounds that it is contradicted by the *Chronicle*, which describes the succession first of Cenwealh's queen, Seaxburh, itself an unusual occurrence, and a year later of Æscwine who is said to have fought Wulfhere at an unidentified site, *Biedanheafde*, and to have died in the following year. According to the *Chronicle* his successor was Centwine who is also named as a king of the West Saxons by Eddius (c. 40). Aldhelm goes further and refers to Centwine's three victories and to his *imperium* over the West Saxons (p. 14). Bede's account of this period of West Saxon history is not, however, inconsistent with these other sources. He states that subkings ruled the West Saxons for about ten years, that is until about 682. As Cædwalla only ruled for two years before his abdication in 688 there is an interval of about four years in which Centwine could have made himself master of the West Saxons. It is indeed likely that one of the consequences of Centwine's success was Cædwalla's exile. Æscwine was therefore a subking who was probably remembered because of his victory against Wulfhere, an event which places him firmly in the ten years after Cenwealh's death. This interpretation not only shows that the West Saxons were less united in the seventh century than the *Chronicle* makes them appear, it also yields another example of Bede's selectivity. He was writing ecclesiastical not secular history, and he was more interested in the bishops of the West Saxons than in their kings. He emphasized Cædwalla not because of his *imperium* – he only makes two brief references to Ine despite his long period of rule – but because of his part in the conversion of the last of the pagan English, in the Isle of Wight, and because he died at Rome very soon after his baptism on Easter Saturday 689, an event commemorated in an epitaph fully reported by Bede.

Many, but not all, of the kings who were remembered as rulers of the West Saxons, and who are therefore mentioned in the West Saxon *Chronicle*, were those who like Cædwalla and Ine acquired an *imperium* over the West Saxons. This would explain why so many of the kings who are named in that source do not seem to have been close kinsmen of their immediate predecessors. Cædwalla was at best only distantly related to either his predecessor Centwine or his successor Ine. Their kinship, as reported in the *Chronicle*, is as likely to be fictional as real. Later generations liked to think of them all as descendants of Cynric, or of Cerdic, but that does not prove that they were (Dumville, 1977b). The most satisfactory explanation of the West Saxon situation revealed by the

Chronicle is that there were several kingdoms, each with a royal family, and that the *imperium*, or overlordship, was not, in the seventh and eighth centuries, held for long by any one of the constituent dynasties.

The provinces, or kingdoms, over which these subkings ruled are never distinguished, although we may suspect that some survived as the later shires of Wessex. Some were conquered from the British during the seventh century, a continuation of the process described in the *Chronicle* under the year 577 when three British kings lost their kingdoms. The West Saxons also expanded at the expense of the English. Bede gives an unusually detailed account of one example in his description of Cædwalla's conquest of the Isle of Wight:

After Cædwalla had gained possession of the kingdom of the *Gewisse* he also captured the Isle of Wight, which until then had been entirely given up to idolatry, and endeavoured to wipe out all the natives by merciless slaughter and to replace them by inhabitants from his own kingdom, binding himself, or so it is said, by a vow, though he was not yet Christian, that if he captured the island he would give a fourth part of it and of the booty to the Lord ... among the first fruits of the island who believed and were saved were two young princes, brothers of Arwald, king of the island, who were specially crowned with God's grace. When the enemy was approaching the island they escaped by flight and crossed over into the neighbouring realm of the Jutes. They were taken to a place called *Ad Lapidam* [Stoneham?] where they thought they could remain concealed from the victorious king; but they were betrayed and condemned to death. On hearing this, Cyneberht, an abbot and priest whose monastery was not far away at a place called *Hreutford*, that is, the ford of the reed [Redbridge], came to the king who was living secretly in those parts while he recovered from the wounds which he had received during the fighting on the Isle of Wight. The abbot asked the king whether, if the boys must needs be killed, they might first be instructed in the mysteries of the Christian faith. The king agreed, so Cyneberht instructed them in the word of truth and baptized them in the fount of salvation and thus made sure of their entry into the eternal kingdom. When the executioner arrived, they gladly submitted to temporal death through which they were assured that they would pass to the eternal life of the soul. In this

way after all the kingdoms of Britain had received the faith of
Christ, the Isle of Wight received it too. (*HE*, iv. 16)

This ruthless treatment of a conquered province and its ruling dynasty
must have been repeated many times in the competition for power that
lies behind Bede's rather bland account of dynastic history. It also
confirms that what he elsewhere describes as a province (p. 40) was in
fact a kingdom. Bede's terminology is thus consistent with the interpretation of West Saxon dynastic history offered here.

Northumbria, Mercia and Wessex were therefore all overlordships.
They each consisted of a number of subkingdoms, or provinces, in
varying degrees of subjection. Some were so completely absorbed that
by the seventh century their former independence had been forgotten,
but others were ruled by men who were occasionally called kings or
subkings. The Northumbrian and Mercian overlordships were held
for most of the seventh century by the same families. Once the Mercian
overlordship had been won by Penda it was retained by his sons and
grandsons until the succession of Æthelbald in 706, and he was believed
to be a fourth-generation descendant of Penda's father. The overlordship of Northumbria was held for most of the seventh century by
the sons and grandsons of Æthelfrith, but Edwin's family were rivals
with a very powerful claim and even after his immediate kin were no
longer a threat to the Bernicians the independent traditions of Deira
could not be ignored.

These Northumbrian, Mercian and West Saxon overlords all
attempted to enlarge their resources by extending their authority well
beyond their native kingdoms. They may indeed have seen very little
difference between a neighbouring and a distant kingdom. To the
Bernicians, Lindsey must have appeared as desirable as Deira and
both were legitimate objects of ambition. The only significant difference was that the Bernicians found it more difficult to retain control
of Lindsey than of Deira. Had they been more successful we would
probably have found it less convenient to talk about the Northumbrians. The kingdoms that we recognize, and read about in the
sources of the seventh and early eighth centuries, were those that
succeeded in preserving their independence. It was East Anglian
resistance to Mercian domination that saved them from reduction to the
provincial status of the Hwicce and the *Magonsæte*.

There are some indications that other English kingdoms besides

Northumbria, Mercia and Wessex also comprised several kingdoms, but as they were not expanding in the seventh century the process of their creation cannot be so easily studied. It is, however, significant that they were all, at some time, ruled by more than one king or *dux*, and, as we have good reason to believe that Bede omitted the names and deeds of many kings who were not relevant to his theme (p. 46), it is probable that multiple kingship was a more common phenomenon in the seventh century than his narrative reveals. Sæberht of the East Saxons, who died in 616 or 617, and Wihtred of Kent, who died over a century later, were both succeeded by three sons ruling jointly, and there is another example of joint kingship among the East Saxons later in the seventh century (*HE*, ii. 5; iii. 30; v. 23). After Æthel-wealh's death the South Saxons were ruled by two *duces* and there is also a reference in Bede to a case of joint kingship among the East Angles (*HE*, iii. 18; iv. 15). There is nothing to suggest that these joint kings divided their kingdoms as though they were private property to be shared among heirs (cf. Wood, 1977) but Bede's state-ment that Ecgric ruled over part of the East Angles and that Sigehere apostasied with part of the East Saxon people suggests that they had distinct, and probably well-defined, areas over which they had rights and responsibilities. It is worth noting that even in Northumbria our sources often name a king without specifying his kingdom. Eddius, for example, simply states that the kings Ecgfrith and Ælfwine were present at the consecration of Ripon; it is a deduction from other evidence that Ælfwine ruled Deira alongside, or possibly under, his brother. The most satisfactory explanation for the shared kingship of Kent, the East Saxons and the East Angles, and for the division of the rule of the South Saxons, is that these kingdoms, normally treated as units, were in fact formed of separate provinces or districts, possibly former kingdoms, which from time to time, perhaps frequently, had their own kings, or subkings, either as a means of satisfying the am-bitions of princes, or to appease the separatist tendencies of provinces which had once been independent kingdoms. The Heptarchic king-doms were therefore probably much less united than appears in con-temporary sources, whose authors tend to be more interested in the actions of kings than subkings, and of overlords than kings.

The distinction between British and English kingdoms in the seventh century depends in large measure on whether they were ruled by British or English kings, and the contrast between British Elmet and English Deira seems clear. There are, however, some difficulties; Deira and Bernicia are both British names, even if their meaning is uncertain. On the other hand the name of the Hwicce is thought to be English, if equally obscure, but there are good reasons for thinking that its boundaries were already old when the English first gained control of that area (p. 146). What is more, the royal genealogies of the English kingdoms contain such British names as Cerdic, an English form of Ceredig or Ceretic, as the early seventh-century king of Elmet was called, and the Lindsey genealogy includes the British name Cædbæd. Most remarkable of all is the name Cædwalla, that prince of the *Gewisse* who acquired *imperium* over the West Saxons. It is a variant of the name Cadwallon, borne by the famous king of Gwynedd, who himself briefly acquired *imperium* over the northern English. There are therefore some grounds for suspecting that the Britons may have played a significant part in the making of the English kingdoms. The relatively late absorption, or conquest, of some British kingdoms by the West Saxons may explain the importance of Cerdic in their royal ideology, and it may also account for the similarity between West Saxon and Irish kingship (p. 70).

Unfortunately, Bede had a profound contempt for the Britons. He appears to have been deeply affected by the gulf of misunderstanding that separated the British and English clergy, for which Aldhelm provides vivid and independent testimony. According to Aldhelm, the clergy of Wales treated the English with what seemed to be arrogant discourtesy. They disdained to eat with them, insisted on the thorough cleansing of any vessels that they had used for eating or drinking, and even refused the customary form of greeting. Aldhelm further explains that if any Englishman went to live among the Britons, he had to undertake 40 days' penance before the British clergy would have any dealings with him (p. 484). If such behaviour towards the English clergy was characteristic, and some leading members of the Roman mission were treated in a remarkably similar manner by the Irish priest Dagan, it is hardly surprising that Augustine's meeting with the British clergy ended in failure or that Bede considered the British failure to preach the faith to the English one of their 'unspeakable crimes'. Aldhelm does, however, incidentally show that there were contacts between the English and the Britons. He must have known about, and probably participated in, feasts at which the British clergy behaved in the manner he describes and he himself wrote a letter to King Geraint of Dumnonia, addressing him as 'the most glorious Lord, wielder of the sceptre of the western kingdom' (Aldhelm, p. 480). Bede reports similar correspondence with the Picts, and wrote approvingly about contacts with the Irish; but if we were dependent on his *Ecclesiastical History* we would have no knowledge of the contacts revealed by Aldhelm's correspondence.

Although Bede clearly gives the impression that English princes would rather spend their exiles and arrange their marriages with the Picts, Scots, Irish and English than the British, he does refer to some examples of friendly relations between the British and the English. If the instances he mentions, Cadwallon's alliance with Penda and Hereric's exile in Elmet, do not show the British in a favourable light, they were probably not intended to. Bede also omits to mention Oswiu's marriage to Rhiainfellt of Rheged, and, if Edwin did spend part of his exile in Gwynedd, Bede conceals it. Penda had British allies long after Cadwallon's death, and according to Felix it was while Guthlac was in exile with the Britons that he learned 'to understand their sibilant speech' (c. 34).

Bede's attitude has also tended to obscure the close similarities between British and English society in the seventh century. In both there was a fundamental distinction between men who were free and those who were not, and in both there were men of intermediate status, the half free. Free society was hierarchical, the higher status of the noble being expressed in a higher value or price, called in English *wergeld*, 'man value', and in Welsh *galanas*, 'honour price'. This determined not only the value of a man's oath and the scale of compensation due to him for injury or less, but was also the sum that had to be paid to his family if he were killed. In both societies the fundamental unit was the family, which extended beyond the nuclear group of father, mother and children, important though that central unit was, to include more distant kinsmen. The protection of British and English freemen from violence against their persons or attacks on their households and property depended on the support of such groups of kinsmen. A man's status also depended on his wealth, in particular his wealth in land, and the maintenance of both status and landed wealth was a major concern of his family. Inheritance was a family matter; there were rules against alienating family land, and a man's sons might all expect to inherit a share of their father's property, the eldest having the main residence. Neither society was, however, fossilized. War was the main agent of change for it could result in the loss of both land and freedom, and equally both could be granted all the more readily by rulers who were successful in war. The prohibition on the alienation of family land made it difficult, if not impossible, to reward faithful service with land, but there were no such restraints on the disposal of conquered land. When Cædwalla attacked the Isle of Wight he 'endeavoured to wipe out all the natives by merciless slaughter and to replace them by inhabitants from his own kingdom'. Conquests were not always or necessarily followed by such wholesale slaughter, but they did naturally create opportunities for the victor to be generous to his followers.

An alternative or supplementary protection for an individual could be provided by a lord, and lordship was highly developed in both British and English society. The lords about whom we hear most, and who played the key roles in contemporary affairs, were naturally the great nobles with their retainers and companions, but lordship was not the exclusive preserve of the high aristocracy; in seventh-century Kent all freemen could be, and probably were, lords with their own dependants (p. 174).

Another institution common to both societies was kingship; there are indeed few discernible differences between British and English kings. In the seventh and eighth centuries they were chosen from men who claimed to be the descendants of the founders of their kingdoms. Several English examples have been given, and the same phenomenon is well evidenced in Wales. Welsh genealogists traced the ancestry of many of their rulers back to Magnus Maximus, or in Gwynedd to Cunedda from whose 'sons' the ruling dynasties of the subkingdoms of Gwynedd claimed descent. When a ruler died his successor was normally chosen from among his close kinsmen and some kings attempted to ensure that result by killing all collaterals whose claims might be considered strong. No wonder so many members of royal families lived much of their lives as exiles, or attempted to renounce their claims by entering a religious community. The power of a king, British or English, depended in large measure on the loyalty of his companions and that in turn depended on his ability to reward them. It is therefore not surprising that one of the main activities of these rulers was to lead their followers on what can reasonably be described as treasure hunts. A successful king would have no difficulty in attracting warriors from far afield. The band commemorated in the

Gododdin included men who came to the court of Mynyddog from many parts of Britain including the lands north of the Firth of Forth, Elmet, Gwynedd and Anglesey, while, according to Bede, nobles from many kingdoms (*provincia*) flocked to serve Oswine of Deira (*HE*, iii. 14).

The poets of the seventh century presented a highly idealized view of their world but, significantly, the same ideals appealed to British and to English audiences. Despite the great differences in language and metre, English and British poetry had much in common. The subject of both was the aristocratic society of kings and nobles who treasured their armour, weapons and horses and whose most highly prized virtues were courage and generosity, to poets as well as to warriors. The poems commemorate not only great fights but also feasts in which a favoured drink was mead, the Dark Age equivalent of champagne. Under its influence the heroes of the *Gododdin* behaved in much the same way as those of *Beowulf* in making proud boasts or promises which it was their ambition to fulfil and by 'earning their mead' win a glorious reputation that would, thanks to the poets, live after them.

British and English societies in the seventh century were therefore very much alike both in their structure and in the heroic ideals of their aristocracies. There was, however, another and more fundamental similarity: they had a common system of social values based on a principle of reciprocity. The implications of this principle have been briefly and clearly stated by Thomas Charles-Edwards with particular reference to English society in the seventh and eighth centuries:

The honourable man was required to maintain and continue any exchange in which he participated, whether this exchange was in itself good or evil. Thus he was expected to answer injury with injury, benefit with benefit. These exchanges could not be honourably ended within the lifetime of the participants, but an exchange of injuries could, with difficulty, be converted into an exchange of benefits. The conversion was accomplished by different forms of compensation for injury followed by the initiation of an exchange of benefits. By contrast, it was not honourable to convert an exchange of benefits into an exchange of injuries. These moral concepts were applicable to all active relationships; it was not thought possible that any active relationship could be merely neutral in value, and it was dishonourable to mix benefit and injury in one relationship. Consistency in love and hatred alike was the mark of the honourable man. Through these principles all relationships were assigned to two categories, friendship and hostility. (Charles-Edwards, 1976a, p. 180)

It was this code of conduct, this system of reciprocal obligations, that underlay the heroic ideals portrayed so vividly in the poetry. Just as Beowulf is made to declare:

'In that fray fortune granted that I might repay Hygelac with my bright sword for the treasures he had given me; he had bestowed land on me, a domain to enjoy and leave to my heirs. . . . I would always go before him in the marching host, alone in the van,' (lines 2490–7)

so many heroes in the *Gododdin* clearly regarded themselves under an obligation to fight, and if necessary to die, in return for all the hospitality and gifts they had received from the ruler on whose behalf they fought at *Catræth*. This principle of reciprocity was not, of course, confined to the British and the English; it was, and is, a common characteristic of pre-literate societies, but it was their common acceptance of it that facilitated relations between these two peoples. The fact that they both accepted this principle of reciprocal obligations as the basis of honourable conduct made it possible for them to establish friendly relations as well as the more familiar hostile ones. It was this common code of conduct that made it possible to form alliances and dynastic marriages between the British and the English, and it also made it possible for English princes to be received as exiles in British courts as easily as in English ones. We may, indeed, suspect that many of the conflicts of the seventh century were caused by breaches of this code of honour. It is, for example, likely that Edwin's conquest of Elmet was at least in part a response to the betrayal of his nephew Hereric while an exile there. Bede underlines the contrast between the treatment of Hereric and of Edwin. Æthelfrith attempted to persuade Edwin's host, Rædwald, to kill him, but Rædwald's queen 'warned him that it was in no way fitting for so great a king to sell his best friend for gold, when he was in such trouble, still less to sacrifice his own honour, which is more precious than any ornament, for the love of money'. If Edwin had spent part of his exile in Gwynedd, his attack on it may have been regarded as a particularly serious breach of the current code of conduct, and would explain the apparent ferocity of

Cadwallon's revenge. These relationships were fundamentally personal and, although there might be some pressure on an individual to continue the friendships or enmities of his father, they were inevitably weakened by the death of one party.

The campaigns and plundering expeditions reported in our sources appear superficially to be disordered conflict in which only the fittest survived, but they were in fact regulated to a remarkable extent by a code of conduct that was probably recognized by all, if disregarded by some. Just as the life of a royal or noble household was regulated by this code of conduct, so too were relations between households, and between kingdoms. There were of course breaches of the code, but the fact that some men break laws is no proof that the same laws are not regarded as binding by the majority.

Overlordships were one form of relationship between kings, British as well as English, and they implied some consent, however obtained. Bede had little direct knowledge of what overlordship meant to a subject people, but he does describe in highly emotional terms what Northumbria suffered from Cadwallon during his short rule over the Northumbria kingdoms 'not ruling them like a victorious king but ravaging them like a savage tyrant, tearing them to pieces with fearful bloodshed'. A little earlier he explains that Cadwallon,

> although a Christian by name and profession, was nevertheless a barbarian at heart and by disposition and spared neither women nor innocent children. With bestial cruelty he put all to death by torture and for a long time raged through all their land, meaning to wipe out the whole English nation from the land of Britain. (*HE*, ii. 20)

This British king appears to have behaved in much the same way as his namesake in the Isle of Wight later in the century, although the latter's conduct was not condemned by Bede, and it may be that it was similar behaviour by Oswald in Lindsey that left such a persistent and unpleasant memory at Bardney. We may indeed suspect that the contrast between the conduct of a victorious king and a savage tyrant depended very much on the status and situation of the observer. Bede's words do, however, indicate that a victorious king, once his conquest was accepted, was not expected to continue behaving like a tyrant. He might grant estates to religious communities, as Cædwalla did in the Isle of Wight, and he would certainly expect some form of regular tribute from his subject kingdom.

The basis for the collection of tribute in both English and British society was normally the same, the holding of one free family, called in English a hide. Bede was consequently able to indicate the size or resources of Anglesey and Iona in the same terms as the Isle of Wight by giving the number of family holdings in each, and Ine's laws show that the holding of a Welshman, that is a Briton under English rule, was, like that of an English freeman, assessed in hides. There is abundant evidence from Ireland and Dál Riata to show that this system was common in Celtic society, and cannot therefore be explained as an English innovation.

There are therefore many similarities between British and English society, and others can be recognized in later if not in seventh-century sources. Some were the result of English influence on the British, but others reveal ways in which the British affected their conquerors. There were also similarities due to their common Indo-European origin. In the course of time these, like other Indo-European peoples, had developed in different ways, the most obvious being linguistic, but many fundamental similarities persisted and are only concealed behind superficially different terminology. It was these similarities that facilitated the transformation of British into English society. The Britons had, however, been subjected to one major influence that did not affect the English before their migration to Britain, the authority of Rome, and before attempting to assess the British contribution to the making of England it will be desirable to consider some of the ways in which British society had been affected by four centuries of Roman rule.

3 *Britain and the Romans* *

When Caesar invaded Britain in 55 B.C. his opponents were the Belgae, a Celtic people who had themselves crossed from the continent in the recent past and seized control of the south-eastern part of the island. The people conquered by the Belgae, like the other inhabitants of Britain south of the Firth of Forth, were also Celts and they all spoke a language now called British, closely related to the language spoken in Gaul. Language is, of course, no guide to the ethnic composition of

* This section is based on Frere (1967), Rivet (1964) and, for Scotland, Duncan (1975) supplemented by the references given in the text. I am grateful to my colleagues Professor Harold Mattingly and Dr John Hind for their advice, and to Dr Richard Morris for information about churches.

a population, a truth that needs no emphasis in modern Britain or America, but whatever contribution was made to British society of the first century B.C. by earlier inhabitants of the island, it was, in Caesar's time, fundamentally Celtic. The similarity between Britain and Gaul was not limited to language but extended to their material culture, art and social organization. In this Celtic society a key role was played by *druides*, learned men with priestly and scholarly functions. Caesar describes them in Gaul, and in Ireland they may have survived the conversion to Christianity as *filidh*, men who, thanks to Christianity, lacked a priestly role but maintained their scholarly tradition and preserved poetry, genealogies and historical and geographical lore. The other dominant group in Celtic society were what Caesar called *equites*, warriors whose status was reflected in the number of their retainers or clients (Dillon and Chadwick, 1972). Archaeology has shown that forts, sometimes very large and frequently on hill-tops, were occupied at that time and it is reasonable to assume that at least some housed the courts of the kings mentioned by Caesar. Coins were used, and produced, by the Belgae and some other British rulers, and these not only confirm Caesar's reports of multiple kingship, they also suggest the existence of ephemeral overlordships. According to Caesar the Cantiaci, the people of the south-east whose name is preserved in Kent, were ruled by four kings, and their coins reveal several kings ruling at the same time and that after Caesar's withdrawal the area was ruled successively by the kings of different neighbouring kingdoms.

North of the Forth lived a people called Caledonians in the first century, but later described as the Picts. What little is known of their language, thanks to place- and personal names and to a few mysterious inscriptions, distinguishes them from their Brittonic neighbours, and so, too, do their art and their matrilineal royal succession. They may represent an earlier stratum of the island's population that was elsewhere obscured by later immigration and conquest; their ruling class, or part of it, may have been Celtic. Irish society was certainly Celtic, and the language spoken there in historic times, that is from the sixth century, appears to have preserved more archaic (i.e., Indo-European) features than British.

Caesar left no garrison in Britain, but he could claim that Roman authority had been asserted and accepted there. The Claudian invasion of A.D. 43 was in fact caused by the renunciation of that relationship and was intended to be a permanent conquest. Within forty years the

Romans controlled the greater part of the island. When, in 84, Agricola was recalled after six years as governor of the new province, the military occupation of Wales, including Anglesey, was complete, the northern frontier lay between the Forth and Clyde and he had begun offensive operations farther north. Agricola's northern forts were not, however, garrisoned for long and the legionary fortress at Inchtuthil, near Dunkeld, was never completed. By the beginning of the second century the frontier had been withdrawn to the line between the estuaries of the Tyne and Solway, and it was here that an elaborate fortification was constructed in the years 122–8. This Roman wall was more than a barrier against attack from the north, it also served as an internal division that hampered, if it did not completely prevent, concerted action by the potentially hostile natives either side of it. The experiment was not an immediate success and by 145 a turf wall was built on the line of Agricola's frontier. Eventually the combination of these two walls, both garrisoned, together with the many forts constructed in the Pennines and the Lowlands of Scotland, reduced the north Britons to a more or less reluctant submission. The frontier was breached more than once at the end of the second century by the unpacified Caledonians who, in 196, took advantage of the withdrawal of troops by the governor of Britain, Albinus, in support of his claim to be emperor. The invaders found that the Brigantes who lived south of the wall were willing allies, and there was much destruction. The restoration of the frontier was not completed until the end of 207, and it was only then that the Emperor Septimius Severus was able to launch punitive expeditions against the Caledonians. These appear to have achieved their purpose and resulted in a century of peace, making it possible to withdraw the main forces to the southern wall, and to improve the amenities of some northern forts, for example by the construction of bath-houses.

Relations with the Britons north of the wall were then apparently regulated by treaties which, to judge by similar arrangements elsewhere on the Roman frontier, would have provided for the payment of subsidies by the Romans in return for troops and a cessation of inter-tribal hostilities. The peace was supervised by small military units called *exploratores* whose functions probably included the supervision of native assemblies and markets at designated sites, or *loca*, including *Maponi*, which is probably the Clochmabenstane near the Solway; *Taba* on the Tay; and *Manavi* probably to be identified as Clackmannan, 'the stone of Manu'. As a result of Roman activity many hill-forts were abandoned and some were left unfinished, but others were still occupied, if not continuously. The most remarkable example is the forty-acre fortress of Traprain Law, about twenty miles east of Edinburgh, whose ramparts were reconstructed several times before it was finally abandoned in the early fifth century.

Roman influence in the north and in Wales was therefore predominantly military. It was through such forts as Housesteads and *Vindolanda* by the Wall, or Carnarvon with associated civilian settlements, that Roman objects and ideas passed to the natives. Some of the most significant imports were tools, including scythes, a major innovation that revolutionized methods of cattle-farming by making it easier to gather hay for winter feed, and it is likely that farmers also benefited from the peace that Rome imposed. Highland society may not have been Romanized but it was certainly affected by centuries of Roman influence and rule.

The lowland area of Britain was, in contrast, pacified within a relatively short time of the invasion, and before the end of the first century the work of civilizing the new province was well under way. A provincial capital was established at London and self-governing cities called *coloniae* had been created for veteran soldiers at *Camulodunum*, now Colchester, as early as A.D. 49, and later in the century at Lincoln (*Lindum colonia*) and Gloucester (*Glevum colonia*). The natives were organized in *civitates* which, subject to the superior authority of the Roman government, regulated their own affairs. Some of these *civitates* were based on native kingdoms existing at the time of the conquest, while others were the result of Roman reorganization. The *civitas* of the Atrebates, for example, covering what is now Berkshire with parts of Wiltshire, Hampshire and Surrey, consisted of the northern part of the territory of the Belgic kingdom of the Atrebates. The southern parts were formed into two separate *civitates*, the Belgae, with Winchester as capital, and the Regnenses, 'the people of the Regnum', the kingdom created for Rome's loyal ally King Cogidubnus. The Romans encouraged the establishment of urban centres to serve as the capitals of these *civitates*. These were sometimes on the sites of pre-Roman settlements that may have served a similar function, Leicester and Silchester are examples, but others appear to have been on new sites, replacing earlier centres; thus Chichester may well have been the Roman successor of the native 'capital' at Selsey. Some native centres replaced by new Roman towns had been in hill-forts. Thus, the capital of the Cantiaci at Canterbury appears to have been the Romanized successor of the fort at Bigbury, a mile and a half to the west, and a similar relationship has been suggested between Maiden Castle and Dorchester, between the fort on St Catherine's Hill and Winchester, and between Bagendon (in which Dobunnic coins were produced) and *Corinium Dobunnorum*, now Cirencester. Other hill-forts abandoned in the first century included Ham Hill in Somerset, to which Ilchester may have been a successor, Eddisbury in Cheshire and Bury Hill in Hampshire (Applebaum, 1972, p. 35).

Inscriptions and early lists furnish the names of eleven native capitals established in the first century of Roman rule, all distinguished by the incorporation of the name of their *civitas*:

Calleva Atrebatum	Silchester
Venta Belgarum	Winchester
Isurium Brigantum	Aldborough
Durovernum Cantiacorum	Canterbury
Ratae Coritanorum	Leicester
Viroconium Cornoviorum	Wroxeter
Corinium Dobunnorum	Cirencester
Isca Dumnoniorum	Exeter
Venta Icenorum	Caistor-by-Norwich
Noviomagus Regnensium	Chichester
Venta Silurum	Caerwent

This list is certainly incomplete for it omits the capital of the Catuvellauni, that is *Verulamium*, now St Albans, which probably lacked a tribal suffix because it had a higher status as a *municipium*. There must also have been capitals for the Durotriges, that is Dorchester, and for the Parisi, probably *Petuaria*, now Brough-on-Humber. Later subdivisions created new capitals which are also not recorded as such. Thus, before the third century the Durotriges were divided in two, with a second capital at *Lindinis*, now Ilchester.

These towns, whether established for the conquerors or the conquered, were centres of Roman influence as well as of administration and were equipped with the basic apparatus of civilized life: a water-supply, baths, temples, an amphitheatre and a forum or marketplace together with a basilica, the meeting-place of the town's governing council. The native aristocracy normally continued to live on their estates in villas or country houses but they were encouraged to build town-houses and to play an active part in urban affairs. There were also smaller settlements of merchants and craftsmen that grew up naturally in the right circumstances, most commonly in the vicinity of military garrisons, as at Housesteads and *Vindolanda*; and if these prospered sufficiently they could acquire a degree of independence and even become important enough to be considered small towns despite the absence of the regular lay-out that was characteristic of officially planned towns. Other small towns developed on sites that may have had some role as religious or market centres before the Roman conquest. In the second century such small towns appear to have been called *vici*, a word with a wide variety of meanings ranging from a part of a large household to a street or a quarter of a town (Johnson, 1975). According to a late second-century Latin writer called Festus the most important meaning of *vicus* was a closed community, and he explains that 'some *vici* have citizenship and the rights of law, but others have none of those privileges and are merely places where markets are established for trading purposes and involve the annual appointment of magistrates of the *vicus* in the same way as magistrates of the *pagus*'. In other words, most *vici* were administratively part of the *civitas* to which they belonged. There is direct evidence for the use of the term *vicus* for only two British towns outside the military zone; some second-century pottery is stamped to show that it was made in *vico Durobrivis*, that is Chesterton near Peterborough, and a theatre constructed in the second century at Brough-on-Humber had an inscription describing it as dedicated by an official of the *vicus Petuarensium* to the *civitas Parisiorum*. It is, however, likely that most if not all small towns were *vici*. Many were later fortified and were then sometimes called *castra*, a development that explains why they were often gives names like Chesterton or Chesterford by the English. There are, however, reasons for thinking that in the fourth and fifth centuries in Britain the word *vicus* was still used, if only in common speech, to describe small Roman towns, whether or not they were fortified. By the fourth century the word *civitas* was acquiring its modern sense in being applied to the 'city' and its inhabitants rather than to the territory of which it was the capital. In Gaul the *civitates* were subdivided into rural districts known as *pagi*, and it is likely that similar divisions existed in Britain although none is known by the term *pagus*. Like the *civitates*, *pagi* were commonly formed from earlier units and they may therefore have preserved traces of native kingdoms or subkingdoms which were, either before or after the Roman conquest, incorporated in larger political units. A *pagus* was not independent of its *civitas*, and must normally have contained at least one *vicus* which served as its administrative, economic and perhaps religious centre. By the fourth century several *pagi* had been raised to the status of *civitates* with former *vici* as their capitals; that is at least the implication of Gildas's assertion that there were twenty-eight *civitates* in Britain (Stevens, 1937). The names of most of the additional *civitates* are unknown but there is some evidence to suggest that *Durobrivae* was the capital of one, and Carlisle may have been the capital of another, the *Civitas Carvetii*, attested by third-century inscriptions from Old Penrith and Brougham. In the south-east the *civitas* of the Cantiaci probably consisted of two *pagi* one of which became a separate *civitas* with Rochester as its capital, much as Ilchester appears to have become capital of a *pagus* of the Durotriges which was then elevated to the status of *civitas* before the third century.

Away from the towns and military installations the most obvious and universal sign of Roman influence was the elaborate network of roads constructed to facilitate the movement of troops and administrators. Milestones erected on these roads show distances from provincial or *civitas* capitals and these can help to determine the extent of some of the political units of Roman Britain. Thus a milestone found at Thurmaston measuring a distance from *Ratis* shows that it lay in the territory of the Ratae and that the distance was measured from their capital at Leicester. It is also a milestone that indicates the elevation of *Durobrivae* to the status of a *civitas*. The boundaries of the *civitates* are, despite such clues, largely unknown. There is, however, a possibility that some may be preserved as the later boundaries of shires or dioceses, a possibility suggested by the frequency with which *vici* occur on these later bounds (Phythian-Adams, 1977b, esp. p. 77). In a tribal society in which an individual's security depended in large measure on the support of kinsmen, there were great advantages in holding markets on tribal boundaries so that people from either side could attend without having to enter territory in which they would be strangers. This consideration applied in early English society and it is, therefore, possible that early English boundaries were determined in part by the location of established markets. It is, however, possible, and perhaps more likely, that these markets existed before the Roman

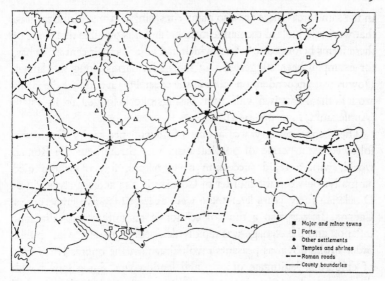

Figure 4 Roman settlements and county boundaries in south-eastern England (pp. 62–3)

Roman features are taken from the Ordnance Survey *Map of Roman Britain*, 3rd edn. The county boundaries are those existing before 1974, and for Middlesex before 1889, as used in the Domesday Geography, cf. Darby (1977, p. 381).

conquest and that their location was determined by the political structure of pre-Roman Britain. Under Roman rule such limitations on movement no longer applied but, in so far as the Romans based their *civitates* and *pagi* on earlier tribal divisions, some *vici* would be on boundaries which in their turn provided the framework for later English political and ecclesiastical organization.

One of the early results of the Roman conquest was the construction of villas, houses or groups of buildings in the Roman style (Percival, 1976). Some, like the early and elaborate villa at Eccles, near Rochester, may have been made for imperial officials or other immigrants who arrived in the wake of the army, but most were certainly built for native aristocrats who abandoned their traditional styles and adopted the new rectilinear style of their conquerors. A large number of these villas is known and many more are being discovered with the help of aerial photography. They are generally found in the lowland parts of Britain, most commonly in areas that were well suited to arable farming.

In the same areas there are also many sites, single farms or nucleations, that were still built in the native manner, and it is possible that some of these farms belonged to estates which had villas as their centres. It has, for example, been suggested that the native farms along the Sussex Downs were dependent on villas in the coastal plain and that the farms around the Newtown villa near Basingstoke belonged to its estate (Applebaum, 1972, pp. 41–4).

The second century was a time of general prosperity but it was followed by a period of political instability throughout the Roman world, with a rapid succession of emperors, few of whom died naturally. Between the murder of Gordian in 244 and the accession of Diocletian forty years later there were at least fifty-five emperors or Caesars. It was also a time of economic disruption with dramatic inflation and the coinage was rapidly debased. In parts of Gaul public order broke down as peasants revolted against the oppressive régime of emperors, legitimate or not, and landowners. Some joined with deserters to form bands of marauders: these terrorized town and country alike. The situation was made more serious by Germans and other barbarians who seized this opportunity to cross the frontier in search of plunder. Britain was fortunate to escape the worst of the crisis; its northern frontier was secure and peaceful and the sea hindered barbarian attacks. It did not, however, prevent them. A sudden and large increase in the number of coin-hoards deposited (and not recovered) after 268 suggests that there were serious disturbances in those years (Frere, 1967, pp. 188–9). As coins of the decade after 274 are scarce in Britain, many of these hoards could have been deposited rather later than their most recent coin, possibly on the eve of Carausius's rebellion in 286 (Robertson, 1974). It was at this time that several coastal sites were destroyed, including the great villa at Fishbourne. The response of the Roman government was to fortify the towns – which were until then simply defended by earthen banks, ditches and palisades – and before the end of the century a series of forts was constructed, or reconstructed along the south and east coasts, from Portchester to Brancaster south of the Wash. Some of this work, including the construction of a stone fort at Richborough, was undertaken not by the imperial government but by a rebel régime established in 286 by Carausius, commander of the Channel fleet, who in that year fled from the continent and proclaimed himself emperor of Britain. He was assassinated in 293 and shortly afterwards the imperial government recovered control, but the rebellion had provided an opportunity for uprisings in the north which necessitated extensive reconstructions not only of the frontier defences but also of some Pennine forts. The construction, at this time, of a new fort at Lancaster and reconstruction work at Chester suggests that the west coast was also being attacked, by the Irish. Like the Germans in the east, the Irish were a persistent threat requiring constant vigilance, and some time before the end of the fifth century several Irish colonies had been established along the western coasts, in south-west and north-west Wales, in Devon and Cornwall and also in what is now Argyll where they founded the kingdom of Dál Riata. Most of these Irish colonists in Britain were eventually absorbed, leaving little trace other than memorial stones, but the Irish of Dál Riata preserved their identity and when, in the ninth century, they conquered the Picts they gave their name to the new enlarged kingdom, *Scotia* or Scotland.

The emperor responsible for the reorganization after the rebellion of Carausius was Constantius Chlorus who died at York in 306, having restored the frontier and subdued the Picts. Britain then enjoyed a time of renewed prosperity. Many villas were rebuilt on a larger and more elaborate scale and it appears that some Gauls crossed the Channel to the relative security of the island. The situation was, however, transformed by the rebellion of Magnentius, a barbarian who seized power in Britain in 350 and proclaimed himself emperor of the western provinces. He probably weakened the frontier defences by with-drawing troops for his unsuccessful attempt to make good that claim and before long the Picts and Scots took advantage of the new situation. Attacks by them are reported in 360, 365 and most seriously in 367 when they were joined by Saxons in what a contemporary historian, Ammianus Marcellinus, described as a *barbarica conspiratio*. The defences were overwhelmed and at least two leading military com-manders were killed. The *exploratores* failed to give warning of the attack and were suspected of collaboration with the raiders; there were also desertions among the regular troops. The apparent support for the rebellion of Magnentius suggests that there was some discontent in Britain with the imperial government; the reprisals taken after this downfall may have induced fear but are unlikely to have increased British enthusiasm for Roman rule.

The situation was saved by very rapid action. A recent study of the account given by Ammianus Marcellinus has shown how quickly the Roman government moved (Tomlin, 1974). Before the end of the year Theodosius arrived in Britain with reinforcements that included units drawn from garrisons in north-eastern Gaul. He drove the invaders from the province, rounded up deserters and reorganized the army. Many forts in the north, but not all of them, were repaired and arrangements were made to man them with native militia. Now that bitter experience had shown that the frontier was not impregnable, and that once it was breached raiders could range throughout Britain, there was increased emphasis on the defence of individual towns. The walls of many of them were strengthened by the addition of projecting bastions from which artillery could be fired at anyone attempting to scale the walls. The army in Britain at this time included many Germans. The Romans had always used auxiliary units of barbarians but in the first and second centuries these normally served well away from their home territories and they were also under the control of Roman officers. After the crisis of the third century the barbarian element at all levels of the army grew and the defence of Britain against Saxon, that is German, raiders was largely in the hands of Germans. The two commanders killed in 367 both had German names. The presence of German troops in many parts of Britain is indicated by the discovery of late fourth-century metal buckles from leather belts which were part of the uniform worn by Late Roman officers, civilian as well as military. The fact that some of these buckles were of continental origin and had distinctive Germanic designs has led to the reasonable conclusion that at least some were worn by Germanic warriors who were transferred to Britain from the continent, first under Theodosius after the crisis of 367 and finally in the last years of the century when Stilico reorganized the defences. Buckles of this kind have been found in the Roman fort of Richborough, where a full burial of a German soldier has also been discovered, at Bradwell, and also in several of the walled towns, including London, Leicester and Winchester. The absence of such buckles from sites north of Catterick confirms the suggestion, made by C. E. Stevens (1940), that the frontier was then manned not by regular units drawn from the continent but by native levies (Hawkes and Dunning, 1961; Hawkes, 1974).

The Roman authorities may also have recruited German warriors, not organized in regular military units, to reinforce the defences of some key centres. Roman pottery decorated to suit Germanic taste has been found at Caister-by-Yarmouth, Colchester, Richborough,

Aldborough, York, Ancaster, Brancaster and Leicester, all in the east and all vulnerable to English raids. Other cemeteries near Roman towns and forts contain purely Germanic pottery that appears to be very early, some even of the late fourth century and it has been suggested that many of these burials were of German warriors (Myres, 1969, pp. 66–81; cf. Morris, 1974).

It is clear, therefore, that in the second half of the fourth century the Roman government put less trust in the frontier defences than formerly and concentrated its efforts instead on improving the defences of the towns that still flourished. By strengthening the walls they did not fundamentally change the character of the towns, but the dispersal of troops in such places was a significant change of policy, and the use of German warriors was in fact the first step towards the making of England.

Another fundamental change that occurred in the fourth century was the official acceptance of Christianity throughout the empire. The early history of this religion in Britain is very obscure. The first martyr was Alban whose cult was at *Verulamium*, but virtually nothing is known about him or the date and circumstances of his death. The church in Britain was sufficiently well organized to send three bishops and representatives of a fourth to attend a council at Arles in 314, a year after the Toleration Edict. Two were from London and York, and all probably attended as metropolitans of the four provinces into which Britain was then divided (Mann, 1961). Three British bishops also attended a council at Rimini in 359. The involvement of Britons in the wider church was not limited to attendances at councils. It was a Briton, Pelagius, who was responsible for a heresy, named Pelagianism after him, which attracted a great deal of attention, and the condemnation of St Augustine, in the early years of the fifth century.

It was not until the fourth century that buildings were specifically constructed to serve as churches and for some time after the official acceptance of Christianity worship must commonly have taken place in buildings designed for some other purpose. A set of rooms in the villa at Lullingstone in Kent was decorated with Christian wall-paintings and appears to have been set aside for Christian worship. One of the main rooms in that villa had a large pagan mosaic which the owner clearly did not consider inconsistent with his new religion. Indeed the faithful could recognize hidden Christian symbols in many pagan patterns; the four winds, for example, could be accepted as representing the four evangelists. This combination of pagan and Christian motifs is well shown in some other fourth-century mosaics from the villas of Hinton St Mary and Frampton in Dorset, in which scenes such as Bellerophon slaying the Chimaera are found alongside a depiction of Christ or a *chi rho* symbol representing him (Toynbee, 1968).

It has naturally been assumed that Christianity flourished best in the most highly Romanized part of British society, in particular in the villas and the larger towns, but there are now some indications that it was more widespread. The recent discovery in a small unwalled Roman town at Icklingham in Suffolk of a group of buildings, including what is apparently a small stone font, in a cemetery which was in use from about 350, shows that a Christian community was well established in this *vicus* during the last century of Roman rule. The Christian associations of this site are shown very clearly by the discovery close to the 'font' of a lead tank, 87 cm in diameter and 37 cm deep, decorated with a *chi rho*, symbolizing Christ. A similar tank, with *alpha* and *omega* either side of a *chi rho*, was discovered in the same field in 1939, and one with a capacity of about 16 gallons was found somewhere in Icklingham in the early eighteenth century (West and Plouviez, 1976).

These tanks are far too heavy and structurally too weak to be portable fonts, and the discovery of several on the same site suggests that they were not themselves fonts but served some as yet unrecognized ritual purpose. These tanks have a wider significance than confirming the existence of a Christian community in fourth-century Icklingham, for similar tanks have been found elsewhere, including a pair found in 1976 near Peterborough (West and Plouviez, 1976, pp. 76–9). No trace of church buildings has been found at these other sites and it has been assumed that they were associated with villas, but at least three sites, Wiggenholt, Bourton-on-the-Water and Icklingham, have proved to be small towns, and a recently discovered tank from Ashton in Northamptonshire comes from the perimeter of a major Roman site at Oundle. If there were churches at all these places it is clear that Christianity was far more deeply rooted in the life of fourth-century Britain than has sometimes been supposed.

Archaeology has vastly increased our knowledge of the material culture of Roman Britain and has made it possible to recognize many ways in which the island was physically influenced by four centuries of Roman rule. It is, however, less easy to study the impact of Rome on social institutions. As Professor Rivet neatly expressed it: 'You can dig up a villa but you cannot dig up its land tenure.' Attempts have been made to deduce tenurial systems from the physical remains of fields and farms but these necessarily depend on assumptions about Celtic society in Britain which are difficult, if not impossible, to test. Far less is known about the law of Roman Britain than about continental law. Many of the barbarian law-codes of the continent were compiled at a very early date; they were in many respects closely based on current legal practice and were written in Latin. In Britain the earliest law-codes were compiled in the seventh century and are English in both language and content. Welsh laws have some archaic Celtic features as well as clear signs of Roman and English influence, also shown in the earliest Welsh charters; they therefore have a very limited value as a guide to the legal and tenurial system of third- and fourth-century Britain or the part Rome had in shaping them. We may be certain that Roman legal procedures and concepts greatly affected British law, although we may suspect that in large areas of the province the society they regulated remained, in many respects, more Celtic than Roman.

One aspect of Roman influence on Britain that can be studied in some detail was the effect of the conquerors on the language. The situation is best summarized in the words of Professor K. Jackson:

Latin was the language of the governing classes, of civil administration and of the army, of trade, of the Christian religion, and very largely (but perhaps not entirely) of the people of the towns. The rural upper classes were bilingual; the peasantry of the Lowland Zone, who constituted the great bulk of the population, spoke British and probably knew little Latin; and the language of the Highland Zone (apart from the army and its native camp-followers) was to all intents and purposes exclusively British. (Jackson, 1953, p. 105)

This conclusion, modified but not fundamentally changed by more recent work (Mann, 1971; Hamp, 1975), was based in part on a study of the Latin words borrowed into the British language and surviving in its derivatives, Welsh, Cornish and Breton; there are some 600 in Welsh. Professor Jackson's preliminary comment on this list of loan-words is worth quoting in full:

As would be expected, the Latin words borrowed are in many cases the names of objects or ideas belonging to the higher civilization, for which the Britons could only use foreign terms because they had none of their own. Such would be *abecedarium, grammatica, papyrus, calendae, (dies) Lunae,* and so on. In other instances, though the Britons probably had a similar object, the Latin word expressed a better or at least a different variety. So *pontem* drove out *briva,* perhaps because the Roman bridge was an impressive work of engineering whereas the Celtic one would be a rough affair, and all the main bridges on roads and in cities would be of Roman construction. Often, though, it is hard to see why the Latin name should have been borrowed at all, when the Britons had a perfectly good one already; why, for instance, *piscis* should have come to be the exclusive word for 'fish' instead of the British one which was probably **escos.* (Jackson, 1953, pp. 77–8)

In attempting to assess Roman influence on Britain it is helpful to consider the political and social structure revealed by early Irish sources (p. 19). There were in sixth- and seventh-century Ireland many small kingdoms, perhaps as many as 100, each called a *túath,* meaning 'people', 'tribe', and each *túath* had a king, *rí,* a word cognate with Latin *rex.* There were larger groupings, for the king of one *túath* could also rule several others and be an overking, *ruiri,* and he in turn could make himself a king of overkings, *rí ruirech.* A king was the representative of his people, his *túath,* and the inauguration of a king involved a symbolic mating of the king and the land. The good fortune of a *túath* depended on the fortune, or 'justice', of their king. The fruits of a just king are vividly portrayed in a text called the *Last Testament of Morand* which Professor Binchy has argued is, in its earliest recension, pre-Christian. Binchy summarizes the long catalogue it contains

> of the blessings that accrue to the *túath* from *fír flathemon,* literally 'the prince's truth', or the just rule of a righteous king. Through *fír flathemon* come prosperity and fertility for man, beast and crops; the seasons are temperate, the corn grows strong and heavy, mast and fruit are abundant on the trees, cattle give milk in plenty, rivers and estuaries teem with fish; plagues, famines, and natural calamities are warded off; internal peace and victory over external enemies are guaranteed. (Binchy, 1970a, p. 10)

One of the main functions of a king was to lead his people in war and, as their representative, his victory or defeat was theirs. Over-kingships were achieved by kings who, by violence or some other means, gained the submission of other kings, and therefore of their *túatha*. The subjection was personal and did not result in the permanent incorporation of one *túath* in another; there was normally no territorial loss and each subordinate *túath* had its own king. Kings had little to do with the administration of justice or the resolution of disputes among their people. An individual's life or property was protected not by the king but by his lord, possibly but not necessarily the king, or by his family, a group consisting for most purposes of the male descendants of a common great grandfather. Rights were protected and if necessary vengeance exacted by a man's kinsmen or by his lord, who could himself be a kinsman. These relationships had a stabilizing effect in Irish society; so too did the custom of fosterage which created a bond between foster-parents and foster-children that was very close and life-long. The law was conserved by men specially learned in it, the *brithemhain*, and among the things they remembered were the elaborate procedures which included the systems of pledges and suretyship. Pledges were normally valuable objects that were intimately connected with the pledgor so that he was symbolically committing himself. The giving of a real pledge was often a preliminary to the pledging of a surety, a familiar legal procedure that was developed most remarkably in Irish law. Sureties were needed for virtually all legal actions and were of various kinds. The simplest, and most common, was that offered by an individual who undertook to pay in case of default. There was also the personal surety who might be obliged to pay with his freedom, and thirdly the *naidm* or enforcing surety who was pledged to compel the debtor to fulfil his obligations, if necessary by force. A surety could in his turn recover what was due to him by resorting to another fundamental procedure, distraint, that is the seizing or im-pounding, after due warning, of the goods or cattle of another to force him to come to law. Distraint could, of course, become a political action when taken by one king against another. Perhaps the most remarkable of all Irish legal procedures was the archaic process of fasting. This was the only remedy available against the king himself and was apparently effective because to disregard a fasting claimant meant loss of honour, or face, which no king could afford. All free men had honour, *enech*, a word that originally meant 'face', 'countenance', and a man's status was expressed in terms of his honour-price. This was the compensation due to him for offences which caused him to lose face. It also defined the limits of his legal competence, for example as an oath-helper or a surety. A man could not act as surety for more than his own honour-price, and the oath of a man of high status was of more value than, and could therefore override, the oath of an inferior.

The wealth of a king came from his own estates as well as those that belonged to the office of king. He could also expect renders from his own *túath* and if he were an overking, from other *túatha*. Like his nobles he had clients who rendered him tribute and services of various kinds. The gulf separating a king from others was clear, but not wide. A systematizing lawyer who wrote in the early eighth century prescribed the length of a king's house as 37 feet while that of a noble was to be 30 feet. Whatever force such a rule had, the fact that it could be stated at all serves as a corrective against thinking of Irish kings in anachronistically exalted terms. The retinue of a king was similarly simple: 12 were prescribed for public and 9 for private business, and the number was reduced to 3 during 'the month of sowing'. Kings were chosen from the male members of the royal family, commonly but not always from among the late king's brothers or his sons, who might be numerous thanks to the Irish custom of polygamy. The man chosen had theoretically to be unblemished, but as some of them had such names as 'the one-eyed' what counted was probably not so much bodily perfection as ability to fight. Once chosen a king would take hostages from potential rivals, as he would from subordinated *túatha*.

Ireland was at that time a coinless society; values were expressed in terms of cattle and renders were made in kind. There were no towns but there were regular fairs or assemblies at which buying and selling could occur along with traditional games and the transaction of public business.

The differences between Britain and Ireland were certainly not all due to Rome. Some Britons had begun to produce, and use, coin before Caesar's invasion, and by then there were already some very large British settlements that resembled towns. The political units in the last century B.C. were already much larger in southern Britain than they were to be in Ireland for many centuries. With the absorption of the British *toutas (the equivalent of the Old Irish *túatha*) into larger and permanent kingdoms which became *civitates*, the equivalent of a *rí túaithe* did not survive in Britain except as the personal name Tudor.

It was replaced by a word that has become the Modern Welsh *brenhin*, 'king', which has been interpreted as belonging to a complex of words and names of which Brigantes, the name of the largest British *civitas*, is best known (Binchy, 1970a, pp. 12–14; Charles-Edwards, 1974). This new term applied especially to the larger type of political units of which the Brigantes were an especially good example, comprising as they did at least twelve kingdoms, dominated by one based in the West Riding of Yorkshire.

Some of the changes wrought by the Romans are obvious: they introduced monumental architecture, well-engineered roads and regularly planned towns and farms, but they also influenced the machinery of government, for example the collection of tribute. The empire, from Syria to Gaul, was in the fourth century assessed in terms of *iuga*, or yokes, units that were applied to all sorts of land, vineyards and forest as well as the arable in which yokes would be appropriate. The survival of an assessment based on ploughs and yokes in Kent shows that it was introduced into Britain, and that at least some of the British, and later English, rulers of what had been Roman Britain retained Roman systems of assessment.

Four centuries of Roman rule transformed the basis of power in Britain, and in the fifth century the rulers of post-Roman Britain had resources very different from those available to their Irish counterparts, whether these were acquired by imperial grant or simply taken over by the successors of imperial government. It was not simply a difference of scale. Some *civitates* were indeed much larger than Irish *túatha*, but after the collapse of Roman authority in the island some of the *civitates* broke up into smaller units; the Brigantes disappeared and their place was taken by smaller kingdoms including Elmet and Rheged. The Romans did, however, impose a degree of stability on the political divisions of Britain. The Brigantes were preserved as a *civitas* until the fifth century and other *civitates* were similarly based on the units existing when the Romans conquered Britain. Despite the later subdivision of some *civitates*, the political pattern of Britain was, in effect, fossilized by Rome.

The changes in the rights and prerogatives of rulers were even more significant. The rulers of fifth-century Britain certainly retained control of what had been public land and their successors used some of it to endow churches. They also appear to have maintained some right to toll at *Salinae*, later called *Saltwic* or Droitwich by the English, and possibly at other *vici*, some of which were markets that had been institutionalized by Rome's authority.

The effect of Rome was probably more marked in the Romanized lowland zone than in the highlands, where older habits persisted. In the north, hill-forts like Traprain Law survived and in Wales the forts at Dinas Emrys and Degannwy were reoccupied in the fifth century, while the fort called Parc-y-Meirch on Dinorben was reoccupied in the fourth (Jones, 1972, pp. 289–91). The highland rulers may consequently have had an advantage over those in the lowlands when Roman imperial government was no longer able to provide the military support on which the Britons had come to rely, but the rulers of the lowlands had certainly acquired significant rights and privileges, some of which survived the turmoil of the fifth and sixth centuries to provide a basis for the authority of English kings.

The reorganization by Count Theodosius after the crisis of 367 must have appeared to contemporaries very much like the earlier achievement of Constantius after the rebellion of Carausius, with the significant difference that more emphasis was placed on the defence of individual towns and forts than on the northern frontier. Britain was, of course, threatened not only by its traditional enemies north of the wall but was under increasing pressure from across the North and Irish Seas. The use made of the reinforcements brought by Theodosius shows how seriously the threat to the east coast was taken. One reason for the growing Saxon pressure was the changing water level along the North Sea coasts of Frisia and Germany, technically known as the Dunkerque II transgression, which was reducing the amount of permanently dry land available on that coast (Roeleveld, 1974, p. 15), a gradual change which must have made the opportunities offered by Britain – for plunder or even settlement – appear ever more attractive. The Picts remained a menace and when, in 383, a military commander in Britain called Magnus Maximus proclaimed himself emperor and crossed with his forces to the continent, they seized their chance and the consequent war lasted until after his defeat and death in 388. The Picts attacked again ten years later but were repulsed by the legion then in Britain, but in 401 this was withdrawn to help meet the threat posed to the empire by Alaric and the Visigoths (Miller, 1975d).

Six years later another soldier was appointed emperor by the army in Britain and he assumed the name Constantine III. It has been reasonably suggested by the late C. E. Stevens (1957), whose account of these events is followed here, that the intention was to organize an effective defence for Britain against a barbarian invasion that appeared imminent after a massive breach of the Rhine frontier late in 406. To achieve this end Constantine crossed to the continent and secured Boulogne and other Channel ports just in time. The barbarians had apparently seized Amiens, Arras, Thérouanne and Tournai, but were persuaded, or forced, to submit to Constantine's authority. His actions even before leaving Britain make it clear that he had larger ambitions, possibly modelled on the achievement of Constantine I who had been proclaimed emperor by an army in Britain only a century earlier. Constantine III moved south to Arles, attempted to gain control of Spain, and early in 410 invaded Italy but retreated, probably after suffering a defeat. Stevens argued that these events help explain what was happening at that time in Britain. According to Zosimus, during Constantine's usurpation the Britons took up arms, and 'fighting for themselves freed the cities from the attacking barbarians'. He also reported a rebellion at that time in which the Britons freed themselves, expelled Roman officials and 'established a sovereign constitution on their own authority' (Thompson, 1977, p. 306). Stevens suggested that this revolt was against the administration of Constantine and that his officials were expelled after Constantine's withdrawal from Italy, but Thompson (1977) has alternatively suggested that this rebellion occurred in 409 before Constantine entered Italy. Zosimus also reports that the legitimate emperor Honorius sent a letter to the *civitates* of Britain, an address that agrees well with the proposed interpretation because in normal circumstances an imperial letter would have been sent to an official, not to *civitates*. According to Zosimus, Honorius urged the *civitates* of Britain to defend themselves, in effect a reaffirmation of the imperial decision made four years earlier to allow provincials to take up arms in their own defence, something hitherto prohibited by the *Lex Iulia de Vi Publica*. It may even have been this letter, or something based on it, that Gildas cited when he wrote 'the Romans urge the Britons to accustom themselves to arms and fight bravely, so as to save their liberty and life ... have their hands ... provided with bucklers, swords and spears' (c. 18). But, as the sixth-century Byzantine historian Procopius wrote, possibly on the basis of an early fifth-century source, 'The Romans, in fact, were never able to recover Britain, but it remained from that time under tyrants.'

4 *Britain after the Romans*

The letter sent by Honorius in 410 marked the end of Roman authority in Britain, and the suggestion that Roman forces returned is a fallacy based on a misinterpretation of the *Notitia Dignitatum* (Stevens, 1940). The last apparently detailed glimpse of Britain in the fifth century is provided by the *Life of St Germanus*, bishop of Auxerre, written about 480 by Constantius of Lyons. According to this, Germanus made two visits. The first was in response to an appeal by the bishops of Britain for help against the Pelagian heresy that was undermining the faith of Britain (Constantius, cc. 12–18). Germanus, accompanied by St Lupus, bishop of Troyes, crossed the Channel in 429 during winter and, after preaching widely, he took part in a great debate between Catholics and Pelagians in which the Catholics triumphed. After that he healed the blind daughter of a man described as 'of tribunician power', visited the shrine of St Alban and then led British forces against an attack by Picts and Saxons, who fled in panic at the shouts of *Alleluia* that echoed from the surrounding hills. After these adventures Germanus returned to Gaul but another British mission reported a revival of Pelagianism and asked for his help. He agreed and his second visit has been dated between 441 and 448 (c. 25–7). As Mrs Chadwick pointed out (1955, pp. 256–9) 'the second journey looks suspiciously like a duplication of the first, possibly incorporating a variant tradition'. Both were in response to appeals for help against Pelagianism, on both Germanus was accompanied by another bishop, both Channel crossings were marked by flights of demons, and on both visits children of prominent officials were miraculously healed. The second visit, in which Germanus is not said to have accomplished anything apart from the miracle, cannot provide a basis for any discussion of the situation in Britain after 440.

Better evidence that Germanus did visit Britain comes from the contemporary chronicle of Prosper of Aquitaine who was much concerned with the fight against Pelagianism. Under 429 he reports:

the Pelagian Agricola, son of the Pelagian bishop Severianus, corrupts the churches of Britain by the introduction of his doctrine; but at the suggestion of the deacon Palladius, Pope Celestine sends Germanus, bishop of Auxerre, as his own representative, and after the overthrow of the heretics, guides the Britons to the Catholic faith. (*MGH AA*, ix, p. 660; Chadwick, 1955, p. 248)

The details of this visit provided by Constantius are of very doubtful value. He names no places in Britain and clearly had only the vaguest ideas about the island. He was aware of the cult of St Alban but does not say where his shrine was. It is possible that Germanus did help the Britons win a victory – before becoming a bishop he had been a soldier (Constantius, c. 1) – but no more weight can be put on the fantastic details of that campaign than on the 'official' position of the man whose daughter he cured. The most that can be gleaned, and it comes from Prosper rather than Constantius, is that in 429 British bishops appealed to the Pope for help against Pelagianism and that Germanus, a former military officer, was sent and achieved some success.

The first and only reliable source of detailed information about Britain in the fifth and sixth centuries is Gildas, whose account merits careful consideration (p. 15). In chapter 19 he describes renewed attacks by the Irish (*Scotti*) and the Picts who differed in their habits but shared 'the same thirst for bloodshed'. When they heard that the Romans had departed and refused to return they 'became more audacious than ever, and seized the whole northern part of the land as far as the wall, to the exclusion of the inhabitants'. The incompetent defenders of the wall were overwhelmed, and it was abandoned, as were cities.

> Calamities from without were aggravated by tumults at home, because the whole country by pillagings, so frequent of this kind, was being stripped of every kind of food supply, with the exception of the relief that came from their skill in hunting. (Gildas, c. 19)

It was then that 'the miserable remnant' sent a letter to Agitius, 'a man holding high office at Rome', who may be identified as Aetius, a commander of Roman forces in the west. His third consulship was in 446, and fourth in 454, and the letter can therefore be dated within those limits.

> To Agitius, three times consul, come the groans of the Britons ... the barbarians drive us into the sea, the sea drives us upon the barbarians; by the one or other of these two modes of death we are either killed or drowned. (Gildas, c. 20)

But no help came. Meanwhile, famine drove some to submit, but others carried on the fight.

> Then for the first time, they inflicted upon the enemy, which for many years was pillaging in the land, a severe slaughter: their trust was not in man but in God. ... The enemy withdrew from our countrymen, but our countrymen withdrew not from their sins. (Gildas, c. 20)

The Irish (he here uses the word *Hiberni*) went back to their homes but returned before long while the Picts turned their attention, for the first time, 'to the furthermost parts of the island'. The period of peace and prosperity that followed was, in the eyes of Gildas, a time of corruption of secular and religious leaders (c. 21).

In these chapters Gildas appears to have been particularly concerned with northern Britain, with the Picts and Scots and the fate of the wall. In chapter 22, as Dr Molly Miller has shown (1975a), he turns to events in southern Britain beginning with some account of divine efforts to bring correction to his sinning people by 'a deadly pestilence', and also

> a rumour not unfamiliar to them, that their old enemies had already arrived, bent upon thorough destruction, and upon dwelling in the country, as had become their wont, from one end to the other. (Gildas, c. 22)

The response of the Britons was to hold a council

> to deliberate what means ought to be determined upon, as the best and safest to repel such fatal and frequent irruptions and plunderings by the nations mentioned above. At that time all members of the assembly, along with the proud tyrant, are blinded; such is the protection they find for their country (it was in fact its destruction) that those wild Saxons, of accursed name, hated by God and men, should be admitted into the island, like wolves into folds, in order to repel northern nations. (Gildas, cc. 22, 23)

There are good reasons for thinking that the original version of the *De excidio*, including the one used by Bede, may have given the name of the proud tyrant, Vortigern (Dumville, 1977a, pp. 183–4). It has often been assumed that Gildas implies that Vortigern's invitation to the Saxons came after the letter to Aetius but if, as Dr Miller has argued, Gildas only mentioned Vortigern in his account of events in southern Britain, the invitation could have been a response to any attack, or threatened attack, from the north once these had become familiar. Gildas certainly implies that Vortigern's invitation happened after the Romans had finally departed, that is 410, but there is no need to date it after the letter to Aetius, nor is there proof that it was earlier.

Gildas' account of the consequences of the invitation is clear enough, and is worth repeating at some length.

They sailed out, and at the directions of the unlucky tyrant, first fixed their dreadful talons in the eastern part of the island, as men intending to fight for the country, but more truly to assail it. To these the mother of the brood, finding that success had attended the first contingent, sends out also a larger raft-full of accomplices and curs, which sails over and joins itself to their bastard comrades. From that source, the seed of iniquity, the root of bitterness grows as a poisonous plant, worthy of our deserts, in our own soil, furnished with rugged branches and leaves. Thus the barbarians, admitted into the island, succeed in having provisions supplied them, as if they were soldiers and about to encounter, as they falsely averred, great hardships for their kind entertainers. These provisions, acquired for a length of time, closed, as the saying is, the dog's maw. They complain, again, that their monthly supplies were not copiously contributed to them, intentionally colouring their opportunities, and declare that, if larger munificence were not piled upon them, they would break the treaty and lay waste the whole of the island. They made no delay to follow up their threats with deeds. (c. 23)

Gildas then gives a vivid account of the horrors of the Saxon mutiny that devastated 'all the neighbouring cities and lands . . . until it burnt nearly the whole surface of the island, and licked the western ocean with its red and savage tongue' (Gildas, c. 24). Some Britons surrendered themselves into slavery, others fled across the sea, while others 'trusting their lives to the high hills, overhanging, precipitous, and fortified, and to dense forests and rocks of the sea, remained in their native land, though with fear' (Gildas, c. 25). This was not, however, a conquest for 'after a certain length of time the cruel robbers returned to their home', that is their territory in eastern Britain. Some Britons took up arms and challenged the invaders under the leadership of Ambrosius Aurelianus, a man of Roman race and noble birth 'whose offspring in our days have greatly degenerated from their ancestral nobleness' (Gildas, c. 25). The Britons had varying fortunes until the siege of *Mons Badonicus*, probably a hill-fort, but it cannot be identified with any confidence. Gildas associates that siege with what he calls 'almost the last great slaughter inflicted upon the rascally crew', and says it happened in the year of his birth, that is forty-three years before he wrote, making it possible to show that the battle occurred between 491 and 516 (Miller, 1975c). This victory did not mean the restoration of the former state of Britain. Gildas' description of Britain after *Mons Badonicus* is especially valuable because he is here writing of his contemporary circumstances:

> Not even at the present day are the cities of our country inhabited as formerly; deserted and dismantled, they lie neglected until now, because, although wars with foreigners have ceased, domestic wars continue. (c. 26)

As long as men remembered the tragedy and the miraculous recovery

> kings, magistrates, private persons, priests, ecclesiastics [*reges, publici, privati, sacerdotes, ecclesiastici*] severally preserved their own rank. As they died away, when an age had succeeded ignorant of that storm, and having experience only of the present quiet, all the controlling influences of truth and justice were so shaken and overturned that, not to speak of traces, not even the remembrance of them is to be found among the ranks named above

with the sole exception of a few men of noble life, monks,

> by whom my weakness is supported so as not to fall into entire ruin, by holy prayers, as by columns and serviceable supports. (c. 26)

This account by Gildas, supplemented by the few references to Britain in continental sources, is in general agreement with the archaeological evidence, which tends to be more abundant for the English than for the Britons and consists principally of grave goods, pottery from cremations and ornaments, weapons and other equipment from inhumations. There is also a small but growing number of early settlement sites (listed by Rahtz, 1976). The pottery has been systematically studied by Dr J. N. L. Myres, and his interpretation has been widely accepted. In his view the great cremation cemeteries of the east coast and the east Midlands, some of which were associated with Roman forts or towns, began to be used in the late fourth century (Myres, 1969, esp. p. 74). Some pots that are dated to the later fifth century are more widely distributed. Myres noted 'no less than twenty-seven additional sites, with no obvious relationship to the Roman administrative pattern, now appear for the first time and to anyone familiar with Romano-British affairs the whole balance has thus a different look' (p. 103 and map 4a; cf. map 8 which also shows finds of other material, in particular brooches, that have been dated to the fifth century and have a very similar distribution). The argument is developed with many refinements, including the suggestion that the absence of pottery earlier than the last quarter of the sixth century in parts of east Suffolk and most of Buckinghamshire suggests that that region long remained in British hands, while the recovery after the battle of *Badon* is recognized in the lack of sixth-century pottery in such areas as Sussex, Essex and Hertfordshire, which have all yielded fifth-century material (pp. 110–12).

The main outlines of this interpretation may prove to be right, even if its starting-point may have been put too early (Morris, 1974). But, as Myres himself acknowledges, archaeological arguments from negative evidence are especially dangerous, and the blanks on distribution maps may be filled by new discoveries. Some blanks will, however, probably remain, not because there were no burials, but because continuous ploughing has destroyed most of the evidence (p. 159). It would therefore be best, at this stage, not to press the archaeological evidence too far in tracing the changing fortunes of the English, although it would be reasonable to accept the general pattern it reveals of early settlements associated with Roman sites, especially in the east, with a more general spread thereafter.

The value of the archaeological evidence is not, however, exhausted by such a general conclusion. Two contributions in particular should be noted. First, similarities between ornaments, pottery and other objects may provide clues to the continental homes of the invaders and their later contacts. The earliest pottery and brooches found in Kent and, it must be admitted, elsewhere in England, are best paralleled in Jutland, south Scandinavia and Frisia (Myres, 1969, map 7; Hawkes, 1969, p. 190) which is some confirmation of the tradition reported by Bede that the people of Kent were of Jutish origin (*HE*, i. 15). Bede's statement is made in a famous passage in which he describes the threefold origin of the English: Angles, Saxons and Jutes. This attempt to locate them on both sides of the North Sea is to some extent supported by the archaeological evidence (Myres, 1970) although it is increasingly clear that these groups, as archaeologically defined, often overlapped; the neat distinction between Saxon and Anglian areas is not always very clear.

Another author who recognized three elements in the British population was the Byzantine Procopius who asserted that the *Angiloi*, *Frissones* and Britons, each with their own king, occupied Britain.

> So great appears the fertility of these nations, that every year vast numbers migrating thence with their wives and children go to the Franks, who colonize them in such places as seem the most desert parts of their country, and consequently claim a part of the island. Indeed, not long since, the king of the Franks, sending some of his own people on an embassy to the Emperor Justinian at Byzantium sent with them also certain of the *Angiloi*, thus making a show as though this island was also ruled by him. (Procopius, *Wars*, viii, 20)

This story of emigration from sixth-century Britain to Frankia recurs in later continental sources and archaeological traces of such a movement have been recognized (Myres, 1969, pp. 58–9, 105). That there were links between Kent and Frankia in the sixth century is shown by richly furnished sixth-century Kentish graves which, in Mrs Hawkes' words, 'are hardly ever without some Frankish imports, whether weapons, buckles, brooches, or vessels of glass or bronze, buried alongside goods of Kentish and Scandinavian manufacture' but, as she recognizes, 'the cosmopolitan appearance of these assemblages makes it difficult to interpret them simply as evidence of further Frankish immigration' (1969, p. 191). As such objects passed from hand to hand in many different ways, they are of little use in defining the ethnic origins of the people using them; burial customs, where they can be deduced, are a more reliable guide. There is, of course, good historical evidence for contact between Kent and Frankia in the sixth century in the marriage between King Æthelberht and a Frankish princess (p. 93).

Another important contribution that archaeology can make to our understanding of the relations between the English and the Britons is by revealing areas in which early English settlement was intensive. There is, for example, a remarkable concentration of English material on the south bank of the Thames below Oxford, which is in contrast with the relative scarcity of such finds a little farther south. The fact that Silchester has yielded substantial quantities of late Roman and fifth-century material and the apparent absence of early English settlement in its immediate neighbourhood may mean that, as Myres suggested (1969, p. 89), there was for a while 'some sub-Roman power centred in that area that was in a position to hold hostile barbarians at arm's length, and perhaps to employ more friendly ones to defend its northern frontiers in the Thames valley'. Martin Biddle (1976c) has made a similar suggestion for the neighbouring *civitas* of the Belgae where signs of early English settlement in the countryside are rare, but where recent discoveries at Winchester and Portchester have revealed good evidence of an English presence in both places early in the fifth century.

The interpretation of this material is clearly a highly specialized and sometimes very speculative business but, despite the uncertainties, it is possible to use it to test and supplement the account given by Gildas. The main outline that results can be briefly stated.

When the Roman imperial government relinquished its claim to rule, and any responsibility to defend, Britain, the machinery of government presumably continued for some while. There might be no troop reinforcements or coins, but there were no more imperial taxes. Many signs of the Roman past survived until Gildas' lifetime. In the sixth century the cities may not have been inhabited as formerly but they still stood, as did the wall, even though it was no longer manned. There were men who held some forms of public office or at least its name (*publici*) whether or not they had 'any regard for truth and justice'. What kinds of councils survived so late is uncertain, but a century earlier it was a council that decided to invite the Saxons and enter into some form of treaty with them. But things were changing, and invasions by the Picts, the Irish and the English accelerated the change. Towns decayed, villas were abandoned, and as Britain became less Roman it became more Celtic. Rivalries between different tribes were no longer effectively held in check and Gildas may be believed when he wrote of civil wars. The leaders in such wars were the men Gildas called kings or tyrants like Vortigern, or, in his own day, Constantine of Dumnonia. He calls Ambrosius Aurelianus a leader not a king, but in contemporary eyes the difference, if any, was probably hard to detect. We have no idea what areas Vortigern or Ambrosius ruled, but we may be sure that there were other kingdoms in their day whose rulers Gildas does not name. His letter is addressed to five: Constantine of Dumnonia, Aurelius Caninus, Votipor, tyrant of the Demetae (Dyfed), Cuneglas, and Maglocunus, 'the island dragon', that is Maelgwn of Gwynedd. One of these kings is commemorated on a famous stone from Castelldwyran in Carmarthenshire with its bilingual inscription, in Ogam *Votecorigas* and in Latin *Memoria Voteporigis Protictoris*, in which both language and title, *Protector*, echo the Roman past (Jackson, 1953, p. 169). St Patrick's *Letter to Coroticus* is contemporary evidence for another fifth-century king or chieftain, possibly of Strathclyde (Thomas, 1968, pp. 108–9).

Such rulers not only fought each other, they also had to deal with the continuing attacks by the familiar enemies of Britain, Picts, Irish and Saxons. Gildas was aware that the Irish returned to Britain after the third Pictish War described in his chapter 21, but he does not say when or where. Fifth- and sixth-century inscriptions in the Irish cipher known as Ogam are good indicators of Irish settlements and are found in several parts of western Britain: Argyll, the Isle of Man, Wales, and in Devon and Cornwall. There is also one stray inscription from Silchester (Jackson, 1953, pp. 153–4). It has been suggested that some Irish were encouraged by the Romans to settle in Wales and south-west Britain to help defend those coasts from the attacks of other Irish raiders (Jackson, 1953, pp. 153–6). Unlike the Irish of Dál Riata, who survived as a distinct political unit in south-west Scotland (p. 65), the Irish settlers in Wales, Devon and Cornwall were, in time, absorbed or driven out by native British society (Richards, 1960; Thomas, 1972).

British forces were also reinforced by German warriors. The earliest English graves suggest that they may already have been used to help defend some towns and forts in eastern Britain before the end of the fourth century. This was certainly the policy after 410. The Saxons invited by Vortigern and his council may have been employed in just such a way. We have no idea where they were stationed, or settled, beyond Gildas' statement that it was in the eastern part of the island; there is certainly no sound evidence to show that he meant Kent. There is no good reason to reject Gildas' statement that the first group came in three ships. The archaeological evidence suggests that the first arrivals were not numerous. Gildas and the archaeological evidence agree that many others followed. It is therefore possible that Vortigern and his council were responsible for a limited area, possibly the territory

of one *civitas*; there is certainly no reason to assume that they controlled large areas of eastern Britain. Gildas also says that there was a
treaty with these Saxons under which they received regular monthly
supplies, *epimenia*.

What Gildas says about the early stages of the English occupation of
Britain has far more value than the speculations of those who reject his
testimony as worthless and it seems best to accept the plain implication
of his text that Vortigern was remembered, and later execrated
(Dumville, 1977a, pp. 183–7), because he had initiated a policy that
had such disastrous results for the British. The archaeological evidence
suggests that this policy was followed in several *civitates* and Gildas
implies that, whether or not other British rulers followed Vortigern's
lead, the first Saxons were quickly joined by many others, but they all
appear to have been bound by some form of treaty until their revolt,
an event that cannot be dated. Fifth-century archaeological evidence
can certainly not make good our lack of firm dates and the best that
can be said is that sometime in the fifth century after 410, and probably
after Germanus' visit in 429, German warriors who had been recruited
to assist the defence of British *civitates*, revolted. They caused havoc
throughout Britain and then withdrew. Their activity, as described in
Gildas' chapter 25, looks very much like the invasions of Northumbria
by Cadwallon and Penda as described by Bede. According to Gildas it
was after they had returned to their territory, presumably the areas
they occupied before the revolt, that the Britons under the leadership
of Ambrosius Aurelianus took up arms and gained a victory. It was,
however, not decisive, for the Britons – Gildas calls them citizens,
cives – gained other victories before that of *Badon*. There is no
suggestion that the leader at *Badon* was Ambrosius. Gildas' comment
(c. 25) on the degeneracy of the descendants (*suboles*) of Ambrosius
suggests that more than one generation separated them from him.

The relatively stable situation described by Gildas in his own time
did not last beyond 549 for in that year western Europe, including the
British Isles, suffered from an outbreak of plague that left a terrible
trail of death, comparable with what happened almost exactly eight
centuries later (Miller, 1975c, p. 173n for the date). This plague not
only killed British leaders including Maelgwn of Gwynedd but
must also have affected the English (p. 18). Once the epidemic had sub-
sided, the survivors would have been able to take over any deserted
lands, and this is likely to have been an important stage in the expansion

of English settlements. English leaders certainly extended their territories after 550 and it may well be that the disruption caused by the plague gave them their opportunity to do so.

It was in this period that the later royal dynasties of the English were founded. If the English royal genealogies are correctly preserved so far back, the men who gave their names to the royal families, *Oiscingas* in Kent, *Wuffingas* in East Anglia and *Iclingas* in Mercia, lived in the sixth century (Dumville, 1977b, pp. 91–2). Wuffa would indeed have ruled in the last quarter, which agrees remarkably well with the dates given for him by Roger of Wendover, 571–8. We do not know the dynastic name of the West Saxon royal family but Cerdic, from whom they later traced their descent, would on this basis have flourished at the earliest in the late fifth century, and the West Saxon tradition as reported in the *Chronicle* placed him in the early sixth century. In other words, the English kingdoms at the beginning of the seventh century, including those in areas first settled by the English in the fifth century, were ruled by men whose ancestry was effectively traced back for less, sometimes very much less, than a century. The earlier names in their pedigrees, like Woden in the Anglian pedigrees, or Offa in Offa's, were symbolic rather than biological (Dumville, 1977b). The seventh-century English kingdoms were made in the sixth century, and ruled by the descendants of the men who had seized their chances then.

The transfer of power to an English king did not necessarily mean that there was widespread disruption. There were certainly battles, like that reported near Dyrham in the *Chronicle* for 577 when three British kings were killed and the English captured Gloucester, Cirencester and Bath. They were Roman centres, but six years earlier the West Saxons fought the Britons and captured four places that were less obviously Roman: Limbury, Aylesbury, Benson and Eynsham. When such centres passed from British into English control, their new rulers would naturally expect to receive the renders and services that went with them. This must also have been true in other areas, including those first settled by the English. These early settlements must have been made with the agreement of British rulers. This is implied by the relative distribution of Roman and early English finds in Sussex and in Kent (Welch, 1971, Hawkes, 1969). The same may also have been the case in the *civitates* of the Atrebates and the Belgae (p. 83). The British may possibly have been unable to prevent such settlements but their limited extent does not suggest that the English were all-powerful at first. Their role was, in fact, to help defend the British territories, and when their descendants, or others, enlarged English possessions at the expense of the British they would naturally have hoped to take over going concerns. The areas of primary settlement were no less likely to have been taken over peacefully than anywhere else.

Some relatively peaceful transfer of power is implied by the rights that later English kings had in places that had been in some sense official in Roman times. One of the public functions which appears to have been taken over by English rulers was the right to take toll both at coastal markets, like London, Fordwich and Sarre, and inland at the salt *wīc* of Worcestershire and Cheshire (p. 225). The name Droitwich, although not recorded until the fourteenth century, probably contains, as Ekwall suggested, the element *dryhten*, an archaic word meaning 'lord' and later usually reserved for God; it was certainly a place in which Mercian kings had special rights from a very early date (Sawyer, 1977, pp. 147–8). Sarre, on the Wantsum Channel which then divided Thanet from the rest of Kent, was, as Mrs Hawkes has pointed out, an obvious place for a toll station for it was 'strategically placed where vessels using this inner route had to put in to wait on the double tide, and where traffic on the Roman Road passed over to Thanet by ferry'. She continues:

It is the site of one of the largest and most remarkable cemeteries in Kent: it is set apart from the majority by virtue of the high proportion of male burials with weapons, including numerous swords, far in excess of what is normal even in aristocratic cemeteries such as Bifrons. The only truly comparable case in Kent is the cemetery at Buckland, behind Dover. Here, then, we have two unusually well-armed communities in strategic positions close to known ports, and it is very tempting to think of them as representing, for the 6th/7th century, the military establishments which the king's port reeves must surely have maintained for the execution of their duties in the eighth. The implication is that both ports were already functioning as royal toll stations at latest by the seventh century, if not already in the sixth. The number of Frankish wine bottles and jugs buried with the men at Sarre is another abnormality, and one which conjures up a vivid picture of the king's customs officers regaling themselves with some of the imported French wine which came into Kent through this port of Sarre. (Hawkes, 1969, pp. 191–2)

It is significant that the Kentish system of assessment in the seventh and later centuries was unlike that found in other parts of England; it appears to be a survival of a Roman system (p. 73).

The English did not only take over such centres of Roman government as Gloucester, Cirencester and Bath, they also acquired places like Aylesbury and Benson that were still royal estates in the eleventh century and served then, as they had done in Roman and probably pre-Roman times, as centres for the collection of renders and services. This helps to explain the many points of similarity between the territories dependent on, or 'lying to', such king's *tūn* and the shires of Scotland and Northumbria, or the commotes of Wales (Barrow, 1973; Jones, 1976).

In medieval Wales a payment known as Commorth or *Treth Calan Mai* (the Aid or Tribute of the First of May) was, in some lordships, paid in cattle every two or three years at the time the herds were moved to their summer pastures. The same render, sometimes commuted to a money payment, appears in the Welsh Marches under various names, Cowgeld, Horngeld, Neatgeld. It also occurs in North Lancashire as *Beltancu* and throughout the north as Cornage or Horngeld, a payment in cattle every three years (Rees, 1963, pp. 157–62). In Scotland a similar payment was called Cain (Barrow, 1969, pp. 18–20). Another pastoral render, distinct from Cornage, was *metreth*; the word normally occurs in the formula *vacca de metreth*, which is tautologous, for *metreth* means, according to William Rees (1963, p. 161), 'cow-tribute', and is Celtic in origin. Other services due in northern England, including the responsibility of building, enclosing and victualling the lord's hall for hunting, have close parallels in the Welsh Laws (Rees, 1963, pp. 162–4), and foresters were numbered among the agents of lords who could claim billeting, a custom also paralleled in Wales. The services due from some southern English estates in the ninth century, known only because exemptions from them were granted by charters, show other ways in which English and British societies were alike. In 843 or 844 a Berkshire estate, at Pangbourne, was freed 'from the entertainment of ealdormen and from that burden that we call in Saxon *fæstingmen*; neither are there to be sent there men who bear hawks or falcons, or lead dogs or horses' (S, 1271; *EHD*, 87; cf. S, 186). These obligations are very similar to the *gwestfa*, 'feast or entertainment', that a Welsh prince could demand when on a progress. The Welsh evidence is late, but clear, and a thirteenth-century jury from west Wales reported that:

> each *Westfa* used to feed the lord and his household and bodyguard, the huntsmen with their dogs and the falconers with their birds at their coming, which service is called *Westfa*. (Rees, 1963, p. 157)

The existence in twelfth-century Scotland of a similar obligation to feed a lord, known as 'waiting' or 'coneveth', shows that this, like some other institutions briefly discussed here, was once common throughout Britain (Barrow, 1969, pp. 21–2).

These similarities do not prove that the English took over British institutions with little change; it is possible that their societies were very similar before they met. There is, however, one institution that the English appear to have adopted in Britain, the festival of Lammas, celebrated on 1 August. Its date and its name, which means 'loaf-mass', show that it was connected with the beginning of the harvest season. It was, indeed, a form of the Celtic festival called in Irish *Lughnasa*, celebrated at that time of the year, and its Celtic origin is clearly proved by the absence of a similar festival in other Germanic parts of Europe (MacNeill, 1962, esp. p. 1).

The English certainly made one dramatic and fairly complete change in Britain; they replaced British speech in the areas they controlled by their own language, English. We do not know how long the process took, but its completeness has effectively concealed the antiquity of many features of early English government and society. The relationship between the two languages is best described in the words of Professor Kenneth Jackson.

> Taking together all the evidence on the linguistic relations of Britons and Saxons, though it is of course impossible to generalize, we do seem to observe the following features: the Britons learned the language of their conquerors, and they acquired its sound-system and vocabulary very completely, their own phonetics having no discernible effect on the new language and their own vocabulary very little. There must have been at least some degree of close relationship and intermarriage, through which British personal names were taken into Anglo-Saxon. All this suggests a bilingual stage, when the Britons knew both Anglo-Saxon and British, though

it is not likely to have been a long one, especially in the East; and it is not probable that the conquerors learned much of the language of the conquered. Of the many British place-names which became English, some did so through the mouths of the bilingual Britons . . . others were taken over by the uncomprehending monoglot Saxons. . . . The whole picture is, at any rate, totally incompatible with the old theory of the complete extermination of the British inhabitants. (1953, pp. 245–6)

Jackson drew particular attention to the few cases of names which were plurals in both British and English speech. Two, Dover and Lympne, were on the coast of Kent.

It has been objected, among others by Dr Margaret Gelling, that the linguistic evidence is incompatible with the view that the English conquest amounted to little more than a transfer of lordship.

Neither the Roman occupation of the first century A.D., which brought a Latin-speaking administrative class to Britain, nor the Norman Conquest of 1066, which brought a new French-speaking aristocracy, caused a major replacement of the pre-existing place-names by new place-names in the languages of the conquerors. It seems likely that a replacement of the kind which happened after the end of the Roman period . . . occurs only when the newcomers are farmers rather than, or as well as, overlords. (Gelling, 1976, p. 811)

It is no doubt true that in some parts of England many of them settled and became farmers, but the replacement of British by English speech occurred even in those areas where the English can never have been more than a tiny minority of the population. In Bernicia there is little evidence of the presence of English settlers: only ten pagan English cemeteries are known and they contain few, and poorly furnished, burials. In both Bernicia and Deira there are clear indications that a substantial British population survived the English conquest: native burial customs persisted and there is a significant number of Celtic place-names (Faull, 1977). British speech may have survived longer in Northumbria than in many other parts of England but there is no evidence for its general survival into the ninth century. Professor Jackson is cautious enough to admit the possibility that it may have survived in some places but he emphasizes that there is good evidence for its virtually complete disappearance in Dumfriesshire (1963, pp. 79

84). The situation was complicated in the north-west by the re-introduction of British speech into northern Cumberland in the tenth century where it may have survived until the twelfth century (Jackson, 1963, p. 84). The disappearance of British speech in large areas of Northumbria proves that this particular linguistic change cannot be taken as a measure of ethnic change. There need not have been much or any English blood in many of the men and women of the north who spoke English in the ninth century and gave most places their English names. In parts of eastern Britain the number of known English graves shows that there must have been many settlers. The apparent desertion of settlement-sites in Jutland and Frisia in the fifth century is consistent with the large-scale migration which was believed in Bede's time to have left Angeln empty (*HE*, i. 15). The linguistic evidence from northern England should, however, serve as a warning against assuming that there were few British survivors in areas of relatively dense English settlement. If English speech replaced British where there were few English, it was even more likely to do so in areas where there were many. It is therefore possible that significant numbers of Britons survived the English occupation of Kent, East Anglia and similar areas and that, with the loss of their language, they have left virtually no trace.

5 *The conversion of the English*

Gildas shows that in his day the British church was well established and flourishing, although he considered it was desperately in need of reform. We do not know the fate of the church in areas then under English control, but such bishoprics as London, Lincoln and York are unlikely to have survived the great fifth-century revolt. The presence of bishops, and perhaps of other clergy, would not have been tolerated by the pagan English, faced as they were by Christian enemies. In areas that remained British the church probably continued in some form. Bede shows that the cult of St Alban survived at *Verulamium*, and we have no reason to think that it was unique. A recent survey of the rural churches of medieval Essex has shown that almost half were connected in some way with Roman sites; some incorporate Roman building material, Roman finds have been found in some churchyards or nearby and a few, like Alphamstone, East Mersea and Brightlingsea, lie directly over Roman buildings (Rodwell and Rodwell, 1977). Elsewhere, as at

Frocester and Woodchester in Gloucestershire, Widford in Oxfordshire and Flawford in Nottinghamshire, medieval churches stand on
villa sites, Lullingstone church in Kent may be directly over a Roman
mausoleum, and a tessellated pavement lies underneath the nave of
Wimborne minster in Dorset (Morris, 1978). Evidence like this may
mean no more than that settlements continued, or were re-established,
on these sites and that churches were later constructed on Roman
foundations which would have made the land inconvenient for cultivation, or were built of materials found nearby. In some places, such
as Lullingstone or Flawford, where the walls of a pre-Conquest church
exactly follow the alignment of the underlying Roman building, some
structural, and possibly some functional, continuity is possible. The
occurrence in Norfolk and Kent of the place-name Eccles, from Late
Latin *eclesia*, shows that some churches did survive long enough to be
given distinctive names by the English, whether they learned the word
directly from Latin speakers or first heard it as a British word, the
predecessor of Modern Welsh *eglwys* (Cameron, 1968; Gelling, 1977).
Other Eccles names tend to be found in areas that were taken over by
the English relatively late (map, p. 24). Some probably refer to churches
like those which had recently been abandoned by the British when
they were granted to Ripon shortly before 680 (p. 23).

The Britons made no attempt to convert the English, and heavy
penances were prescribed for Britons who helped their pagan enemies
(Bieler, 1963, pp. 68–9). It was their failure to 'preach the faith to the
Saxons and Angles who inhabit Britain with them' that was, in Bede's
eyes, one of their greatest crimes (*HE*, i. 22). The British church even
remained aloof when friendly relations were established between
British and English rulers; Penda's alliance with Cadwallon does not
seem to have encouraged the British clergy to undertake missionary
work among their allies. The English did, however, have contacts with
other peoples, some of whom had been recently converted to Christianity and were, for different reasons, willing to undertake missionary
work among the English. Æthelberht's marriage to a Frankish
princess, Oswald's exile in Iona and Sigeberht's in Gaul are contacts
mentioned by Bede, and there were probably more.

In seventh-century Ireland voluntary exile undertaken as an act of
renunciation converted what had been a punishment into a form of
ascetism that gave the *deorad Dé*, 'exile of God', the highest moral
status as, in effect, God's representative on earth, and such men eagerly

undertook God's work abroad (Charles-Edwards, 1976b). Bede devotes some space to St Fursey, an Irishman who established a monastery at Burgh Castle in East Anglia in about 630 but later went on to Gaul. Irish exiles also went direct to Gaul. Columbanus who arrived there in about 590 is the most famous, but there were others and their activity may well have led to some movement of Christians from Gaul to Britain, much as Fursey had crossed the other way. One missionary from Gaul mentioned by Bede was Felix of Burgundy who was invited by Sigeberht of East Anglia and became the first bishop of that kingdom.

The contacts between Britain and Gaul emphasized by Bede were connected with the mission sent by Pope Gregory but, as both Bede and Gregory make clear, there were contacts before Augustine arrived in Kent. It is in fact likely that the papal mission was a consequence of earlier Frankish interest in Kent. Æthelberht married Bertha, daughter of the Frankish king Charibert, sometime before 588 and according to Bede the marriage was on condition

> that she be allowed to practise her faith and religion unhindered, with a bishop named Liudhard whom they had provided for her to support her faith. (*HE*, i. 25)

The letters written by Gregory before his mission reached England show that he had received reports that

> the English nation by the will of God wishes to become christian but the priests who are in the neighbourhood are negligent and fail to enflame their desire by encouragement. (*EHD*, 162)

Gregory's knowledge of the situation in Britain probably came from the Franks who accompanied Bertha. Frankish rulers presumably realized that the connection created by Bertha's marriage would be greatly strengthened by the conversion of her husband. Even if, as seems likely, Augustine was made a bishop before he reached England, the missionaries would have been under the ecclesiastical jurisdiction of a Frankish archbishop; Gregory was not attempting to subvert the established order of the church. After 601, when Augustine became an archbishop, and Rome had direct responsibility over the English church, it was still considered an extension of the church in Gaul. When a great reform council was held in Paris in 614, there were among the twelve metropolitans and sixty bishops attending at least two representatives from England: Justus, bishop of Rochester, and Peter, abbot of Canterbury (*MGH Legum*, III. i. 192).

The Roman mission appeared initially to be a great success and by 604 bishoprics had been established at Canterbury, Rochester and London. This achievement depended, however, on the power of Æthelberht, and his death in 616 was followed by a pagan reaction which caused the bishops of London and Rochester to flee to Gaul. The conversion of Æthelberht's son and successor came in time to save the continuity of the church in Canterbury and it was from Kent that Paulinus was sent to King Edwin in Northumbria. He preached, baptized multitudes and built churches both there and in Lindsey; he also made some beginnings in East Anglia, but he, too, was dependent on a king, and when Edwin died Paulinus fled. The Roman mission in the north collapsed.

The Irish proved to be more effective missionaries, possibly because the conduct of these 'exiles of God' had a greater appeal to English kings than men whose traditions derived more directly from Rome. The obstinate refusal of these holy Irishmen to conform to the accepted conduct of English society distinguished them as men of power, and success made their appeal hard to resist. Bede presents Aidán as a 'great contrast to our modern slothfulness' but he must have seemed extraordinarily different from the secular nobles, and Roman prelates, of his own day.

> And if it happened, as it rarely did, that he was summoned to feast with the king, he went with one or two of his clergy, and, after taking a little food, he hurried away either to read with his people or to pray. . . . Neither respect nor fear made him keep silence about the sins of the rich, but he would correct them with stern rebuke. He would never give money to powerful men of the world but only food on such occasions as he entertained them; on the contrary he distributed gifts of money which he received from the rich either, as we have said, for the use of the poor or for the redemption of those who had been unjustly sold into slavery. (*HE*, iii. 5)

Aidán rarely travelled on horseback but king Oswine of Deira gave him a 'royal horse' so that 'he could ride if he had to cross a river or if any other urgent necessity compelled him'. When the King heard that Aidán had given it to a beggar he was naturally surprised and pointed out that 'we have many less valuable horses or other things which would have been good enough to give to the poor'. Aidán's rebuke, 'Surely this son of a mare is not dearer to you than that son of God?', so moved the King that he gave his sword to a thegn and prostrating himself before Aidán promised never to question his gifts to the 'sons of God'. 'When the bishop saw this he was greatly alarmed', and he had good cause to be. The rejection of accepted norms of gift-exchange was appropriate for 'holy men', not for kings.

English churchmen trained by Aidán learnt a similar contempt for the material things, and the powers, of this world. Chad preferred to go on foot rather than on horseback and was reluctant to obey Archbishop Theodore's command to ride when undertaking long journeys:

> but Chad showed much hesitation, for he was deeply devoted to this religious exercise, so the archbishop lifted him on to the horse with his own hands since he knew him to be a man of great sanctity and he determined to compel him to ride a horse when necessity arose. (*HE*, iv. 3)

Chad's brother Cedd behaved with dramatic boldness when he rebuked Sigeberht, king of the East Angles, for disobeying his order not to enter the house of an excommunicated noble, or to take food with him. Cedd met the King as he was leaving the forbidden house.

> When the king saw him, he leapt from his horse and fell trembling at the bishop's feet, asking his pardon. The bishop, who was also on horseback, alighted too. In his anger he touched the prostrate king with his staff which he was holding in his hand, and, exercising his episcopal authority, he uttered these words, 'I declare to you that, because you were unwilling to avoid the house of this man who is lost and damned, you will meet your death in this very house.' (*HE*, iii. 22)

Sigeberht was duly killed, by his own kinsmen, for

> they were angry with the king and hated him because he was too ready to pardon his enemies, calmly forgiving them for the wrongs they had done him, as soon as they asked him pardon.

The Christian message did not find ready acceptance in a society in which an eye, or suitable compensation, had to be given for an eye.

As Mr James Campbell has pointed out (1971, pp. 23–4), the conduct of Aidán and Cedd has close parallels with that reported by Jonas in his *Life of Columbanus*. This holy man's refusal to bless the illegitimate children of King Theuderic was marked by a clap of thunder. When Queen Brunechildis, Theuderic's grandmother, and a supporter of the 'Roman cause' – she was one of those thanked by Pope Gregory for helping his mission to England – attempted to control the Irish monks of Columbanus with regulations foreshadowing those later imposed in England by Archbishop Theodore, Columbanus used the only process that was, in Irish law, available against a king, 'fasting'. Theuderic sent him 'food and drink prepared with royal magnificence' but Columbanus refused it declaring, 'It is written "The Most High is not pleased with the offerings of the wicked"' and the dishes broke, spilling the food and drink on to the ground. The queen and her grandson, according to Jonas, begged forgiveness, but their continuing hostility led Columbanus to prophesy the destruction of their kingdom and family (Jonas, c. 32).

Very little is known about English paganism. It certainly had idols of wood or metal, and in times of distress, as when plague struck, men resorted to incantations and amulets. The miraculous release of a prisoner from his chains was thought to be due to magic spells. There was apparently some hierarchy of pagan priests, some of whom were subject to taboos. 'A chief priest of their religion was not allowed to carry arms or to ride except on a mare' (*HE*, ii. 13) and when Coifi, who was a chief priest, set out to defile the temple at Goodmanham he armed himself with sword and spear and mounted a stallion. 'The common people who saw him thought he was mad.' A few place-names have pagan associations: some include the names of gods, like Tiw in the Surrey place-name Tuesley, and others refer to a shrine or sanctuary, like Harrow in Middlesex, originally *hearg*, 'a temple'. The English names of days from Tuesday to Friday derive from the names of gods and some of the pre-Christian names of months as listed by Bede had some pagan significance, including *Eosturmonath*, from which Easter comes (Gelling, 1961 and 1973; Mayr-Harting, 1972, pp. 22–30).

The Christian missionaries had their own magic writings and strange rituals but they had more effective ways of appealing to kings. As kinless strangers, missionaries depended on kings for their protection and it was to these rulers that their mission was particularly addressed. Kings doubtless shared with their people that preoccupation with the after-life which is implied by the elaborate burial customs revealed by archaeologists. They also had a more immediate and earthly interest in power, which was thought to depend on divine support. Christianity had much to offer on both counts: the promise of eternal life and many proofs that the God of the Christians was more powerful than other gods. Kings, including overlords, soon saw the advantages of this new religion, and by 660 almost all English kingdoms had accepted it and had their own bishops.

Within the English church there were significant differences of discipline and observance. Some of the differences were instantly obvious, as between Irish and Roman tonsures. There was a more fundamental disagreement over the method of calculating the date of Easter, the principal feast of the Christian year, but that was resolved in 664 at a council at Whitby summoned by the Northumbrian king. Five years later the pope sent a new archbishop, Theodore, to bring Roman order to the English church. He did this by means of councils of bishops, at the first of which, held at Hertford in 672, it was ruled, among other things, that bishops should be content with the government of the people committed to their charge and not interfere in the dioceses of other bishops, and that monks and clergy should not wander from place to place without permission. Some of the churchmen who belonged to the Irish tradition accepted the new order and conformed, while others went abroad, to Ireland or elsewhere, but the English church long retained signs of the Irish influence which was so important in shaping it – its art, scripts and penitential discipline – and many monasteries continued to be under more of an Irish than a Roman discipline, to Bede's dismay (p. 237).

Theodore had also to contend with a Gallic attitude to episcopal authority. His attempt to create smaller dioceses by division was opposed by bishops like Wilfrid who belonged to the Gallic tradition in which bishops were expected to be powerful, rich and to preside over their dioceses with great splendour. Wilfrid himself, as a young man, spent three years in the *familia* of Annemundus, bishop of Lyons, and for his own episcopal consecration went to Gaul with

a force of men as well as a large sum of money, so as to enable him to enter Gaul in great state. Here at once there took place a large meeting consisting of no less than twelve catholic bishops, one of whom was bishop Agilbert (of Paris). When they heard the testimony to his faith they all joyfully consecrated him publicly before all the people with great state, and raising him aloft in accordance with their custom as he sat in the golden chair, the bishops unaided and alone carried him with their own hands into the oratory, chanting hymns and songs in chorus. (Eddius, c. 12)

Agilbert had earlier been bishop of the West Saxons but King Cenwealh

who knew only the Saxon language, grew tired of his barbarous speech and foisted upon the kingdom a bishop who had been consecrated in Gaul but who spoke the king's tongue. He divided his kingdom into two dioceses and gave Wine an episcopal seat in the city of *Venta* which the Saxons call *Wintancæstir*. Agilbert was deeply offended because the king had done this without consulting him and returned to Gaul, where he accepted the bishopric of Paris and there died 'being old and full of days'. (*HE*, iii. 7)

At the Synod of Hertford a proposal to increase the number of bishoprics was discussed but no decision was reached. Wilfrid was not present and was represented by proctors, but there were others who shared his views. Theodore had to wait for opportunities to implement his policy, and when Wilfrid went into exile in 678 he divided his diocese into three and later, in 681, into five: Lindisfarne, York, Ripon, Hexham and, for the Picts, Abercorn (Mayr-Harting, 1972, pp. 130–9).

The English church was thus slowly brought into conformity with Roman tradition. English churchmen did, however, exhibit a missionary zeal that owed much to the example of the Irish 'exiles of God' and, almost before Christianity was secure in England, English missionaries had begun their work among the still pagan Germans on the continent.

II

The making
of one kingdom

1 *The Mercian hegemony*

The hegemony established by Penda and enlarged by his sons was not
finally destroyed until the ninth century, and then as much by Viking
invaders as by rival English rulers. In those two centuries there were, of
course, many changes, especially in the frontier areas; Kent and East
Anglia vigorously resisted Mercian overlordship, and the middle
Thames valley was debatable land in which the boundary frequently
changed with the fluctuating fortunes of the West Saxons over whom
the Mercians were never able to assert their authority for long. From
time to time a Mercian king could claim to be overlord of all the southern English kingdoms. That was the situation when Bede completed
his *Ecclesiastical History*. He ended it with a survey of the state of
Britain in 731 in which he listed the bishops of the southern kingdoms
and then noted that 'all these kingdoms and the other southern kingdoms
which reach right up to the Humber, together with their various kings,
are subject to Æthelbald, king of Mercia'. Offa had a similarly extensive
authority in the years before his death in 796 but none of his successors
could claim so much, and from the accession of Egbert as king of the
West Saxons in 802, Wessex permanently escaped Mercian control.

Our knowledge of the southern kingdoms of Kent, Sussex and
Wessex in those years is fuller than for others, thanks largely to the
relative abundance of charters surviving from them, and the eventual
success of the West Saxons has helped to preserve their historical tra-

ditions. The lack of any early charters or chronicles for East Anglia, Lindsey and most other kingdoms dominated by Mercia, or even for Mercia itself, apart from its subkingdom of the Hwicce, means that most details of Mercian history will always be obscure. The surviving charters are in fact the most valuable source of information. The titles charters give to kings show what claims were made for them; the lands or rights that were granted, and the people or churches to whom grants were made, are a good indication of the extent of the authority of royal donors; and the witness lists reveal who attended their courts. The charters of Æthelbald, for example, confirm Bede's statement about the extent of his power. An original, dated 736, describes him as 'king not only of the Mercians but also of all provinces which are called by the general name *Sutangli*', that is the South English, and his subscription made the even larger claim that he was *rex Britanniae* (S, 89; *EHD*, 67). This charter granted land by the river Stour in Worcestershire, in the territory of the Hwicce, and one of the witnesses was Æthelric, *subregulus et comes*, 'underking and companion of the most glorious king Æthelbald'. Some of the charters attributed to Æthelbald are spurious, but the genuine texts include grants of land in Middlesex as well as in Herefordshire, Gloucestershire, Warwickshire and Worcestershire, and his authority in London is shown by a series of charters issued between 732 and 748 remitting toll on ships at that port, the beneficiaries including Worcester Cathedral, St Paul's in London, and several Kentish churches. In a charter issued shortly before his death he granted land in north Wessex, near Tockenham in Wiltshire, and this was witnessed by Cynewulf, who had very recently succeeded as West Saxon king, and by several of his nobles, secular and clerical, including the bishops of Winchester and Sherborne. His control of the middle Thames valley was shown by his gift of the Berkshire monastery of Cookham to Christ Church, Canterbury. He also appears to have maintained peaceful relations with the Welsh; at least, no conflict is reported between the English and the Welsh in his reign after battles in or about 722 noted in the Welsh annals (Lloyd, 1939, p. 197). His success as a ruler made it possible for Archbishop Boniface, who deplored many aspects of his life and rule, to say, in a letter of 746–7, that he had heard 'that you repress robbery and wrongdoing, perjury, and rapine with a strong hand, that you are famed as a defender of widows and of the poor, and that you have established peace within your kingdom' (*EHD*, 177).

Æthelbald's assassination by his household at Seckington, near Tamworth, in 756 or 757 was followed by civil war in which Beornred was briefly successful; but he was quickly overthrown by Offa who was at best a distant kinsman of Æthelbald – both Æthelbald and Offa traced their descent from a brother of Penda. Very little is known about the first part of Offa's reign and there is no warrant for assuming that he quickly acquired the extensive authority that he certainly had in the ten years before his death in 796. It does appear, however, that his over-lordship was acknowledged in Kent and in London soon after his accession. Before 764 he confirmed one of Æthelbald's charters to Minster in Thanet granting freedom from toll for one ship at London (S, 143) and his first charter to survive in contemporary form was a grant, dated 767, of land near Harrow in Middlesex in exchange for land that possibly lay in the Chilterns (S, 106). It was only witnessed by three bishops but the fact that Iænberht, archbishop of Canterbury, was one of them (the others were of Leicester and Lichfield) suggests that he already had some authority in Kent. Two later grants to Iænberht, of land in Kent, dated 774, in which Offa is described as *rex Anglorum*, were written in the tenth century and therefore cannot be used as evidence for contemporary usage (S, 110–11; cf. Stenton, 1970, pp. 60–1). By the end of his reign, his court was certainly attended by bishops from all parts of England south of the Humber, and already by 781 he presided over a synod attended by bishops from Kent, Sussex, Wessex and East Anglia as well as from the Mercian sees of Lichfield, Worcester, Hereford and London. These late texts are in marked con-trast to the charter of 767 with its three bishops, or even a grant of land in Gloucestershire in 779 (S, 114) in which the only bishops witnessing were from Mercian sees. It is therefore possible that Offa initially had little authority outside Mercia (and its constituent kingdoms) and Kent. His power in Kent was not unchallenged and in 776 a battle was fought at Otford between the Mercians and the people of Kent after which Offa lost control of that kingdom for about ten years. The com-plicated history of his relations with Kent, which can be traced in some detail thanks to the archives preserved at Canterbury and Rochester, are worth fairly full consideration not only as an illustration of what Mercian overlordship could mean but also because of their wider sig-nificance, for Kent played an important, and possibly vital, role in the later triumph of the West Saxons.

After Wihtred's death in 725 the kingship and perhaps the kingdom of Kent was divided between his sons Æthelberht and Eadberht, both of whom were still alive in 762. It is possible that Eadberht's son Eard-wulf ruled at the same time as his father, and that he also survived him for a few years (S, 31). In or shortly before 764 Sigired, described as king of half Kent, made a grant to Rochester that was confirmed by an otherwise unknown Kentish king called Eanmund and this grant was in turn confirmed at Canterbury by Offa in 764 with the approval of Archbishop Bregowine and another Kentish king, Heahberht. In the following year a grant of some property at Rochester by a King Egbert was confirmed by Heahberht and then taken to Offa at Peterborough Abbey for his approval. Offa's insistence on this point has left traces in other parts of the country. When in 770 Uhtred, subking of the Hwicce, made a grant of land it was 'with the advice and permission of Offa', who heads the witness-list consenting 'to this, my subking's donation' (S, 59; *EHD*, 74). One of the most fortunate survivals from this period is an original charter, dated 780, by Oslac, described as *dux* of the South Saxons and possibly a member of the royal family, grant-ing land to the episcopal church at Selsey (S, 1184). Offa's confirma-tion, made at Irthlingborough, in Northamptonshire, was added on the back of the charter in a different hand. Pierre Chaplais has pointed out to me that this endorsement was added after the parchment was folded; it is therefore reasonable to suggest that the original charter, which was probably written in Sussex, was taken to Offa for his approval.

Offa's rule in Kent was certainly opposed, and after the Battle of Otford Egbert was able to issue charters without Offa's confirmation. One of these, a grant to the bishop of Rochester in 778, fortunately survives in its original form (S, 35). In 784 another Kentish king, Eal-hmund, similarly made a grant to the church of Reculver without Offa's consent (S, 38), but by the following year the Mercian king must have recovered his power in Kent for he then began to issue charters con-cerning land there (S, 123; 128–31) and the series of charters by Kentish kings was interrupted for twenty years, until Cuthred, himself a Mer-cian, issued some in 805 as king of Kent (S, 39–41).

The later collapse of the Mercian hegemony has obscured Offa's achievement and historians have tended to concentrate on such violent events as the execution of Æthelberht and 'the blood shed to secure the kingdom on his son' (*EHD*, 202). There is, however, ample evidence to show that he was one of the most remarkable of all early English kings. Charlemagne's *imperium* was more extensive and is better recorded, but the style of government of the two great kings was very similar. West Saxon and Kentish sources emphasize his aggressions, and it is true that he seized every opportunity to enlarge his dominions and extend his resources, but he also provided for the defence of his territory against enemies, both old and new. He was praised by Alcuin for being 'intent on education, that the light of wisdom, which is now extinguished in many places, may shine in your kingdom' (*EHD*, 195), and appears also to have had an interest in the pagan past. The emphasis on his putative ancestor Offa of Angeln in the poems *Beowulf* and *Widsith* suggest that they were composed in his reign, perhaps even for his court (Whitelock, 1951, pp. 58–64). A similar interest is revealed by the Anglian collection of royal genealogies that were compiled in Offa's reign although it is possible that the collection, as it stands, had a Northumbrian rather than a Mercian origin (Dumville, 1975, esp. pp. 45–50). Offa's reign also saw notable developments in coinage and his moneyers produced some of the finest coins minted in England. Some of them, in gold, appear to have been produced in order to pay the alms that Offa promised for the relief of the poor and the maintenance of lights in Rome (*EHD*, 205). Such gifts were only one sign of his respect for Rome. It was in his reign that the first papal legation since the conversion came to England. The legates were George, bishop of Ostia, and Theophylact, bishop of Todi, and their report has survived (*EHD*, 191). They visited several parts of Britain and drew up some decrees for the reform of the church that were approved first by a Northumbrian council and then by a Mercian council attended by the bishops of southern England together with Offa and his nobles, described as *senatores*. Patrick Wormald has suggested that the decrees of this Legatine Synod were the laws of Offa that Alfred used in compiling his own code (Wormald, 1977b). It is clear that Offa, and his advisers, exploited all the available resources of kingship with remarkable skill.

When Offa died in July 796 the people of Kent were eager to be rid of the Mercians and elected as king Eadberht Præn, described by the pope as an apostate clerk (*EHD*, 205), which may mean that he was a member of a Kentish royal family who had taken orders during Offa's reign to avoid death. No charters attributed to him survive but he did issue coins as Offa had done (Blunt, Lyon and Stewart, 1963); Mercian hostility and papal condemnation do not mean that he was not a legitimate king of Kent. The Mercians clearly regarded him as a rebel and in 798 King Cenwulf ravaged Kent in punishment and Eadberht was, according to the *Chronicle*, 'brought in fetters to Mercia'. According to one version of the *Chronicle* (F), written at Christ Church, Canterbury in about 1100 and preserving some Kentish material, he was mutilated; 'and they had his eyes put out and his hands cut off'. For the next nine years Cenwulf ruled Kent jointly with his brother Cuthred; they both issued coins from the Canterbury mint, and there are charters recording grants made by them individually and jointly; but after Cuthred's death in 807 Cenwulf ruled as the sole Kentish king. He was succeeded in 821 by his brother Ceolwulf who issued charters as *rex Merciorum vel* (or *seu*) *etiam Cantwariorum*. The generosity of the Mercian kings to Kentish religious houses was doubtless partly designed to make their rule more acceptable but Mercian authority did not long survive Ceolwulf's deposition as king of Mercia in 823. His place was taken by Beornwulf who presided over two councils to resolve Kentish disputes at *Clofesho* in 824 and 825 (S, 1434; 1436). Kentish coins were not, however, issued by Beornwulf but by a king called Bealdred and there is numismatic evidence to suggest a period of political confusion at Canterbury during Ceolwulf's reign before Bealdred's accession, which was probably in 823 (Blunt, Lyon and Stewart, 1963). He was certainly king of Kent in 825 for in that year, according to the *Chronicle*, the West Saxon king Egbert defeated Beornwulf in a battle at Wroughton, near Swindon, and then

> he sent from the army his son Æthelwulf and his bishop Ealhstan (of Sherborne) and his ealdorman Wulfheard to Kent, with a large force, and they drove King Bealdred north across the Thames; and the people of Kent and of Surrey and the South Saxons and the East Saxons submitted to him because they had been wrongfully forced away from his kinsmen.

Taken together this evidence suggests that Kent remained a Mercian dependency under Beornwulf but with its own king, Bealdred, who was probably a Mercian. This may well have been an attempt to meet the Kentish wish to be independent, a determination which had already cost the Mercians so much, and may have been a factor in the quarrel between Cenwulf and Wulfred, archbishop of Canterbury, which led to the archbishop's suspension from his see from 817 to 821. The *Chronicle*'s claim that Egbert was a kinsman of earlier Kentish kings suggests that his father, Ealhmund, was the king of Kent who made a grant to Reculver in 784 (S, 38). Whatever the basis of his claim to rule Kent, he certainly proved more acceptable than the Mercians, and Kent was from that time ruled by West Saxons. The Kentish kingdom remained distinct for most of the ninth century but its king was normally the son or brother of the reigning West Saxon king. Thus Æthelwulf was king of Kent until he succeeded Egbert as king of Wessex in 839, and then Kent passed to his son Athelstan, who survived until at least 850.

Æthelbald of Mercia was regarded with some favour by Felix in his *Life of St Guthlac*, and presumably also by Ælfwald, the East Anglian king (713–49) to whom that work was dedicated. This suggests that there were friendly relations between these two kings, but after Æthelbald's death there are many signs of East Anglian opposition to the Mercians. It became explicit in 825 when the *Chronicle* reports that:

> the same year the king of the East Angles and the people appealed to King Egbert for peace and protection because of their fear of the Mercians. And that same year the East Angles killed Beornwulf, king of the Mercians.

There must have been some very serious difficulty, unexplained by the *Chronicle*, which made it necessary for Offa to behead Æthelberht, king of the East Angles, in 794. A King Eadwald issued coins from the East Anglian mint between those produced there for Offa and Cenwulf, and it is therefore probable that rebellion broke out in East Anglia, as well as in Kent, on Offa's death.

The *Chronicle* says that the East Anglians in 825 appealed for Egbert's help, not that he gave it, and there is nothing to suggest that he had any part in the campaign that ended in Beornwulf's death. The East Anglian mint struck coins for the next Mercian king, Ludeca, but after his murder two years later, the coin evidence suggests that East Anglia was again independent, for there are coins issued there for two kings, Athelstan and Æthelweard, who would otherwise be unknown (Blunt, Lyon and Stewart, 1963).

The West Saxons were rather more successful than the people of Kent or East Anglia in resisting Mercia, but they did not escape entirely. The *Chronicle* has few entries for the years of Offa's rule, most of which do not refer to West Saxon events, and although coins were produced at *Hamwih* (p. 224) throughout the period, the king's name was only given towards the end of Egbert's reign.

West Saxon charters from this period are, unfortunately, too few and too badly preserved to contribute much to our knowledge of West Saxon relations with Mercia. Under Æthelbald the Mercians controlled the middle Thames valley, and the monastery of Abingdon, a West Saxon foundation, looked on him as its protector (Stenton, 1913, pp. 22–3). As already mentioned, he controlled Cookham and was also in a position to make grants of land in Somerset to Glastonbury abbey (S, 1679). There was some vigorous resistance under Cuthred who defeated Æthelbald at an unidentified site *Beorhford* in 752, but Cuthred died in 756 and was succeeded by Sigeberht who was soon deposed by his successor, Cynewulf. Cynewulf immediately accepted Æthelbald's overlordship and attended the Mercian court with his leading followers, but he did not as readily accept Offa and only once, in 772, appears in a Mercian witness-list, and then in a charter concerning Sussex (S, 108).

The *Chronicle* reports that Offa recovered Benson, in Oxfordshire, from Cynewulf in 779, which means that the West Saxons must have won back at least some of the territory they lost to Æthelbald. Cynewulf was killed in 786 in the course of a quarrel that the *Chronicle*, in a famous entry (s.a. 755, *recte* 757), traced back to his own accession twenty-nine years earlier. The next West Saxon king was Beorhtric, who soon formed an alliance with Offa, and in 789 married his daughter Eadburh who, according to Asser (c. 14), lived after the tyrannical manner of her father. The *Chronicle* (839) suggests that this marriage led Beorhtric to help Offa and it may have been to that end that Beorhtric drove Egbert, the man who eventually succeeded him as king, into exile. Charlemagne's friendly reception of Egbert may help explain why relations between the Frankish and Mercian kings were strained in 790 and for some time afterwards (*EHD*, 192; Asser, pp. 206–8). Offa's friendly relations with Beorhtric did not, however, amount to an overlordship and he did not issue charters for Wessex as he did in Kent. With Egbert's accession in 802, Mercian influence in Wessex ended.

The Northumbrians appear to have been more successful than any other kingdom in resisting Mercian pressure. There is no suggestion that either Æthelbald or Offa had any authority north of the Humber and it is worth noting that the legatine decrees of 786 were presented to a Northumbrian council before a Mercian one (p. 103). Indeed, in 801 the author of the *Historia Regum* (attributed to Simeon of Durham), who was here drawing on some fairly detailed earlier annals, reports that:

> In these times Eardwulf, king of the Northumbrians, led an army against Cenwulf, king of the Mercians, because of his harbouring of his enemies. And the latter king collected an army and led many forces from other provinces with him. When there had been a long campaign between them, they finally made peace by the advice of the English bishops and nobles on both sides, by the grace of the king of the English. And an agreement of most firm peace was made between them, which both kings confirmed with an oath on the gospel of Christ, calling God as witness and surety that in their life-time . . . a firm peace and true friendship should persist between them. (*EHD*, 3)

This annal has many points of interest – the cause of the quarrel, its resolution by a treaty that was to last for their lives, the invocation of God as surety – but it is perhaps most important for the light it casts on the relative power of Northumbrian and Mercian kings at the beginning of the ninth century. The initiative in the conflict was taken by Eard-wulf; Cenwulf, who had brought a Kentish king to Mercia in fetters, gathered an army, like other overlords before him, from many pro-vinces, but the campaign was long and was certainly not ended by a Mercian victory. The text says that it was *per gratiam regis Anglorum*, which has been variously interpreted as a reference to Egbert, which is incredible, or as a mistake for 'the king of the angels', which is unneces-sary; its natural meaning is 'the king of the Northumbrians'. It implies no claim to overlordship, and a century earlier Bede had called Aldfrith *rex Anglorum* (*HE*, v. 15). This also makes more sense in the context, for the ending of the quarrel naturally depended on Eardwulf's 'grace' if Cenwulf could not defeat him.

The violence of Northumbrian politics at this time had led to the death or expulsion of several kings – Eardwulf was himself temporarily driven into exile during 808 – but that does not mean that they were impotent while they ruled. The fragmentary evidence for Northum-brian history after Bede, and the dynastic instability that it reveals, should not mislead us into thinking that Northumbrian society was un-stable or that the kingdom was on the verge of collapse. The Northum-brian achievement in maintaining the frontiers that had been settled in Bede's lifetime was remarkable, and in this the Northumbrians were

rather more successful than their Mercian neighbours. It was the Vikings who destroyed the Northumbrian hegemony; the Mercians had
begun to collapse long before the Vikings seized any Mercian territory.

The Mercians, as has been seen, were bounded on the north by a
frontier that was well preserved, their eastern neighbours were, in and
after Offa's time, increasingly reluctant to accept their overlordship
and, with the accession of Egbert, Wessex was also hostile. To the
west their neighbours were the Welsh, who had a long tradition of
opposition to the English invaders. The Welsh annals report Welsh
victories in 722, but Æthelbald's reign appears to have been untroubled
by attacks from that quarter. Conflict was, however, renewed soon
after Offa's accession. Welsh annals report a battle at Hereford between the Mercians and the Welsh in 760 and expeditions by Offa to
Dyfed in 778 and to some unnamed part of Wales in 784, and according
to one version of the Welsh annals (*Annales Cambriae* C) in 795 Offa
devastated *Rhieinwg*, probably meaning Brycheiniog, and surrounding
areas (Bartrum, 1970). The threat of attack by the Welsh is probably the
reason why Hereford appears to have been fortified before the Viking
period. Its defences were a natural development of those which had
long been normal around *burhs*, great houses with their associated
buildings, traces of which have been discovered at the royal villa of
Tamworth (Rahtz, 1977).

Far more remarkable, and undisputably related to the Welsh, is
Offa's Dyke. This bank and ditch marked the boundary from the north
coast of Wales to the mouth of the Wye. It was probably continuous,
with breaks only where either the rivers Severn or Wye or dense woodland made it unnecessary, but the northern section has now disappeared.
Early excavations by Sir Cyril Fox (1955) demonstrated that it was a
post-Roman earthwork and there is no reason to doubt the traditional
association with Offa, already mentioned by Asser within a hundred
years of his death. It is impressive enough as it stands but was probably
made more effective by a timber palisade; only modern excavation
techniques could hope to detect what would inevitably be faint traces of
such structures. Fox's work has, however, revealed how carefully and
skilfully the line of the dyke was chosen to command the Welsh
approaches. It certainly hindered the movement of cattle and if manned
it must have been a formidable barrier; no one, Welsh or English,
could claim that he did not know he had crossed it.

A shorter earthwork, called Wat's Dyke, runs from Basingwerk on the Dee as far south as Oswestry. Like Offa's Dyke to the west, it is a unitary work and both appear to have been built in much the same way. Fox suggested that it was built by Æthelbald to defend a particularly vulnerable part of Mercia, apparently on the assumption that Offa's boundary would have been an advance on his predecessor's. There may be good archaeological reasons for dating them both in the same period, but Wat's Dyke could well be later than Offa's and represent a retreat. It has even been suggested that the northern part of Wat's Dyke represents the missing section of Offa's (Hill, 1974).

Whatever the relationship between these dykes, and the other short dykes in the region, their construction was a remarkable undertaking, and explains the attention which Mercian kings paid to the exaction of a universal obligation to build fortifications. The military effort needed to suppress rebellions and to protect territory against attack led the Mercians to make great demands, further enlarged by the need to build and man fortifications like those at Hereford or like the dykes themselves. Whatever the basis of their armies, the Mercian kings made great efforts to obtain as much service as possible for the construction of fortifications. Æthelbald was criticized by Boniface for the demands he made on the Church and for the violence and servitude imposed by his reeves and gesiths on monks and priests (*EHD*, 177). Another letter from Boniface, written at about the same time to the archbishop of Canterbury, shows that his agents had been forcing monks to do servile work on royal buildings. Shortly afterwards Æthelbald responded by freeing monks from such servile tasks, but he then insisted that their estates, like all others, would without exception be required to contribute to the building of fortifications against enemies. By 792 the threat of Viking attack had led Offa to make the same demands in Kent, and the West Saxons followed his lead later in the ninth century, no doubt for the same reason (Brooks, 1971).

The obligation to build and man fortifications may have been new, but it was based on the traditional assessment on which all royal dues were collected. The assessment of particular estates of communities would obviously have been known locally; they were traditional and may indeed have derived from arrangements that were already old when the English came to Britain (p. 56). The assessments could of course be altered, but rulers and their agents would in any case need to know what they were, and when new territories were acquired they would have to discover what the assessments were, or to impose new ones. Plunder was one thing but the regular collection of tribute had to have some legal, recognized basis. This information was, of course, initially kept by word of mouth, but from the seventh century it could be written down and Bede's information about the assessment of different kingdoms implies that he knew about and may even have seen at least one assessment list.

A text, known as the *Tribal Hidage*, has been interpreted as a pre-Conquest assessment list. It survives in seven medieval manuscripts, the earliest being of the eleventh century, and lists some thirty-five kingdoms or peoples, giving a number of hides for each. It begins by assigning 30,000 hides to 'the area first called Mercia' and continues with groups of very different sizes, some of which cannot now be identified. Those that can include the 'Wrekin-dwellers' of Shropshire, the Hwicce and the men of Lindsey with Hatfield, each assessed at 7000 hides, the 'Peak-dwellers' of Derbyshire with 1200 hides, and the 'El-met-dwellers' with 600. It ends with the kingdoms of East Anglia (30,000), Essex (7000), Kent (15,000), Sussex (7000) and Wessex (100,000). The full list is given on p. 113 and those that can be identified are mapped in figure 5. It has generally been interpreted as a product of the Mercian hegemony (Stenton, 1971, p. 297; Davies and Vierck, 1974; Hart, 1971). The fact that Kent is assigned 15,000 hides is particularly instructive, for Kent was never assessed in hides, a fact which shows that these totals are not necessarily based on the internal assessments of the kingdoms in the list. They could, of course, be figures determined by an overlord who was optimistic or extortionate or, as Maitland suggested (1897, pp. 510–11), simply mistaken. It does, however, seem likely that some of the figures given for the kingdoms had a symbolic significance. The assessments of 7000 are reminiscent of the endowment given by King Hygelac to Beowulf. In addition to a vast treasure

> he gave him seven thousand, hall and throne. To both of them in that nation belonged land naturally transmissible, homeland, rightful ancestral property; but the larger region, the broad kingdom itself, was for him whose rank was higher. (lines 2194–9)

The poem also has a reference to a gift of 'a hundred thousand of land and of treasure-rings' (line 2994). These poetic gifts may be compared with the *Chronicle*'s annal for 648 which records that Cenwealh gave his kinsman Cuthred 'three thousand of land'. It is likely that in all these references hides were either meant or, at an early stage, understood. Seven thousand (hides) were therefore considered an appropriate endowment for a prince who had proved himself, and these units in the *Tribal Hidage* and in Bede (Hart, 1971, p. 146) may have simply been a way of expressing the status of kingdoms or provinces. Thus Kent's 15,000 may imply a higher status, a 'greater kingdom' or, alternatively, some awareness that it was formed by the union of two kingdoms. It certainly seems likely that the very high figure for the West Saxons, 100,000, is an expression of their superior status as a kingdom. This in turn suggests that the *Tribal Hidage* in its present form was compiled in the ninth or tenth century by a West Saxon. The survival of so many versions of this text would be less surprising if it was produced then than if, as has sometimes been supposed, it was compiled in the time of Offa, or even earlier. The *Tribal Hidage* was, nevertheless, based on an earlier list that must have been Mercian and the names may have come from an assessment list. Many of the peoples listed lived around the heartland of Mercia, and the order in which many of them are given appears to be a systematic circuit of Mercia's neighbours, in a clockwise direction. Knowledge of some of these peoples would hardly be expected anywhere else than in Mercia.

The *Tribal Hidage* may, therefore, be accepted as a monument to Mercian power but on a more limited scale than has sometimes been supposed. It does not portray the interest of a *rex Britanniae* in all the kingdoms of the *Sutangli*, so much as the interest of a Mercian king in the peoples who lived between the Humber and the Thames, and west of the Fens. The original list was probably made at a very early date. The inclusion of Elmet may point to Wulfhere, who may have controlled it briefly before his defeat by Ecgfrith, or to his brother Æthelred after his victory at the Battle of the Trent (670–4; 679–704). On the other hand, the assessment given for the *Elmedsætna* is surprisingly small and may only refer to a section of that people. An early date is also suggested by the obscurity of so many of the names, and possibly by the omission of others for whom we have good, independent evidence.

The *Tribal Hidage* may reflect an early stage in the development of Mercian power. By the middle of the ninth century that power was in full decline and in 829 Egbert of Wessex, the man Offa drove into exile, ruled briefly, but fully, as king of Mercia (Dumville, 1977b, p. 100). In the early ninth century almost the only successes gained by the

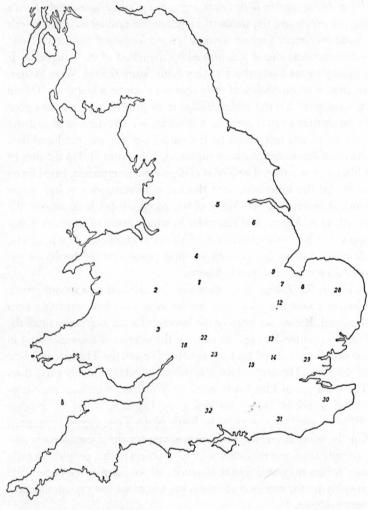

Figure 5 The *Tribal Hidage*

Figure 5   The *Tribal Hidage*   (key)

The text followed is in B.L., MS. Harley 3271. The identifications have been discussed recently by Wendy Davies (with Vierck 1974) and Hart (1971).

No.		Hides	Possible identifications and related names
I	Myrcna landes	30,000	'the area first called Mercia'
2	Wocen saetna	7,000	'Wrekin-dwellers'
3	Westerna	7,000	? = *Magonsaete*
4	Pec saetna	1,200	'Peak-dwellers'
5	Elmed saetna	600	'Elmet-dwellers'
6	Lindes farona mid Haethfeld land	7,000	Lindsey with Hatfield Chase
7	Suth Gyrwa	600	Medeshamstede 'in the region
	North Gyrwa	600	of the Gyrui' (*HE*, iii. 20)
8	East Wixna	300	Wisbech, Cambridgeshire
	West Wixna	600	
9	Spalda	600	Spalding, Lincolnshire
10	Wigesta	900	?
11	Herefinna	1,200	?
12	Sweord ora	300	Sword Point, Huntingdonshire
13	Gifla	300	River Ivel, Buckinghamshire
14	Hicca	300	Hitchin, Hertfordshire
15	Wihtgara	600	?
16	Noxgaga	5,000	?
17	Ohtgaga	2,000	?
18	Hwinca	6,000	Hwicce
19	Ciltern saetna	4,000	'Chiltern-dwellers'
20	Hendrica	3,500	? Berkshire
21	Unecung ga	1,200	?
22	Aro saetna	600	River Arrow, Warwickshire
23	Faerpinga	300	Charlbury, Oxfordshire
24	Bilmiga	600	?
25	Widerigga	600	?
26	East Willa	600	?
27	West Willa	600	?
28	East Engle	30,000	East Angles
29	East Sexena	7,000	East Saxons
30	Cantwarena	15,000	Men of Kent
31	Suth Sexena	7,000	South Saxons
32	West Sexena	100,000	West Saxons

Mercians were at the expense of the Welsh but when, in 853, Burgred of Mercia hoped to bring the Welsh under his control he appealed for West Saxon help. Fifteen years later he made an even more urgent plea for help against the Vikings who had begun their seizure of eastern England, and were then based on the Trent at Nottingham, close to the heart of Mercia. Even with West Saxon help they failed to dislodge the Vikings and, as the *Chronicle* reports, 'the Mercians made peace with the enemy'. Worse was to follow. In 874 Burgred abdicated after a reign of twenty-two years and went to end his days at Rome. The Vikings, according to the *Chronicle*, then had control of Mercia and gave the kingdom to 'a foolish king's thegn' called Ceolwulf who

> swore oaths to them and gave hostages, that the kingdom should be ready for them on whatever day they wished to have it, and he would be ready, himself and all who would follow him, at the enemy's service.

That may be West Saxon propaganda, but there is no disguising the collapse of Mercian power.

2   *The Vikings*

Viking raids on Britain began in the last years of the eighth century. The first attack whose date is known, June 793, was on Lindisfarne and in the following year another Northumbrian monastery, possibly Jarrow, was plundered. In 795 Iona was raided and 799 saw the first attack on the abbey of St Philibert on the island of Noirmoutier, near the Loire estuary. The *Chronicle* also reports an attack on the Channel coast of Wessex in the reign of Beorhtric (786–802). The fact that Offa was already arranging for the defence of Kent against pagan seamen in 792 (S, 134) underlines the inadequacy of our sources and shows that the attack on Lindisfarne was not the first. Several early ninth-century Kentish charters specifically mention pagan enemies in clauses dealing with the universal obligation to build defences and perform army service, and two of them also refer to the duty of destroying fortresses, implying that the Vikings already had fortified bases for their plundering expeditions, as they certainly did later. In 804 the monastery of Lyminge, an exposed site just north of Romney Marsh, acquired a site of 6 acres within the walls of Canterbury as a refuge. All this shows that the Vikings were a serious threat, especially to the defenceless churches whose treasures and men were a tempting target, and that our sources certainly give an incomplete account of the raids.

The first Vikings were Norwegians and their attacks were a by-product of the Norse colonization of Shetland, Orkney and the Hebrides that had begun a little earlier. They soon established bases on the Irish coast, Dublin was the first in 841, and from these they plundered the monasteries and strongholds of Ireland and the coasts of Britain. They were soon joined by Danes, the most famous of whom was Ivarr who, with his brother Halfdan, led the Danish army that arrived in East Anglia in 865. Ivarr did not stay in England, for in 870 he joined Olaf, the Norse ruler of Dublin, in a famous expedition to Strathclyde during which they took Dumbarton after a siege of four months and, according to the *Annals of Ulster*, they returned to Dublin the following year 'with a great multitude of men, English, Britons and Picts, in captivity'. When Ivarr died in 873 the *Annals of Ulster* described him as 'king of all the Scandinavians in Ireland and Britain' implying that he had some claim to authority among the Danes in England.

It was about this time that the Norse colonization of Iceland began. Many of the colonists came from Norse settlements in the British Isles and this emigration may have contributed to a reduction in Viking activity in Ireland between 873 and 913, later known in Ireland as 'the forty years' rest'. Control of Dublin was vigorously contested, among others by Ivarr's sons, but there were other challengers, including Scandinavians newly arrived in the British Isles; in 902, however, the Irish succeeded in expelling the Vikings from Dublin. Some went to Scotland, others to north-west England, but about ten years later they returned to renew their pillaging of Ireland, under the leadership of Ivarr's grandsons, one of whom, Sitric, recaptured Dublin in 917.

It was in the first years of the tenth century that Norse colonization in Britain spread south of the Solway Firth, and although some of these settlers may have come from Ireland, it is likely that the majority came from the Hebrides and western parts of Scotland. The lands west of the Pennines appear to have been relatively free of Viking attacks in the late ninth century, and in 875 the community of St Cuthbert sought shelter from the Vikings near Carlisle, but early in the tenth century leading Englishmen from that area, including the abbot of Heversham, fled eastwards in the face of Viking invasion (*HSC*, c. 21; *EHD*, 6). The district north of the river Ribble had already acquired its Scandinavian name Amounderness, 'the headland of Agmundr', by 934 and it was against threats from this quarter that the Mercians refortified Chester in 907, and built *burhs* at Eddisbury in 914 and at Runcorn in 915 (figure 9 p. 202). It is even possible that the Scandinavian colonists in Wirral were settled there by agreement with the Mercians to assist the defence of the area against other Scandinavians.

The Vikings from whom the English suffered most were Danes. Their attacks began in 835 with a raid on Sheppey, a year after they first plundered Dorestad on the Rhine. In the next fifteen years attacks are reported on many parts of the English coast from Somerset and Dorset to Lindsey, and on such towns as London, Rochester and *Hamwih*. The removal of the relics of St Cuthbert from the exposed island of Lindisfarne to the relative shelter of Norham on the Tweed, in the time of Bishop Ecgred (830–45) suggests that the Northumbrian coast did not escape (*HSC*, c. 9). The sources rarely note the nationality of the raiders and it is likely that some attacks after 835 were the work of Norwegians, especially those in the south-west. Some of the Danes had bases in Frisia, but in 850 they began to winter in England, at first in Thanet, and in 865 what the *Chronicle* describes as a 'great army', *micel here*, arrived in East Anglia with the intention of conquering land on which to settle. Their activities can be followed in some detail in the available chronicles, supplemented by incidental references in charters and other sources, but no attempt will here be made, in William of Malmesbury's words, to follow them all round the island. It is, however, important to note the main stages of their advance.

They conquered York in 866. Some Northumbrians, including Archbishop Wulfhere, were prepared to collaborate with them and three English kings, Egbert, Ricsige and a second Egbert, ruled southern Northumbria 'under their domination' (*EHD*, 3; 4). King Edmund of East Anglia opposed them but was killed in 870, and by 869 they had seized control of Lindsey and the eastern part of Mercian territory, and in 869 held Nottingham against the combined efforts of the Mercians and the West Saxons to dislodge them. They were vigorously opposed in Wessex by King Æthelred and his brother Alfred, who succeeded as king in 871. The *Chronicle* reports that:

During that year nine general engagements were fought against the Danish army in the kingdom south of the Thames, besides the expeditions on which the king's brother Alfred and single ealdormen and king's thegns often rode, which were not counted.

The chronicler has, however, to admit that the West Saxons neverthe-less made peace with the enemy, as the Mercians, the East Angles, Northumbrians and the men of Kent had done earlier. The Vikings then controlled the greater part of eastern England from York to London. In 874 the 'great army' divided and one part under Halfdan went north to the Tyne, 'and the army conquered the land and often ravaged among the Picts and Strathclyde Britons'. It was this that forced the community of St Cuthbert to leave Norham and seek a safer re-fuge, at first near Carlisle. In the following year the *Chronicle* reports the beginning of the Scandinavian colonization: 'And that year Halfdan shared out the land of the Northumbrians and they proceeded to plough and to support themselves.' The evidence of place-names shows that this settlement was south of the Tees, in the East and North Ridings of Yorkshire (p. 161). Other groups from the 'great army' settled in Mercia in 877 and in East Anglia under their King Guthrum in 879. Guthrum had attempted to settle in Wessex shortly after Christmas 877 but Alfred, who had retreated to Athelney, organized a successful counter-attack and forced the invaders to accept his terms, which in-cluded the baptism of Guthrum and his leading followers. Five years after they had settled in East Anglia they broke their agreement with Alfred, and in the subsequent campaign the West Saxons took London. Alfred then concluded a new treaty with Guthrum, the terms of which have survived, including a definition of the frontier which was to run 'up the Thames, and then up the Lea, and along the Lea to its source, then in a straight line to Bedford, then up the Ouse to the Watling Street' (*EHD*, 34). Alfred marked his occupation of London by mint-ing some magnificent coins there; he then granted it back to the Mercians.

In 879 a new group of Vikings appeared in the Channel. For thirteen years they concentrated on plundering or extorting tribute from Frank-ish churches and rulers, with occasional attacks on England. They were at Fulham in 879 and in 885 unsuccessfully attacked Rochester. After suffering a severe defeat at the hands of the East Frankish king Arnulf near Louvain in 891, they crossed to England. For three years they attempted to win land on which to settle, but the English defences were too well organized and in 896 they split up, some settling in East Anglia and Northumbria, areas already under Viking control, 'and those who were moneyless got themselves ships and went south across the sea to the Seine', a move that eventually resulted in the formation of Normandy.

East Anglia and Northumbria were Viking kingdoms, but the area between does not appear to have been under the control of one individual. In the English campaigns in the early tenth century the Scandinavians are described in such terms as 'the army of Cambridge', or 'the army of Northampton'. The main centres that remained under Danish control longest were Leicester, Nottingham, Derby, Stamford and Lincoln, later known as the Five Boroughs. Some, perhaps all, of these existed before the Viking conquests, and there are reasons to think that the districts associated with them, which later became English counties, were also old (p. 197). There is, in fact, little significant difference between a Danish army or *here* based on a *burh* and an English county *fyrd* led by an ealdorman who was also responsible for its *burh*.

Although it is in general possible to distinguish Danish and Norwegian Vikings in the ninth century, their great mobility led to many contacts between them. They sometimes co-operated, as for example in the attack on Dumbarton in 870, and some groups were mixed. The predominantly Danish Vikings who settled Normandy were led by a Norwegian, Hrolf. This mobility means that the movements of particular groups, generally identified by their leaders, can only be studied by using a wide variety of sources, Frankish, English, Welsh and Irish. There are also traditions that were preserved in Iceland, but these were modified too much before they were written down in the twelfth century and later to be much use for the ninth and tenth centuries. There have recently been great advances in the study of this source material as a group, largely thanks to the work of Dr Alfred Smyth. He has shown, for example, that the Sigrid who, according to Æthelweard, led a Northumbrian fleet in attacks on Wessex in 893 was probably the man who attacked Dublin in 894 and who later returned to Northumbria, where he minted the first Viking coins of York. The most important result of this work has been to demonstrate that the kings of the Dublin Vikings in the tenth century were a Danish dynasty that also had claims to rule the Danes of York, deriving from Ivarr's kingship of both. Thanks to this, the complex and confusing history of early tenth-century Northumbria, and the links with Dublin Vikings, are now more comprehensible than hitherto, and can be summarized in tabular form, as in figure 6.

In Britain, as in Ireland, some were ready to welcome Vikings as allies. On several occasions the Vikings helped the Britons of the

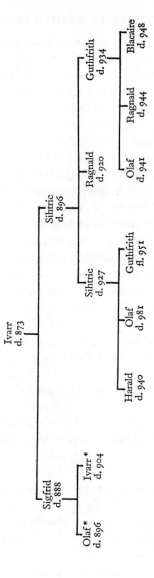

*Probably a son of Sigfrid, certainly a grandson of Ivarr.

Figure 6 The family of Ivarr

I am indebted to Alfred Smyth for generously providing this table in advance of his publication (1978).

south-west in their long struggle against West Saxon pressure, and it is possible that there were many people in East Anglia and Deira who were willing to collaborate with these new rulers. There may even have been some in Wessex, for in 878 some West Saxons submitted to the Vikings, and one of Alfred's great achievements was to attract the loyal support of enough West Saxons to resist this threat. The potential danger was shown very clearly on Alfred's death, when his son Edward succeeded. Æthelwold, son of Alfred's brother and predecessor, clearly thought he had a better claim and when he was disappointed he joined the Vikings as one of their leaders; some versions of the *Chronicle* say, indeed, that the Danish army of Northumbria accepted him as king. He was not the only member of an English royal family to join the Vikings. Brihtsige, son of the ætheling Beornoth, who was killed in 902 along with Æthelwold, was certainly royal, and possibly a member of a Mercian royal family (as suggested by Whitelock, 1961, p. 60).

There is no doubt that much destruction was caused by the Vikings in what Alfred later called 'the time when everything was ravaged and burnt'. In the early tenth century a number of charters that had been lost by fire, water or theft had to be replaced (e.g. S, 225; 367; 371; 395). The best indication of the time that Alfred meant is provided by coin hoards, that are particularly frequent in the decade after 865. In contrast, the great campaigns of 892–6 were not particularly destructive; only three coin hoards that could have been deposited at that time are known from the whole of England, from London, Erith and Leigh-on-Sea, and this confirms the chronicler's judgement that the English people had not been afflicted very greatly (Dolley, 1966a, pp. 48–9 and map 2).

The Vikings were, of course, not the only agents of destruction. They certainly had no respect for the spiritual sanctions on which churches depended for their safety, but churches were sometimes attacked by Christians; Ripon was destroyed by King Eadred in 948. Nor was Viking conquest necessarily a disaster except, of course, for the displaced dynasty; the Northumbrian church survived, and converted its conquerors. We can hardly avoid seeing the Vikings in England through the eyes of the men who successfully resisted them, the West Saxons, and in particular their kings, but we should not expect them to be unprejudiced, nor should we forget that some of their contemporaries, even churchmen, did not regard the invaders with unqualified hostility.

3 *The West Saxon empire*

The foundations of the later West Saxon domination of England were laid by Egbert who, having been king for twenty-two years, emerged in 825 leading the West Saxons to victory against the Mercians. Four years later he displaced Wiglaf as king of Mercia for about a year during which time he issued coins as *rex Merciorum* from the London mint. Wiglaf soon recovered his kingdom, and more. One of his charters, dated 836, was witnessed by the bishops of Selsey, Rochester and Sherborne, described as 'my bishops' (S, 190; *EHD*, 85), showing that the situation was far more complicated than the *Chronicle* implies and that Egbert's control of southern England was neither complete nor continuous. The West Saxon victory of 825 did, however, mark the end of Mercian control of the south-east. After that Egbert was acknowledged as king of Kent, Surrey, Sussex and Essex and issued coins from the mint of Canterbury.

Egbert was also active in the west. A campaign in Cornwall is reported in 815 and there was a battle between the men of Devon and the Britons in 825. It was in the west that the first Viking raids on Wessex are reported and in 838 Egbert successfully defeated a combined force of Vikings and Cornish Britons at Hingston Down.

When Egbert died in 839 he was succeeded by his son Æthelwulf, the first time a son had followed his father as king of the West Saxons since the seventh century. The reason for this break with tradition was, of course, Egbert's success. He had prepared the way for Æthelwulf's succession by making him king of Kent sometime before 838 but that would not alone have been enough. Our evidence is too slight to show whether he was as ruthless as Offa in destroying potential rivals but his family's later monopoly of the kingship would be easier to understand if he had done so. In any case Æthelwulf had a decisive advantage thanks to the new territory that his father had won. He himself continued the expansion by gaining control of Berkshire sometime before 849, when Alfred was born at Wantage, and it thereafter remained West Saxon. Æthelwulf's will, as reported by Asser (c. 16), and described in Alfred's will, shows that he expected to be succeeded by his sons, four of whom were kings in succession: Æthelbald (855–60), Æthelberht (860–5), Æthelred (865–71) and Alfred (871–99).

The success of Egbert's family in retaining the kingship did not ensure that his kingdom would remain united. Kent was in some respects treated as a separate kingdom until about 851, and there were also very disruptive family disputes. In 855, while Æthelwulf was visiting Rome, a revolt which broke out in Somerset put his son Æthelbald on the West Saxon throne. When Æthelwulf returned in 856 he had to be content with the kingdom of Kent, which he had ruled in his father's lifetime. As Asser put it in his *Life of Alfred*,

> where the father ought to have reigned by rights, the wicked and stubborn son reigned; for the western part of the Saxon land has always been more important than the eastern (c. 91),

implying that the main objection was not to the division itself but to the loss of the 'more important part' by the senior man. The cause of this opposition to Æthelwulf is unknown. Asser says that some men blamed 'the royal pride, because that king was stubborn in this affair and in many other wrong acts'. By 'this affair' Asser probably meant the visit to Rome on which the king 'lingered for some little time'. There were precedents for royal visits to Rome: Cædwalla and Ine had both done so, but they abdicated first. Æthelwulf did not, but such a prolonged absence from his kingdom on a pious pilgrimage at a time when it was being attacked by Vikings must have appeared to some an abdication of responsibility.

Men had good cause to fear the Vikings. In the lifetime of Æthelwulf's sons these invaders conquered two English kingdoms and dismembered a third. The main credit for their failure to do the same in Wessex undoubtedly belongs to Alfred. He realized that it was not enough to fight battles, for the Vikings would always have the initiative, and raiders would too often have to be met by local levies who could be mobilized in time. He therefore had ships built 'neither on the Frisian nor on the Danish pattern, but as it seemed to him that they could be most useful' (*Chronicle*, 896). They were twice as long as Danish ships with sixty or more oars, and were therefore faster and higher. They were also deeper, and could be cumbersome, as was shown in a battle reported by the *Chronicle* under 896, but for most defensive purposes they had an advantage over the raiders. The vulnerability of former Roman cities was repeatedly shown between 851 when the defences of London and Canterbury failed to stop the raiders and 877 when the Vikings 'built booths in Gloucester' (Æthelweard). Alfred therefore improved the defences of such places, constructed

other forts elsewhere and arranged for their permanent manning
(pp. 226–9). In 885 the defences of Rochester held. The core of the
king's army had to be mounted, otherwise it could not keep up with the
enemy, nor could it move fast enough to counter threats in good time.
In 885 it was the arrival of Alfred with his army at Rochester that
caused the attackers to flee, abandoning their prisoners and their
horses. There was also a need for local forces, under the command of
ealdormen, to counter threats to their districts, and Alfred took care
not to make excessive demands. According to the *Chronicle* (893) he
divided the army into two, 'so that always half its men were at home
and half on service'.

In all this he had to inspire confidence and overcome apathy. It was
obviously easier to raise an army for an offensive campaign than a defensive one. The time, place and objectives could be determined well in
advance and all participants could hope that success would yield rewards. Defence was a more demanding and less profitable business, and
Alfred had to persuade his people to make efforts 'for the common
profit of the kingdom'. His ability to do this was perhaps his greatest
achievement. He gained the respect and confidence of the leading men,
and reinforced it with success.

> He most wisely brought over and bound to his own will and to the
> common profit of the whole kingdom his bishops and ealdormen
> and nobles and the thegns who were dearest to him, and also his
> reeves, to whom, after God, and the king, the control of the king-
> dom seems rightly to belong, by gently instructing, flattering, urg-
> ing, commanding them and, after long patience, by punishing
> sharply the disobedient and by showing in every way hatred of vulgar
> folly and obstinacy. (Asser, c. 91)

He had particular difficulty in overcoming apathy in the construction of
fortresses; Asser says that he could tell of fortresses ordered by the king
and not begun or begun too late (c. 91), but when they were complete
and proved successful all those who had co-operated in the construction and defence shared the achievement.

Alfred also recognized the importance of spiritual support. His
father's gifts to the church and his pilgrimage to Rome were the acts of
a conventionally pious man, but there was nothing conventional about
Alfred's piety. His sincerity is manifest in his writings, and his concern
for the spiritual welfare of his people led him to arrange for translations

of important works to be made for the benefit of his clergy. He himself translated Pope Gregory's *Pastoral Care*, the *Soliloquies* of St Augustine and Boethius' *Consolation of Philosophy*. He recognized the importance of reformed monasticism and founded a monastery at Athelney for which he recruited monks from the continent because his own people were unwilling to accept such novelty. He also founded a nunnery at Shaftesbury, and made his daughter Æthelgifu abbess. He did not neglect the unreformed monasteries of his own kingdom and Mercia, devoting a fourth part of his revenues to them:

> and in some years he also either made gifts, according to his means, to churches in Wales and Cornwall, Gaul, Brittany, Northumbria and sometimes even in Ireland, in turn, and to servants of God dwelling in them, or else proposed to give them later on, provided his life and prosperity continued. (Asser, c. 102)

It is therefore possible that he made gifts to the shrine of St Cuthbert, as his successors certainly did. Like Charlemagne before him, he recruited scholars and clergy from many places: Asser from Wales, Wærferth, bishop of Worcester, who translated Gregory's *Dialogues*, and another Mercian, Plegmund, whom he made archbishop of Canterbury in 890. Some men came from the continent: Grimbald from the household of the archbishop of Rheims, and John, from Saxony, to be abbot of Athelney. It was perhaps Grimbald's help that made Alfred's propaganda so effective. Its most notable product was the *Chronicle*, compiled sometime after the invasion of 892 to proclaim Alfred's success. There were other more tangible elements in his display of royal power. According to Asser he not only restored cities and towns but also built new ones, and ordered the building of royal halls and chambers 'constructed admirably in stone and timber' (c. 91), and some impression of what they were like may be gained from the remains of the palace at Cheddar, although they mainly date from the early tenth century. Coins also proclaimed his power and, in the London coin, his achievement.

Alfred was acknowledged as the overlord of Mercia and of the princes of south-east Wales, who feared the Mercians and the dynasty of Gwynedd, and he took care to encourage Eadwulf, the 'high-reeve' of Bamburgh who maintained English authority in the North beyond the Viking conquests. By 883 Mercia was ruled by Æthelred, who never called himself *rex*, only *dux*, and issued no coins. He did, however, make grants by charter and clearly exercised royal authority. Before 889 he married Alfred's daughter, Æthelflæd, who continued to rule the Mercians as their lady, *domina*, after her husband's death in 911, as she had done for some years before while he was incapacitated by illness.

Æthelred and Æthelflæd followed Alfred's example by fortifying Worcester and in the early tenth century Æthelflæd collaborated with her brother in constructing many other *burhs* with which Mercia could be defended and the Danish-occupied territories brought back under English control. Before Æthelred's illness he had joined Edward in ordering English thegns to buy land from the pagans. Later charters of Athelstan show that this happened at least twice, the land being in Bedfordshire and in the Peak District (S, 396–7).

When Æthelflæd died in 918 Edward was chosen by the Mercians as their king, and he took care to secure his position by depriving Æthelred's daughter, Ælfwyn, of all authority and removing her to Wessex. After he had constructed a number of other *burhs*, including one at Bakewell, probably on the estate earlier bought from the Vikings (Sawyer, 1975a),

> the king of the Scots and all the people of the Scots, and Ragnald, and the sons of Eadwulf (of Bamburgh) and all who live in Northumbria, both English and Danish, Norsemen and others, and also the king of the Strathclyde Welsh and all the Strathclyde Welsh, chose him as father and lord. (*Chronicle*, 920 A)

This overlordship was inherited by his son Athelstan in 924 who, within a few months, had arranged a marriage between his sister and Sihtric, Ragnald's successor as king of Northumbria. When Sihtric died in 927 Athelstan decided to assume the Northumbrian kingship himself and he drove out Guthfrith, another of Ivarr's grandsons. He 'succeeded to the kingdom of the Northumbrians and he brought under his rule all the kings who were in this island' at Eamont on 12 July (*Chronicle*, 927). This authority could not be taken for granted. Neither the Northumbrians nor the Scots were eager to accept the lordship, direct or indirect, of a southern English king. The archbishop of York, Wulfstan, was granted Amounderness for his church in 934, but after that year he never witnessed any of Athelstan's charters and may not have attended his court. He was certainly openly hostile to later English kings of Northumbria and in 952 Eadred arrested him and deprived him of the archbishopric. Some Scottish opposition caused

Athelstan to undertake a military expedition into Scotland in 934, in the course of which he made lavish gifts to the shrine of St Cuthbert and other Northumbrian cult-centres. The fortunate survival of two charters, an original dated at Winchester on 28 May 934 and another, now only preserved as a copy, issued ten days later at Nottingham, with almost the same witnesses, makes it possible to study the composition and progress of this expedition (S, 407; 425). Athelstan was accompanied by three Welsh kings including Hywel Dda of Dyfed, the two archbishops, fourteen bishops including Wigred of Chester-le-Street, seven ealdormen, six jarls with Scandinavian names, and twenty-four others, eleven of whom are described as king's thegns. The Scots did not offer battle, and Athelstan's forces harried Scotland by land and sea, his fleet going as far as Caithness. He also extorted tribute from the Welsh, which explains their dreams of revenge, given poetic expression at that time in *Armes Prydein Vawr*, 'The Great Prophecy of Britain':

> The warriors will scatter the foreigners as far as
>   *Caer Weir* (?Durham)—
> they will rejoice after the devastation,
> and there will be reconciliation between the Cymry and
>   the men of Dublin,
> the Irish of Ireland and Anglesey (?) and Scotland, the men of
> Cornwall and of Strathclyde will be made welcome among us,
>   the Britons will rise again (?) . . . (*Armes Prydein*, lines 7–12)

What Athelstan's opponents needed was leadership and that was provided in 937 by Olaf, son of that Guthfrith expelled by Athelstan over ten years before. Olaf was king of the Dublin Norse and when, earlier that year, by defeating the Limerick Vikings he had made himself the most powerful Viking leader in Ireland, he hastened to York where he was joined by the Scots for an invasion of Mercia. A hard battle was fought at *Brunanburh*, an unidentified place that is likely to have been, as Alfred Smyth (1978) has suggested, somewhere near the traditional route followed by Northumbrian invaders of the south. Their defeat, and Olaf's flight, was celebrated in the *Chronicle*, and reported widely throughout Britain; it even finds its place in Icelandic tradition. After it, Athelstan could proudly claim, in a charter, that he was *rex Angulsexna and Northhymbra imperator paganorum gubernator Brittanorumque propugnator* (S, 392). His brothers, Edmund and Eadred, also used a similar title but they too had to fight for it. No sooner was Athelstan's death known than Olaf returned to Northumbria, and led another army south. He failed to take Northampton, but was successful at Tamworth and was at Leicester when Edmund met him, and agreed terms that allowed him to keep the territory north of Watling Street. His mastery of the lands south of the Humber, which he marked by issuing coins from Derby and possibly also from Lincoln (Lyon, 1976, p. 192), was short-lived, for in 942 Edmund recovered all Mercia and in 944 regained Northumbria, but southern English control of the lands beyond the Humber was less easily assured and there were several shifts of fortune before the Northumbrians expelled Erik 'Bloodaxe', who proved to be the last Scandinavian king of York in 954.

What appeared to be the united kingdom of England was inherited in 956 by Edmund's son Eadwig, but a rebellion against him a year later led to the choice of his younger brother Edgar as king of Northumbria and Mercia. It was only on Eadwig's death in 959 that the kingdom was reunited under the rule of this sixteen-year-old king. He was celebrated as remarkably successful. This was partly because of his enthusiastic support of reformed monasticism, which earned the praise and support of powerful churchmen. He also made great efforts to combat theft and to improve public security. A panegyric later added to one version of the *Chronicle*, probably by Archbishop Wulfstan II of York, catalogues his virtues and only hints at one great weakness, that he

> loved evil foreign customs and brought too firmly heathen manners within this land, and attracted hither foreigners, and enticed harmful people to this country.

The 'foreign and harmful people' enticed to Edgar's kingdom may have included foreign sea-men. Two sea-kings were among the rulers of Britain who acknowledged his overlordship in 973 (Nelson, 1977, p. 69), a remarkable extension of the list of those who admitted the superior authority of Edward in 920 and of Athelstan in 927. Our sources for the secular aspect of Edgar's reign are too inadequate to rule out the possibility that William of Malmesbury was reliably informed when he described Edgar's naval defences of Britain 'against pirates' (*GR*, pp. 177–8). If Edgar did have a fleet, it is likely that some of the ships were manned by Scandinavians or by men of Scandinavian descent.

Edgar's dominant position was recognized on Whitsunday 973 by his imperial coronation, which took place in appropriately Roman surroundings at Bath, an occasion apparently marked by a special issue of coins from that mint. The ceremony was followed later that year by a dramatic and symbolic demonstration of his power when he was rowed on the river Dee at Chester by eight 'subkings' including Kenneth, king of Scots, Iago of Gwynedd, and Dyfnwal of Strathclyde.

His death in 975 released various tensions that had been suppressed by his effective rule. According to the *Life of Oswald*, written less than thirty years later,

> by his death the state of the whole kingdom was thrown into confusion, the bishops were agitated, the noblemen stirred up, the monks shaken with fear, the people terrified; the clerics were made glad, for their time had come. (*EHD*, 236)

Many, whose resentment at the favour recently shown to monks had been increased by displays of unmonastic arrogance, seized their opportunity and some monasteries suffered serious losses. The consequent conflicts were made worse by a dynastic dispute between rival supporters of Edgar's two sons, the half-brothers Edward and Æthelred. Edward was murdered three years later at Corfe but Æthelred, who was only ten years old, cannot have had any personal responsibility for that crime, and he was not the first king to gain a throne in such circumstances. He clearly expected that he would rule England as effectively as his father had done. His children's names are significant: Athelstan, Egbert, Edmund, Eadred, Eadwig, Edgar. With one exception, the kings after whom they were named were those who had ruled all the English kingdoms and could claim to be, like Athelstan, *rex Angulsexna and Northhymbra imperator paganorum gubernator Brittanorumque propugnator*. Even the exception, Egbert, had been king of Mercia and, according to the *Chronicle*, was acknowledged as overlord by the Northumbrians. Æthelred had stepped into an imperial inheritance. It was only after 1002, when Viking attacks were threatening that 'empire', that he named the sons of his second marriage, to Emma of Normandy, after kings who had successfully resisted an earlier generation of Scandinavian invaders, Edward and Alfred.

It was Æthelred's tragedy that his reign saw the renewal of Viking attacks, led either by Scandinavian kings or by men who hoped to smooth their path to kingship by winning treasure. Their armies were probably larger and better organized than those of the ninth century.

The Danish camps of Trelleborg, Fyrkat and Aggersborg are not directly connected with the raids on England and may not have served a military purpose for long, but they were constructed in the tenth century and reveal a degree of discipline and a potential for organization that must have made Danish armies of that age formidable opponents (Olsen and Schmidt, 1977; Roesdahl, 1977). The failure of the English burghal defences against them may possibly have been because they were not properly maintained, but it is as likely that they were inadequate against such well-organized raiders. There was no difficulty in recruiting warriors for these attacks. England was wealthy and its royal government soon showed that it could gather, by taxation if necessary, vast sums of tribute to buy off invaders.

The problems faced by Æthelred's government in defending the whole of England against such attacks were far greater than those Alfred had faced, and solved, a century before. It was not simply that Æthelred had a larger kingdom to defend, or that his enemies were better organized. There was a more important difference in that Alfred's enemies wanted to settle and, in their new homes, were as vulnerable to reprisals and sudden attack as their victims had ever been. The Vikings of Æthelred's time were simply raiders, and most were eager to return home with the treasure they had won. Against such a threat conventional defences were useless. The problem was not insoluble, as Harold proved at Stamford Bridge, but solutions could not be quickly found, and both Harold and William, who also successfully resisted Danish attacks, owed much to the foundations Æthelred prepared. The recently created unity of the English kingdom was obviously strained by these attacks, and the prominence in many parts of the country of men of Scandinavian descent was an additional source of weakness. The Danish king Swein took care not to antagonize such potential allies by senseless pillage and in 1013 his army did not begin plundering until it had crossed Watling Street. Æthelred has been unfairly blamed for his failure, and the knowledge of that failure has coloured most later comment on his reign. The first, fullest and perhaps least fair was the chronicler whose account of Æthelred's wars against Viking invaders is a remarkable contrast to his predecessor's panegyric on Alfred.

That Æthelred did fail cannot be denied. In 1013 in the face of Swein's violent occupation of the kingdom, Æthelred went into exile with his brother-in-law, the duke of Normandy, but when Swein died early in 1014

all the councillors who were in England, ecclesiastical and lay,
determined to send for King Æthelred, and they said that no lord
was dearer to them than their natural lord, if he would govern them
more justly than before. .... Then during the spring King Æthelred
came home to his own people and he was gladly received by all.
(*Chronicle*, 1014)

Unfortunately Cnut returned to recover what his father had won and,
in April 1016, as he advanced on London, Æthelred died. His eldest
son, Edmund, was immediately elected king but before long was forced
to agree to a partition in which he retained only Wessex.

That proved to be the last time the English kingdom was divided.
When Edmund died later in 1016, Cnut succeeded to the whole and,
although his death in 1035 was followed by a confused situation, there
was no question of partition. His widow claimed to hold Wessex for
her son Harthacnut, while Harald, a putative son of Cnut, was regarded
by some as his regent, but Harthacnut did not return to England until
Harald died and when he himself died in 1042 Æthelred's surviving
son, Edward, inherited the united kingdom.

There were certainly great regional differences in that kingdom.
The unification was too recent for these to have been forgotten, and
they found expression in the great earldoms of the eleventh century,
which were a development of the arrangements of the tenth century
when ealdormen began to hold several counties. These divisions did
not, however, presage a new disintegration of the kingdom. The
groups of counties were not stable, and even Northumbria was occasionally divided; the earls were agents of the king, and among their
functions was the collection of royal revenues; there was only one,
centrally controlled, coinage; and it was the king's forces that the earls
led. The king was not a free agent. He could not appoint anyone as
earl who was unacceptable to the people of that region – as was proved
in 1065 when the Northumbrians forced Edward to make Morcar
their earl in place of Tostig – but no earl was free to defy the king.

That did not, of course, prevent an earl becoming king as Harold,
earl of Wessex, showed in 1066 when he succeeded the childless Edward. There were other contenders. William, duke of Normandy, who
had been promised the succession by Edward, and the Norwegian and
Danish kings also considered they had a right to claim what Cnut had
held. Harald of Norway came first but died at Stamford Bridge on

25 September 1066. On 14 October the victorious Harold was himself killed in battle against William. The English were unable to agree on a successor and reluctantly accepted William who was crowned in Edward's new church at Westminster on Christmas Day. In many parts of England, especially the north and south-west, opposition continued, made more serious by the arrival of a Danish fleet in the Humber. William overcame this challenge and by a combination of force and the offer of tribute he persuaded the Danes to leave and by ruthlessly devastating Northumbria he ensured that it could never again be used as a base for a challenge to his power. There was, however, a later threat from Denmark. In the words of the *Chronicle*:

> In this year (1085) people said, and declared for a fact, that Cnut, king of Denmark, son of King Swein, was setting out in this direction and meant to conquer this country with the help of Robert, count of Flanders, because Cnut was married to Robert's daughter. When William, king of England, who was then in Normandy – for he was in possession of both England and Normandy – found out about this, he went to England with a larger force of mounted men and infantry from France and Brittany than had ever come to this country, so that people wondered how this country could maintain all that army . . . and the king had the land near the sea laid waste, so that if his enemies landed, they should have nothing to seize on quickly.

Coastal waste recorded in Domesday Book in the following year only occurs north of the Wash, which suggests that William feared the invaders would land in the north. The attack was, in fact, never launched and shortly afterwards Cnut was assassinated. This incident shows that, although the wealth of England encouraged the ambition of potential conquerors, it also provided the means with which they could be defeated. England was, therefore, united and relatively secure. William soon re-established the hegemony over Welsh princes and the Scottish king that his predecessors as kings of England had, but that English overlordship now formed part of a far larger 'empire', based on Caen and Rouen as much as London and Winchester.

III

The making
of the landscape

The early history of the English landscape has, until recently, been based on a study of place-names and Domesday Book, supplemented by pre-Conquest charters, especially those with boundary clauses, and some incidental references in contemporary writings. Our knowledge is now being greatly enlarged by archaeological discoveries that have drawn attention to the limitations of these sources, and the consequent re-examination of the evidence has, in its turn, led to some questioning of the assumptions that have hitherto guided discussions of the subject. Prominent among these has been the assumption that medieval English settlement developed by a more or less continuous process of growth from small beginnings made by the early colonists after the collapse of Roman authority until the fourteenth century, when population started to decline and the period of village shrinkage and desertion began. It has, for example, been accepted that, when Scandinavians conquered East Anglia, eastern Mercia and Deira in the ninth century, they found extensive tracts of unoccupied land in which they were able to create many hundreds of new farms and villages. Two centuries later Domesday Book appears to show that there were still large areas with few or no settlements. The fact that Domesday Book records very few places in the Weald, an expanse of woodland that stretches about 100 miles from Kent to Hampshire, led J. H. Round (1899, p. 3) to assert that it 'was still, at the time of the Conquest, a belt some twenty miles in width, of forest, not yet opened up, except in a few scattered spots, for human settlement'. Other blanks on the Domesday map have led to similar conclusions about the extent of settlement elsewhere in the eleventh century. There has, moreover, been a tendency to accept that the first reference to a place gives some indication of the time at which it was first settled, that places first mentioned in the thirteenth or fourteenth centuries were colonized after the Norman Conquest. Further support for this expansionist interpretation has been found in the place-names themselves. A. H. Smith described 'the general picture that we get of the spread of English settlements' as

> a basic nucleus of ancient sites indicated by a limited number of place-names in -ing, of major movements towards the west where names in tūn preponderate and words like cot become more frequent, and of the steady clearing of ground and the growth of outlying farms around all these primary settlements, an expansion first represented chiefly by the use of old topographical names and later by the increasing use of special terms like throp, or stoc or wīc, and last of all by words like rydding, 'clearing', and the like. (Smith, 1956b, p. 88)

This general interpretation of the development of the English landscape in the centuries after Roman rule, apparently supported by so many different kinds of evidence, was well summed up by Professor H. R. Loyn when he wrote that 'the story of Anglo-Saxon settlement, when looked at in depth, yields more of the saga of man against the forest than of Saxon against Celt. It was a colonizing movement in the true sense of the word' (Loyn, 1962, p. 36).

Every year archaeologists uncover remains of English settlements in places that are not named in Domesday Book. Two good recent examples are the ninth-century houses at Goltho in Lincolnshire and at Ribblehead in Yorkshire (Med. Arch., 19, 1975, pp. 223-4, 230). Goltho, about ten miles north-east of Lincoln, is first mentioned in a thirteenth-century ecclesiastical register and was deserted in the following century, but several pre-Conquest houses, some measuring 9 by 4 metres, have been discovered there under early Norman structures that show that the site was still occupied at the time when Domesday Book was compiled. At Ribblehead, between Whernside and Ingleborough, remains of a house, 18 metres long, with associated structures, have been found on the limestone pavement at 1100 feet above sea level. Erosion has destroyed most traces of occupation but several finds have been made and the fortunate discovery of two ninth-century North-umbrian coins in the walls shows that, although no settlement is men-tioned here in any early source, this house was standing when the Scandinavians seized control of the area.

Many other examples could be given of the way archaeological discoveries have revealed the inadequacy of the documentary evidence for settlement, but archaeology alone cannot provide a satisfactory substitute. The possibilities of archaeological investigation are always limited; in many areas modern disturbance has destroyed early evidence and it is normally not possible to explore extensive areas. However large the area excavated, there is always the possibility that other evi-dence lies undiscovered just outside the limits of the dig. One way of extending the area of investigation is by aerial photography. Where ditches or banks have left slight depressions or bumps in the surface, it is sometimes possible to see these more clearly from the air than on the ground; the hillsides near Ribblehead have many traces of struc-tures, some of which may be contemporary with the house already excavated. Even when such traces have been completely levelled, it is still possible, given suitable conditions, to detect them from the air by the crop marks that result from the different rates of ripening caused by varying depths of soil below the surface. In the exceptionally dry summers of 1975 and 1976 many new sites were discovered in this way. Crop marks appear best in light soils, such as sand or gravel; they are much more difficult to detect in heavy soils and, of course, they do not appear at all in grassland or woodland. Unfortunately sites cannot normally be dated without excavation, although sometimes the shape of structures may give some indication of their age. Another method of detecting early settlements is by the discovery of occupation debris, especially fragments of datable early pottery, in cultivated ground. Broken or unwanted vessels once used for domestic purposes can sur-vive more or less permanently in the soil until their fragments are turned up by the action of a plough. The discovery of many fragments of different pots in a limited area is a good indication either of a nearby settlement or of a cremation cemetery, and the presence of such a cemetery implies a settlement in the vicinity. It is true that pieces of pottery could be widely distributed when manure was spread from a farm-yard or byre, but manure-spreading would normally produce a wide scatter of pottery; relatively dense concentrations are more likely to be the debris of pots that were discarded near a house, a conclusion that has often been verified by excavation, most dramatically at Chalton in Hampshire where a large seventh-century settlement was discovered in this way. A concentration of pottery fragments could alternatively come from shattered cremation urns. There is, of course, no hope of discovering such evidence in permanent grassland and even in arable it is more easily found when freshly ploughed soil has been washed by rain. The continuous action of frost and rain may reduce some types of pottery to dust and there is therefore more chance of finding pottery in fields that have been ploughed infrequently than in those that have been cultivated continuously over long periods, perhaps even centuries. The survival of pottery also depends on its quality, and the tendency of well-made pots to survive, while soft friable material disintegrates, partly explains the relative abundance of some Roman pottery in contrast to the less frequent finds of early English vessels, but that difference may also reflect the relative abundance of pottery in the two periods. There is the additional difficulty that sometimes vessels of wood or leather rather than pot were used. The discovery of quantities of datable pottery is therefore a positive indication of the existence of a settlement, or cemetery, at the relevant date, but the absence of such pottery cannot be taken as proof that an area was not settled. The fact that systematic field-walking in parts of Warwickshire, for example, has yielded quantities of Roman pottery but no English material does not prove that those sites were unoccupied after the fifth century.

Not only is archaeological evidence necessarily incomplete, it can never alone explain the evolution of settlements and their surrounding landscape. It may be possible to discover how a building was made, and even what it was used for, but material evidence cannot reveal how many people occupied it, or on what terms; it may sometimes be possible to trace old field boundaries and even to date them, but we cannot discover by archaeological means whether a field was held by one man or many. Archaeological investigations have vastly increased our knowledge of material culture, of buildings and boundaries, of tools, crops and animals, but to understand the customs of inheritance, the relations between members of a community, and the activity of lords, all factors which played a part in the evolution of the landscape, we must depend on the evidence of charters and laws and on the clues that we may discover in contemporary literature.

The natural starting-point for most discussions of early settlement is Domesday Book. This survey, compiled twenty years after the Norman Conquest, describes over 13,000 places south of the river Tees. For some we may be fortunate to have earlier references in charters but for the greater part of the country, and for most places, we have no evidence earlier than Domesday Book. It generally gives not only a valuation and a tax assessment but also details of various assets, including men, plough-teams, mills and woodland. It is arranged by counties and in each the royal estates are described first, followed by the lands of the tenants-in-chief, namely the churches and individuals who between them held the remaining land as tenants of the king. There is no such thing as a typical entry; the information given, its arrangement and even the terminology varies from county to county, and sometimes from place to place within a single county, but some idea of the scope and character of most Domesday entries may be gained from one example. In Wiltshire Odo, bishop of Bayeux, held four estates including Swindon:

> The same bishop holds Swindon, and Wadard of him. Leofgeat held it in the time of King Edward, and it paid geld for 5 hides. Of these one is in demesne and there is one plough and four serfs. There are five villeins and 2 bordars with 2 ploughs. There is a mill worth 4 shillings, and there are 30 acres of meadow and there is as much pasture. It was worth 40 shillings; it is now worth 4 pounds. (DB, i. 66)

It is not surprising that this vast accumulation of detail has appeared to make it possible to reconstruct the settlement geography of eleventh-century England. Unfortunately Domesday Book can be most mis-leading as a guide to the extent and character of rural settlement. This can best be demonstrated in Kent, where some eleventh-century lists of places with churches reveal the existence of no fewer than 400 eleventh-century churches, 159 of them in places that are not even mentioned in Domesday Book. Omissions are revealed in all parts of the county (see Figure 7) but they are particularly significant in the Weald, where there were over thirty places with eleventh-century churches in addition to the eighteen settlements named in Domesday Book. The Weald has always been an area of dispersed settlement and each of these churches must have served a number of separate farms and hamlets, how many we shall never know. If we had similar lists of churches for Sussex and Surrey, they would certainly show that the Weald in those counties was far more thoroughly settled than Domesday Book suggests. Domesday Book itself sometimes implies the omission of places by recording the existence of two or more churches on one estate. The Kentish Domesday mentions 186 churches and chapels in the descriptions of 147 estates, showing that some places had more than one. Multiple churches in such urban centres as Dover, with four, or Canterbury, with several, are not surprising, but most of

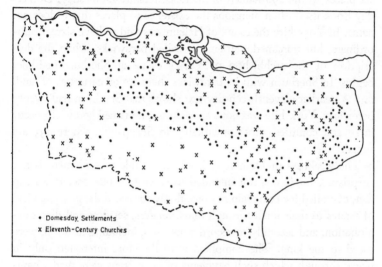

Figure 7 Domesday settlements and eleventh-century churches in Kent (p. 136)
Taken from Darby and Campbell (1962, pp. 496–7).

the estates were rural and their extra churches probably served unnamed settlements. There were sixteen estates with two, five with three, while Folkestone had eight and Hoo, north of the Medway estuary, had six. Similar references to multiple churches occur in other counties, suggesting that they also had settlements omitted from Domesday. A good example is South Elmham in Suffolk, where the six churches mentioned must mean that the six adjacent parishes of South Elmham, now distinguished by their church dedications, St Peter, St Michael, etc., already existed as separate settlements but were grouped together in Domesday. In Hampshire twelve places had 2 churches, while Alresford had 3, Odiham 4 and Chilcomb 9. Unfortunately, in most counties Domesday only mentioned churches incidentally in a few places but sometimes, as at Worth in Sussex, a pre-Conquest church survives to fill a gap in the Domesday map of churches. Such evidence can in some areas be supplemented by surveys that were compiled within a generation of 1086. These show the existence of places that were omitted from Domesday, as for example the Leicestershire Survey, compiled in 1129–30, which although itself incomplete adds twenty-six places to the 296 named in the Leicestershire Domesday. Domesday Book itself often mentions the existence of places that it does not name. In Yorkshire the estate of Hallam was said to have sixteen subordinate, but unnamed, settlements called berewicks, while the description of the archbishop of York's estate at Sherburn-in-Elmet begins 'In Sherburn with its berewicks there are 96 carucates of land. . . .' An earlier eleventh-century text shows that Sherburn had twenty berewicks. Yorkshire was not a special case; unnamed berewicks occur in several counties, most remarkably in Shropshire, where 135 are noted.

The weakness of Domesday Book as a guide to settlement is not surprising, for it was not intended to serve that purpose. It was, in fact, compiled for two main reasons, firstly to record the possible yield of estates to their lords through rents, renders, services and direct exploitation, and secondly to record what dues, including taxation, were owed to the king. The compilers were therefore interested only in places through which such payments of tax or rent were made; hamlets, farms and even sizeable settlements that rendered their taxes or seigneurial dues through some other estate might well not be named. So, for example, the bishop of Lincoln's 95-hide estate at Dorchester-on-Thames in Oxfordshire included Burcot, Clifton, Chiselhampton, Drayton, Stadhampton and Overy, and most if not all of these settlements must have been in existence in 1086, even though they are not mentioned by name in Domesday. For its purposes the names of these places were irrelevant, what mattered was the bishop's estate of which they were component parts. Detailed local studies can make it possible to argue with some confidence, as at Dorchester, that particular settlements, sometimes first mentioned long after Domesday, probably existed when the survey was compiled, but no elaborate enquiry is needed to justify the general claim that estates with very large assessments, like the 95 hides of Dorchester or the 96 carucates of Sherburn-in-Elmet, must have depended for their effective exploitation on several settlements distributed through the whole estate. Large estates of this kind occur in every county and the problems they pose for settlement history can be usefully illustrated by the great royal manor of Milton, near Sittingbourne, in Kent (DB, i. 2b). This ancient estate, which also formed the hundred of Milton, extended some four miles around the vill. In Domesday it was assessed at 80 sulungs, Kentish units that in this part of the county included some 200 acres of arable, suggesting an arable area of about 16,000 acres or twenty-five square miles, slightly less than the extent indicated by the 170 ploughs recorded, each of which could reasonably be expected to cultivate 100 acres a year. The resources of the estate were not exclusively arable; apart from the six mills there were twenty-seven salt-pans and thirty-two fisheries, most of which must have been along the north shore and around the Isle of Sheppey. Domesday records almost 400 peasants at Milton and these men, with their families, must have lived in settlements scattered throughout this vast estate. Domesday also records that an unstated number of 'men of the Weald' belonged to Milton and owed an annual render of 50 shillings as well as carrying services. Later evidence suggests that these men lived in Marden, a large tract of forest some fourteen miles from Milton. The number of settlements that constituted the manor of Milton will never be known, Domesday only names five places apart from Milton in the hundred, but there were twenty-three churches in it. One of the places in Milton hundred that Domesday does describe is Newington. It was held by the queen before the Conquest and the account, although confused, certainly shows that the rights and obligations of that place were intimately connected with the royal estate, an association that is confirmed by other contemporary evidence. In the Domesday account of Milton itself Hugh de Port is said to hold a little more than 8 sulungs 'which in the time of King Edward were joined with the other sulungs (of Milton) in paying customary dues' and this part was worth £20 'which are reckoned in with the £200 of the whole manor of Milton'. The location of Hugh's 8 sulungs is not indicated, even though they had apparently been in some degree withdrawn from the estate since the Conquest – the implication is clearly that they no longer paid their customary dues through Milton. If, as seems likely, they were the four places in Milton hundred that are elsewhere in Domesday described as being held by Hugh, that is Tonge, Tunstall, Upchurch and *Stapedone* in Norton, they illustrate the scattered character of Milton manor, for Upchurch and Tonge are six miles apart. Milton was therefore not only an extensive estate with an unknown but large number of settlements, it also had important resources on the coast and in the Weald, all of which must have had associated settlements from which they were exploited, but which Domesday had no reason to name.

The Wealden appendages of Kentish estates are well known and can be studied from a very early date, thanks to the relatively abundant documentary evidence preserved by the active interest of the great Kentish religious houses, but the forest and marsh resources in all parts of England were to some extent exploited in the same way by being treated as appurtenant to estates elsewhere. One example from another part of the country may serve to illustrate what was a common arrangement: Brailes in south Warwickshire had, according to Domesday Book, extensive woodland, but this in fact lay some twenty-five miles away at Tanworth-in-Arden which was, until the end of the twelfth century, associated ecclesiastically with Brailes by being a chapelry of it, and administratively by being in the same hundred (Ford, 1976, p. 279). Similar connections, often revealed in the same way by parochial or hundredal associations, are found in all parts of the country, especially where there were extensive resources of wood or marsh on which surrounding areas depended.

Small estates as well as large sometimes consisted of several settlements that were grouped together by the compilers of Domesday Book, and occasionally Domesday itself indicates their existence by an incidental reference, as in its account of Dene-in-Westwell, Kent, which was assessed at one sulung dispersed in three places, *erat dispertita in tribus locis* (DB, i. 10b). Dispersed settlement of this kind must have been a common pattern in many parts of England, especially in regions where the land available for settlement was broken by woodland or hills. In Devon, for example, many of the estates described in Domesday included several small and separate farms, and Professor Hoskins has argued that 'the map of Devon in the eleventh century would have looked very like the map today even on the 1-inch scale. Practically all the thousands of farm-names printed on the modern map would have been on the earlier map, could it have been drawn' (Hoskins, 1963, p. 52).

Places omitted from Domesday Book may well not be recorded until long after the eleventh century. If they were held by religious communities with an interest in recording the obligations of their tenants, settlements might be mentioned in twelfth-century surveys. Casual references also occur in the records of royal government as, for example, when a reference to Hugh of Oxenhope in an Exchequer record of 1191 provides the first evidence of the Pennine community from which he took his name. The first systematic list of settlements rather than of estates was that in the Hundred Rolls of 1279 but these only survive in full for six counties, with fragmentary returns elsewhere, and for many areas the first systematic survey of settlements is in the fourteenth-century taxation records which, because the assessments were then based on the personal wealth of individuals, tended to list the settlements in which people lived. These later records make it possible to determine with some confidence the full extent of medieval settlement. A few of the settlements first recorded in the thirteenth or fourteenth century may have been established after the eleventh century, but the great majority probably already existed at that date and were omitted from Domesday because they were component parts of larger estates. Such omissions are naturally more numerous where settlements were dispersed than where they were normally compact, or nucleated. In Doddingtree hundred in Worcestershire, a woodland area, Domesday Book only names a quarter of the known medieval settlements, while in areas of nucleated settlement, like the East Riding of Yorkshire, Domesday Book names 405, or 79 per cent, of the 510 settlements that are recorded before the sixteenth century, and in parts of the Riding the proportion is much higher, rising to 94 per cent in one area of the Wolds, Buckrose Wapentake. This does not mean that the Yorkshire Wolds were more completely settled in the eleventh century than the woodlands of Worcestershire, only that Domesday Book conceals more settlements in areas where they are dispersed.

When a dispersed estate was broken up and its parts were for the first time treated separately for purposes of lordship or taxation, there was sometimes uncertainty about the proper division of responsibility between the parts. Such uncertainties can be seen in Domesday's treatment of those parts of Milton in Kent that had been separated from the royal estate, and an even better illustration of the difficulties that could be caused is provided by a group of estates in the Sussex Weald that had until the Conquest been appurtenant to estates around Eastbourne and Lewes. By 1086 they had been detached from their parent estates and Domesday was unable to record their assessments because they had never paid geld, not because they had been unusually privileged or because they had only recently been colonized, but because their assessment had formerly been included in that of the distant estates to which they had belonged. The reorganization of Sussex into the six post-Conquest rapes resulted in many similar separations, which explains why more Wealden settlements are named in the Sussex Domesday than in that for Kent or Surrey (Sawyer, 1976, p. 4).

In the twelfth and thirteenth centuries there were many changes in rural society; the population certainly grew, the pattern of cultivation was altered as woodland and pasture were put under the plough to meet the demand for cereals, and both processes led to the creation of new settlements. Most of these were small, however, on the margins of cultivation in woodland or on the fringes of high moorland, and many proved ephemeral. The most extensive changes occurred along the Lincolnshire coast where large areas of land were recovered for settlement in the medieval period. Settlements were also abandoned and many places in Domesday Book are now only represented by deserted sites or cannot even be identified. Most of the desertions occurred after the fourteenth century and the fact that 97 per cent of the 13,000 places named in Domesday can be identified in medieval records, if not on the modern map, reinforces the claim that the changes in the twelfth and thirteenth centuries did not fundamentally alter the settlement pattern that had been established by the time of the Norman Conquest.

The main documentary evidence for the earlier history of settlement is provided by land charters. The first were produced in the seventh century and about 1,500 survive from before the Norman Conquest, but unfortunately they are very unevenly distributed about the country. There are relatively large numbers for such counties as Kent, Hampshire and Worcestershire, where great religious houses existed in whose archives the charters were preserved, but large areas of the country yield few or none. There is also the complication that some charters are later fabrications and most of those which may with some confidence be accepted as authentic only survive in later copies in which alterations may have been made by accident or design. The textual difficulties can be avoided by limiting discussion, in the first place, to the charters which survive in original form, or at least very early copies, and are therefore normally free of later interpolations or alterations. Such a limitation drastically reduces the amount of evidence, for of the 228 charters that purport to have been drawn up before the year 800 only twenty survive in copies written before that date and these illustrate the uneven distribution of this material; seven come from Kent, two from the subkingdom of the Hwicce, two from Essex, eight from Mercia, one from Sussex and none from Wessex, East Anglia or Northumbria.

Some of these charters refer to very small estates, for example the grant by Æthelberht of Kent in 732 to the church of Lyminge of a quarter ploughland by the river Lympne for salt boiling or, more normally, Offa's grant in 788 to his *minister* Osberht of one ploughland called *Duningcland* in Kent (S, 23 and 128). In contrast, several charters, to judge by the stated assessments and, when they are given, the bounds, are grants of very large areas indeed. Late in the eighth century Offa granted 55 hides of land at Westbury-on-Trym in Gloucestershire and in 799 Cenwulf of Mercia restored to Christ Church, Canterbury, 44 sulungs in Kent, 30 of which were at Charing (S, 139 and 155). Neither of these charters describes the bounds but the extent of such grants is indicated by the bounds of 40 hides granted to Barking minster at the end of the seventh century, showing that the estate covered more than 60 square miles around Barking (S, 1171). We are fortunate to have one charter in which the existence of unnamed settlements is made explicit; it is a late seventh-century grant by Cædwalla, king of Wessex, 'of land whose name is Farnham' in Surrey, for the construction of a monastery (S, 235; *EHD*, 58). The original no longer survives and the text is known only in a twelfth-century cartulary of Winchester Cathedral, but misreadings in the copy show that it was based on a version that was written in a much earlier script, although it cannot on that ground be proved to have been originally written as early as the seventh century. It does, however, have some features which are consistent with a very early date and, although it has probably been altered, for example, by the addition of a dating clause using the Incarnation, it is in general a reliable early charter. After giving the assessment of the estate, 60 hides, it continues 'of which 10 are in Binton, 2 in Churt, and the rest are assigned to their own places and names, that is *Cusanweoh*; with everything belonging to them, fields, woods, meadows, pastures, fisheries, rivers, springs.' It is possible that the copyist left out some names after *Cusanweoh*, a word meaning 'the sanctuary of Cusa', but the plural forms of 'places and names' are as clear as the conclusion that there were other places in the estate and that they had their own names. The estate was large, Binton lies four miles east of Farnham and Churt five miles south of it, and the grant may be compared with the description of the same estate in Domesday Book, when it was held by the bishop of Winchester and was still assessed at 60 hides. As Maitland remarked:

> we certainly must not draw the inference that there was but one vill in this tract. If the bishop is tenant-in-chief of the whole hundred and has become responsible for all the geld that is levied there-from, there is no great reason why the surveyors should trouble themselves about the vills. Thus the simple *Episcopus tenet Ferne-ham* may dispose of some 25,000 acres of land. (1897, pp. 13–14)

It is therefore clear that early charters can be as misleading as Domesday Book, for neither was intended to provide details of settlements. The men who drafted charters, like those who compiled Domesday Book, were interested in the total resources of estates, and this was often ex-pressed in the form of an assessment that would be used as the basis for levying royal tribute or other obligations, such as military service, and later for the collection of tax. Before the eleventh century these assess-ments were normally expressed in terms of households or standard holdings for which several technical terms were used, *manentes*, *cassati*, or hides, but all express the same basic unit, the land of one family. The assessments stated in the charters were real; they defined the actual burden borne by the estates and not the potential burden that should be borne. There are very few indications of the dues that were expected from estates but those that are recorded show that the burden could be very heavy. In Ine's laws the food rent from an estate of ten hides is given at 10 vats of honey, 300 loaves, 12 ambers of Welsh ale, 30 of clear ale, 2 full-grown cows or 10 wethers, 10 geese, 20 hens, 10 cheeses, an amber full of butter, 5 salmon, 100 eels and a quantity of fodder (Ine, 70.1). Despite the uncertainty about the size of some of these measures, Sir Frank Stenton was clearly right when he described this as a formidable rent (1971, p. 288). It may be compared with the details given in a charter concerning the tribute payable under Offa from the 60-hide estate of Westbury in Gloucestershire. It was to be

> released from all compulsion of kings and ealdormen and their sub-ordinates except these taxes; that is of the tribute at Westbury two tuns full of pure ale and a coomb full of mild ale and a coomb full of Welsh ale, and seven oxen and six wethers and 40 cheeses and six long *theru* [a word of unknown meaning] and 30 ambers of unground corn and four ambers of meal, to the royal estate. (S, 146; *EHD* 78).

These texts imply that the estates were fully exploited and there would have been little room for unworked resources. When, for example, in 681 the abbess Beorngyth was given 20 hides by the river Cherwell for her monastery she was not being given empty land awaiting exploitation; 20 hides meant that the estate was due to pay a large tribute to the king, or, if he wished to alienate it, to some beneficiary.

The assessments given in early charters show that in those areas with surviving charters, the resources were as fully exploited in the seventh and eighth centuries as they were in the eleventh. Few estates remained intact throughout this period and direct comparison is therefore rarely possible, but the assessment of Farnham was the same in the seventh-century charter that has been quoted as it was in Domesday Book, 60 hides. The figure in that charter may, of course, have been altered by some copyist to make it agree with Domesday but there are several original charters to show that the Farnham case was not exceptional. One concerns Westbury-on-Trym in Gloucestershire and is a grant by Offa of 55 hides to a leading layman. Offa later granted the reversion of the same estate, then assessed at 60 hides, to the church of Worcester and the same church held it in Domesday Book' with an assessment of 50 hides (S, 139 and 146; DB, i. 164b).

It has been argued that the boundaries of estates given in some early charters show that England was only lightly settled in the early English period. In the earliest charters the bounds refer only to major features, a good example being the grant in 736 by Æthelbald of Mercia to a *comes* called Cyneberht 'of a small piece of land, namely 10 hides' bounded on two sides by the river Stour, on the north by the wood 'which they call Kinver but on the west another, of which the name is Morfe, the greater part of which woods belongs to the aforesaid estate' (S, 89; *EHD*, 67). Sir Frank Stenton argued that such boundary clauses reflected

> the conditions of a time when river valleys determined settlement and village communities had not yet defined their rights in the woodland which overshadowed them . . . a comparison of this vague language with the definite place-names and exact boundaries of a late Old English charter indicates the nature of the unrecorded changes which had come over English country life between the eighth and tenth centuries. (1971, p. 285)

It should, however, be noted that in many early charters bounds are not given at all and that sometimes they are simply said to be well known or 'ancient and known by the natives', and in the earliest original of all, Hlothhere, king of Kent, grants land in Thanet 'by the well-known bounds indicated by me and my reeves' (S, 8). A remarkable account of a boundary perambulation in 896 has been preserved. It follows the resolution of a dispute between the bishop of Worcester and Æthelwald over woodland at Woodchester in Gloucestershire that had been granted to the church of Worcester well over a century earlier by King Æthelbald. After Æthelwald, who was himself a priest, had accepted the claims of Worcester, 'he ordered his *geneat*, whose name was Ecglaf, to ride with a priest from Worcester, Wulfhun by name; and Ecglaf led Wulfhun along all the boundaries as Wulfhun read out from the old charters, how they had been determined of old by the grant of King Æthelbald' (S, 1441). There is no suggestion that the bounds of this woodland were uncertain; the dispute was caused by the claims of other estates to have rights in it.

Rights over woodland appear to have been well defined from a very early date. The statement in Æthelbald's charter to Cyneberht that the greater part of the wood of Kinver and Morfe belonged to an estate on the river Stour did not mean that contemporaries were uncertain about the apportionment of that woodland between different communities. The antiquity and thoroughness of the division of such resources has been demonstrated by William Ford in his study of the detached appurtenances of estates in the region of the Warwickshire Avon. Figure 8, based on his work, shows the medieval linkages that can be discovered between detached appurtenances and their parent estates in that area by means of arrows. It is clear that these linkages all lay in well-defined regions around which it is possible to draw boundary lines. This map shows clearly that no estates had any appurtenances outside their own districts as defined by these lines, a feature that suggests that the arrangements were made when those boundaries had some political force. One of them follows the boundary of the medieval diocese of Worcester, and probably therefore of the seventh-century kingdom of the Hwicce. After the Hwicce were absorbed by Mercia, that boundary continued to serve ecclesiastical purposes, but its political and economic significance must have declined. It is, of course, possible that, if the settlements in the valleys of the Avon and the Blythe first established their rights over the woodland of Arden after the seventh century, that traditional boundary would still have been respected, but it is more

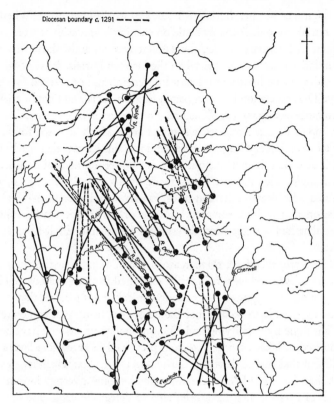

Diocesan boundary c. 1291 — — — —

R. Blythe

R. Avon

R. Leam

R. Itchen

R. Alne

R. Avon

R. Stour

R. Dene

R. Cherwell

R. Evenlode

Figure 8   Linked settlements in Warwickshire
Based on Ford (1976, p. 281).

reasonable to conclude that these arrangements already existed in the
seventh century. There were certainly some late rearrangements of
rights in woodland. The dispute over Woodchester appears to have
been caused by a grant to the church of Worcester of a tract of woodland in which the neighbouring estates of Bisley and Evening as well as
the more distant Thornbury, fifteen miles away, had traditional rights.
It is, however, worth noting that the Woodchester agreement of 896
only recognized the rights of Worcester to the woodland, which remained in the occupation of Æthelwald and his son, and was still a
subject of dispute in the eleventh century (DB, i. 164a). Many small
estates also appear to have had very old boundaries, even though they
are first mentioned in the tenth century or later. This is shown partly

by the use of heathen burials as boundary marks in charters. Whether
the burials were deliberately made on existing boundaries or were later
chosen as boundary marks, these references certainly show that the
boundaries existed at a time when the heathen burials, most of which
have disappeared without trace, were remembered or marked in some
way. The association between pagan English burials and boundaries is
even more clearly seen in Wiltshire. To the west of Stonehenge there is
a group of Bronze Age barrows, only one of which has been found to
contain a secondary English burial, and it is this barrow that marks the
point at which the parish boundary of Winterbourne Stoke turned a
right angle. This discovery was made by Desmond Bonney (1976),
who has also drawn attention to other evidence that confirms the impression that at least some early estate or parish boundaries follow
lines that had already been determined before the English came to
Britain.

There are, therefore, good reasons for thinking that the rural resources of England were being fully exploited from an early date. This
suggestion is supported by palaeobotanical investigations that have
made it possible to reconstruct the ecological history of some areas.
This is done by identifying and counting pollen grains that have been
deposited in lakes or peat bogs and preserved in successive layers of
sediment that can be dated by Carbon-14 assay. The reliability of the
technique has recently been demonstrated by some investigations in the
north of England that have been able to detect the ecological consequences of William's devastation of the area after the Norman Conquest (Bartley, Chambers and Hart-Jones, 1976, p. 466). Pollen dia-
grams from several parts of England have shown that there was no
significant ecological change in the centuries after the end of Roman
rule. There are exceptions, however, and a pollen diagram from Neas-
ham Fen in the middle Tees valley does show that in the eighth century
there was a major local clearance of woodland with the substitution of
grassland and arable (Bartley, Chambers and Hart-Jones, 1976, pp.
438–46, 466), but most investigations have failed to detect a significant
increase in arable cultivation at the expense of either woodland or pasture between the fifth century and the eleventh. A different method of
estimating the extent of woodland in the Dark Ages depends on the
study of the alignment of dykes constructed in that period. Sir Cyril
Fox (1955, pp. 118–23) pointed out that such earthworks could only
be made absolutely straight if the ground were clear and the sight lines

not obscured by trees or undergrowth. He was able to distinguish straight and sinuous lengths of Offa's Dyke and from these to determine which stretches had been constructed on ground that was already clear in the eighth century. He found that in the mountainous areas the northern slopes of valleys tended to be clear, while the southern slopes were not and in Montgomeryshire, either side of the Severn, over seven miles of the Dyke have completely straight alignments, implying large areas of cleared ground.

Full exploitation of the resources and a stable ecology do not necessarily mean demographic stability. Unfortunately the evidence for the size of the English population before the eleventh century is even less satisfactory than that for the settlements in which the people lived. Even the abundant data of Domesday Book allows little hope of a reliable estimate of the population in 1086. The survey enumerates different classes of peasants on most estates but the total number represented by these depends on the size of their households. A reasonable estimate, based on later evidence, is that the average size was five, which would mean a total population of some $1\frac{1}{2}$ million but it is possible that family sizes varied in different areas, and among the different classes. It is, for example, probable that households were larger in towns than in the countryside. A total population of $1\frac{1}{2}$ million in 1086 is therefore a low estimate and the urban element may well have been even larger than Domesday Book appears to indicate. There is, however, an additional complication, for it can be shown that in some areas Domesday Book omitted about half the population. Two surveys of the estates of Burton Abbey made early in the twelfth century show that on those estates Domesday only noted the peasants who owed labour services and, therefore, omitted the wealthier tenants who paid rent and were called *censarii* (Walmsley, 1968). The differences between these surveys and Domesday Book have often been noted but they have generally been explained as an indication of rapidly rising population. Such a dramatic increase in thirty years, followed by apparent stability in the decade that separates the two surveys, is, in any case, implausible and a detailed comparison of all three texts has confirmed the suggestion made as early as 1896 by F. H. Baring (1896) that these surveys show massive omissions from Domesday Book, whose compilers were principally interested in the demesne resources of estates. One of their main purposes was to determine what estates were worth: if peasants paid rent, their contribution was included in the total value; it was therefore unnecessary to note them separately, unless they also helped to cultivate the demesne. This does not mean that all the Domesday compilers interpreted their instructions in the same way. It is indeed likely that in some counties, especially those in which the population densities appear to be much higher than in Staffordshire and Derbyshire, the rent payers were included. The uncertainty is, however, enough to cast serious doubts on all estimates of the population of Domesday England and must also affect discussions about the social composition of that population. It is possible that there was some increase in population during the tenth and eleventh centuries. The apparent growth in the number and size of towns could only have been achieved by drawing on the rural population, but we can never hope to estimate the scale of any such increase any more than we can hope to determine the size of the population at any one time.

Some of the deficiencies of the documentary and archaeological evidence for the history of settlement can be made good with the help of place-names. All settlements, large and small, have names by which they can be identified, and the same is true of most features of the landscape, both natural and man-made. Properly interpreted these names can yield valuable clues to various stages in the development of the landscape and they can sometimes even reveal what men thought about their environment when they first gave the names. People tend to be conservative in the names they use, only devising new names for new places or to describe fields or roads that have been altered in some way. Some important places and landmarks have very old names. Many English cities, for example, have names that go back to the Roman period or earlier and even minor features of the landscape often have names that have been passed on by word of mouth for many generations before being recorded by modern map makers. Major changes have, however, been caused by such linguistic developments as the replacement of British by English or the introduction of Scandinavian elements into the dialects of the Danelaw. The names of small streams, for example, tend to reflect the speech of the people who live nearby and in most parts of England they now have English, not British, names. The general words used to describe them, whatever they are called, are certainly not British. The English introduced *burna* which has survived in Scotland and northern England as *burn*, while in the south this was in its turn replaced long before the Norman Conquest by the word *broc*, now *brook*, and in the Danelaw by the Scandinavian *beck*. Settlement

names have also been affected by these linguistic changes and consequently British names for farms and villages are rare. Some probably
disappeared with the settlements they described but the replacement
of most British stream names suggests that any British settlements
that did survive would also have lost their British names. It is indeed
possible that some English names are translations or adaptations of
earlier British ones. This can rarely, if ever, be proved, but the fact
that many of the earliest English settlement names are, like British
names, based on such natural features as rivers, streams, islands, fords
and woods strengthens this possibility.

Many English settlement names were, however, certainly formed
long after the English conquest. The most obvious examples are the
Scandinavian names. These cannot be older than the ninth century but
there are many place-names outside the Danelaw that were formed in
the tenth century or later. There are, for example, thirty places in
Domesday Book that appear to have been named after the people who
held them in 1065 (von Feilitzen, 1937, pp. 32–3). The pre-Conquest
tenants of Blackmanstone in Kent, Brigmerstone in Wiltshire and
Goodcote in Devon were Blæcmann, Beorhtmær and Godgifu respectively. The relationships are more obvious in the forms taken by
these place- and personal names in Domesday; Blacheman at *Blache-
menestone*, Brismar at *Brismartone* and Godeua at *Godeuecote*. It has
naturally been assumed that these and similar places were first established in the middle of the eleventh century by the people who appear
to have given their names to them. There are many English place-
names that incorporate personal names but we rarely have such good
information about the individuals whose names have been preserved
in this way. One of the exceptions is the Berkshire village of Woolstone,
which originally meant the *tūn*, that is farm or village, of Wulfric. We
are fortunate to have two charters, dated 944 and 958, granting Wulfric
land at *Æscesbyrig* and the bounds show that these two grants together
constituted the parish of Woolstone (Gelling, 1967b). It is a reasonable
conclusion that the village was named after this particular man. There
are, however, grounds for doubting that the individuals commemorated
in this way were the people who first established these villages. According to Domesday Book Blackmanstone had a church, two ploughlands in demesne and thirteen peasants sharing a plough and its value
had increased from £4 before the Conquest to £6 in 1086. It is therefore unlikely to have been a recent creation, and the same may be said

of Brigmerstone, which was assessed at four hides. The assessment of Woolstone was even higher: the charters granting it to Wulfric give its total assessment as 40 hides, a clear indication that this was not empty land awaiting development but a substantial and flourishing part of a much larger estate, or territory, named after a hill-fort Uffington Castle, or Ashbury as it was then called. We do not know what Woolstone was called before Wulfric acquired it, an earlier charter granting its western half to Ealdred describes it in the same terms as in the grants to Wulfric, 'land at Ashbury' (S, 317). We can, however, be reasonably certain that a settlement had already been established on the very desirable site occupied by the modern, and medieval, village. There are a few places where evidence survives to show that the name of a place changed either before or after the compilation of Domesday Book. The Worcestershire village of Bricklehampton appears in Domesday as a ten-hide estate at *Bricstelmestune*, the *tūn* of Beorhthelm, but a century earlier those ten hides were at a place called *Brihtulfingtune*, the *tūn* of Beorhtwulf (DB, i. 174b; S, 786). A good example of a similar, but later, change is *Bedintun* in Staffordshire, an estate of Burton Abbey which is not named in Domesday Book but which does occur in the early twelfth-century surveys of the abbey's property and also in an early charter with bounds showing that it was identical with Pillaton, or Pilton, the name it acquired by the mid-twelfth century and has had ever since (S, 879; Sawyer, 1978a no 26). There are some examples of similar changes long before the Norman Conquest, the best being Wilmington in Kent, about a mile south-east of Sellinge on the road from Hythe to Ashford. This is the subject of two early charters, one of which is an authentic grant, dated 697, of four ploughlands to the church of St Mary at Lyminge. A ninth-century endorsement describes is as *ðæs landes boc æt berwicum*, 'the charter (granting land) at Berwick', Berwick being the name of the adjacent estate to the east (S, 19). Another ninth-century hand has added *nunc wigelmignctun*, 'now Wighelm's *tūn*', showing that it had by then acquired its modern name. In the text of the charter the place is, however, described as *Pleghelmestun*, 'the *tūn* of Pleghelm'. The other charter is an eighth-century copy of the first extending the grant but the first two letters have been altered to *ɣi-*, a contemporary form of *Wi-*, to read *Wieghelmestun*, apparently a clumsy attempt to make it agree with the name it had acquired by the ninth century (S, 21).

It appears that when the estate was first mentioned it could be described as the *tūn* of Pleghelm, and this form is preserved in the copy. By the ninth century it could be described as *æt Berwicum* although later in that century it was called the *tūn* of Wighelm, who is recorded elsewhere in Kent as a landowner in or before the mid-ninth century (see below). There is also a third ninth-century endorsement on the original charter *delhames boc*, 'the charter of Delham', suggesting yet another possible name for the same estate. Wilmington survived as a manor until the nineteenth century but by then it had long been absorbed into the estate of Somerfield and it does not appear on any modern map (Ward, 1936).

Early charters frequently describe estate boundaries in terms of the people who held neighbouring property. This suggests that personal names were commonly used in the centuries before the Norman Conquest to describe or identify estates or settlements. Thus a ninth-century Kentish charter describes the limits of *Wassingwell* as 'in the west, the king's folkland, which Wighelm and Wulflaf held; in the north Cuthric's down and Heregyth's land; in the east Wighelm's land; in the south the bishop's land at Chart' (S, 328; *EHD*, 93). We are fortunate to have an independent reference to Heregyth, who is named in a will (S, 1482) dated between 833 and 839 as having some interest in Challock, immediately north of *Wassingwell*, and Wighelm may be the man who gave his name to Wilmington, less than ten miles away. References of this kind are relatively common in charter boundaries, although we rarely have any other information about the individuals concerned. Dr Margaret Gelling has recently discussed the pre-Conquest charter boundaries of Berkshire and comments:

If the boundary-marks are studied as a whole, and the use of personal names considered together with the use of terms like *biscopes-*, *cinges-*, *ealdormonnes-*, it appears probable that such compounds as *ælfheages gemære*, *ælfsiges mor*, *ælfðryðe dic*, *cyneeahes treow* are shorthand for 'boundary of the estate now or recently in the possession of a thegn called Ælfheah', 'ditch on the boundary of the lady Ælfðryð's estate', etc. This must be so in the boundary marks containing *cyning* 'king'. In the two examples in the bounds of part of Kingston Lisle, *cincges scypene* and *cinges þornas*, it is only sensible to translate 'cowshed and thorn-bushes on the boundary of the royal estate'. There is no likelihood of royal participation in the erection of sheds or planting of thorns, and similarly there is no reason to suppose

that the men and women whose names occur in similar boundary-
marks were responsible for any settling or clearing. (Gelling, 1976,
p. 828)

While some of these names have become permanently attached to estates, others have been completely forgotten. An original charter dated
959 concerning land at Welford in Berkshire defines seven boundary
points in terms of named individuals; Wine's tree, Deora's tree,
Ceolbald's spring, Wulfric's boundary, Cynehelm's stone, Ecghun's
tree and there are references in different parts of the boundary to a
tumulus and an enclosure of Carda. Wine's tree is mentioned as a
boundary point in two other charters and Wulfric may possibly be
identified as having an interest in the neighbourhood at that time, but
none of these people have given their names to local places: there is no
Wine's or Cynehelm's *tūn* here. It may be that such names vanished
because the farms or settlements to which they referred were abandoned
and that some of the early but deserted sites revealed by archaeological
surveys or excavations may have had names of this kind. Another possibility is that places which could be, and sometimes were, described in
terms of individuals also had other, older names and that these have,
for some reason, survived. A similar situation exists today when farms
are locally referred to as belonging to their current occupant and not
by the official name recorded by the Ordnance Survey. The evidence
from Wilmington and elsewhere suggests that some names changed
from time to time, possibly every generation with each new owner or
occupant, but that for some reason the name of one particular tenant
has become permanently associated with the place; Wighelm at Wilmington, Beorhthelm at Bricklehampton and Blæcman at Blackmanstone.

Names of this type are very common and their interpretation is
therefore a matter of some importance in any attempt to understand the
evolution of English settlement. Some names probably became permanent when they were first recorded in writing for the purposes of
taxation or the collection of rent. The compilation of Domesday Book
may itself have been responsible for finally determining the names of
places like Blackmanstone and Brigmerstone. Farms or villages that
were first recorded after Domesday Book was made might well be
named after later tenants; in Devon many were. The records kept by
religious houses may have had a similar effect and it is possible that some

places were named after people who lived in them in the tenth century because it was those people who gave them to the churches. So, for example, Alverstoke in Hampshire was in 948 simply called *Stoce* but later in the century it was given to Winchester Cathedral by Ælfwaru and her name has ever since been prefixed to the old name.* The place occurs in Domesday Book as *Alwarestoch*. Similarly Aughton in Wiltshire is named after Æffe, whose husband left that estate to her for life with reversion to New Minster, Winchester, and it was thereafter known as Æffe's *tūn*, although it was first recorded by name in the fourteenth century (Bonney, 1969). The commemoration of donors is therefore a possible explanation for the naming of some places after individuals.

More important, there was a fundamental change in the concept of land ownership in the course of the eighth and ninth centuries. Before that the land held by individuals was thought to belong either to their families or to their lords. An individual only had a life interest and could not make grants that would in effect disinherit his heirs. Similarly, a retainer might expect to receive from his lord an estate appropriate to his rank and service, but the land was lent, not given, and lords were themselves subject to the same restraints on alienation as anyone else. In such circumstances settlements were more likely to be named after kinship groups than individuals (Charles-Edwards, 1972, p. 30). These early attitudes to land ownership were already changing in the seventh century, largely as a result of the need to endow churches with permanent rights over land, a need met by the granting of royal charters. The earliest surviving original, a grant made in 679 by King Hlothhere of Kent to Brihtwold, abbot of Reculver, and his monastery, conveyed land at Sturry, just outside Canterbury, 'with everything belonging to it' and it was to be 'in the power of the abbot for ever; granted by me, may it be contradicted – which God forbid – by no one, neither by me nor by my kindred nor by others'. In time similar grants were made to laymen and when, thanks to such a grant, an individual was seen to own land it might well be remembered as his, especially if he chose to make it his permanent home. It has been suggested, for example, that Bibury in Gloucestershire, called *Beganbyrg* in a charter of 899 (S, 1279), acquired its name because Beaga established her *burh*

---

* S 532 and, for the benefaction, Reg. John de Pontissara, ed. C. Deedes, ii, Canterbury and York Society, 30, 1924, p. 610. I am indebted to Martin Biddle for this reference.

there in the middle of the eighth century (Gelling, 1976, p. 825). The word *burh*, which commonly occurs in place-names in the dative *byrig*, meant a fortified place, an appropriate description for the houses of important landowners who for reasons of security or prestige must often have surrounded their homes with defences, as happened later with manor houses. Beaga's father, a *comes* called Leppa, was given a lease of Bibury, described as 'by the river called Coln', in the first half of the eighth century (S, 1254). The lease was granted by the bishop of Worcester 'for his life and for hers', and, although it was still a Worcester estate in the eleventh century, it probably has been thought of as Beaga's *burh* since she held it in the middle years of the eighth century. The word *tūn* is even more commonly used in place-names, frequently combined with a personal name. It is likely that many of the place-names of this type were similar in origin to Bibury but refer to un-fortified houses. Woolstone may well be remembered as Wulfric's not simply because he owned it or gave it to Abingdon Abbey but because he made it his home and built a house there. A man's house, whether a *burh* or a *tūn*, was also associated with his 'house' in the sense of lineage, for a principal residence (called in Old English *frumstōl*, meaning first or original seat) was normally inherited by the eldest son.

The new attitude to land ownership was accompanied by, and indeed it contributed to, the fragmentation of many large estates. Some grants were formally confirmed by royal charters but there were also many usurpations. There was a natural tendency for a tenant holding land on lease to regard it as his own, and great landowners sometimes found it difficult to recover the land. The problems they faced are very clearly seen in the century before the Norman Conquest on the very large and well-documented estates of the bishop and church of Worcester. They attempted to limit leases to three lives but sometimes had great difficulty in recovering control after the third, and were in effect forced to make a new lease. The use of personal names in such place-names as Woolstone, Blackmanstone and Goodcote is therefore not evidence for the establishment of new settlements but is rather a natural consequence of the increasing opportunities for individuals to think of themselves, and be accepted, as the owners of estates which they regarded as their homes and on which they built their houses and founded family interests.

While many place-names appear to be relatively late, others can be shown to be early by linguistic features that have left recognizable traces even in their modern forms. Thus the common name Higham is shown to be early because the first element, the adjective *hēah*, meaning high, is not inflected. When the same adjective was used to qualify the word *tūn* it was always in the weak form and generally in the dative *hēan*, and this has resulted in such names as Hampton, Heanton and Henton (Ekwall, 1960, p. xv). Linguistic features can, however, do no more than provide a general indication of the age of a name. A better and more certain indication of early date is the occurrence of names in early texts. Hlothhere's charter of 679 is unimpeachable evidence for the existence at that time of the names Thanet, Reculver and Sturry in the forms *in Tenid, in Sturia* and *in civitate Recuulf,* as well as for an estate called *uuestan æ,* that is 'west of the river'. One of the most important words used in such demonstrably early names was *hām*, which has a wide variety of meanings ranging from 'homestead' to 'large estate'. Its relative frequency in early texts, and its distribution in relation to Roman roads and Romano-British settlements suggests that it was being used to name places at a very early stage of English history (Gelling, 1967a and 1977). There are also some specialized types of *hām* names, notably *wīchām* and *wealdhām. Wīchām* names, which have produced such modern forms as Wickham, Wykeham and Wycomb, are regularly associated with Roman roads and are sometimes found close to major Roman towns or forts. The first element derives from Latin *vicus* and the situation of some of these names on or close to the sites of small Roman towns suggests that when those names were given the towns were still occupied and known as *vici*. The first element of *wealdhām* means 'woodland' and the distribution of this name, now Waltham, is even more limited than that of *wīchām*, and appears only to have been used in the earliest stages of the English conquest (Huggins, 1975).

Another type of early place-name was formed with the common Germanic suffix *-ing* with plural inflection, the nominative *-ingas*, the dative *-ingum* or the genitive *-inga-*, which, combined with other elements, produced such names as Birmingham, Ashington, or, with *lēah*, meaning woodland or a clearing, Chiddingly. Many *-ingas, -inga-* names have a personal name as the first element and these appear to imply the existence of a group of people associated in some way with the person named. It has even been suggested that they refer to groups of colonists dependent on a leader or lord but they could also refer to groups of kinsmen. In any case such a name as Hastings in Sussex, originally *Hæstingas*, described an area settled by people who were the men, or the kinsmen of, *Hæst*. Hastingleigh in the Kentish Weald is probably a detached forest grazing belonging to this group, fifteen miles away.

Detailed studies by John Dodgson (1966 and 1973) of these two early types of name and their relationship with pagan Saxon burials in the south-east of England has led him to the conclusion that *hām* was used in 'the immigration phase' of the English conquest, the stage that is evidenced archaeologically by the pagan burials, while the *-ingas* names represent a later 'colonization phase', during which *hām* was still used both as a separate element and in the combination *-ingahām*. He has argued that this general chronological sequence is confirmed by the rarity of *hām*, *-ingas* and *-ingahām* names in the Weald while other *-inga-* names do occur, a contrast that he considers reflects the later colonization of that area. According to his interpretation *-ingas* names were

> the result of some phase of Anglo-Saxon settlement later than the immigration period, an epoch of territorial expansion and social consolidation, marked by the establishment of colonizing communities, by the recognition of tradition embodied in social structures, and identified as to allegiance, heritage and land tenure with a settlement organization. In this phase a new kind of society emerges characterized by its place-names and its undiscoverable burials. (1966, p. 19)

Where, as in East Anglia and Cambridgeshire, *-ingas* and *-inga-* names do occur in areas where pagan burials are discovered, it has been argued that they must represent 'a new social development in an old immigration area'.

This refinement of the conventional hypothesis of early English settlement depends on the assumption that names can be dated by their proximity to Roman or Romano-British sites or by their occurrence in areas which, to judge by the known pagan burials, were not occupied by the English before their conversion. There are, however, very serious objections to such arguments. The area of Romano-British settlement is not yet fully determined; for, although many villas, towns and military sites have been identified, new discoveries are regularly made and the full extent of native settlement in the Roman period has certainly not been determined. Occupation debris from the Roman period has been found in many parts of the country well away from the Romano-British sites that are known by excavation or aerial photography, and it is therefore misleading to assume that the blank areas on the modern map of Romano-British settlement were in fact devoid of settlement in the fifth century. Even more seriously misleading is the assumption that the areas of English colonization before the seventh century were limited to the districts in which pagan English burials have so far been discovered. Such burials may certainly be accepted as good indicators of areas that were occupied before the conversion, but their absence should not be taken to mean that there was no pagan settlement in those areas. In Lincolnshire, for example, English pottery of the pagan period, found as occupation debris, has revealed many settlement sites in areas that have so far not yielded any pagan burials, possibly because continuous ploughing has destroyed the evidence (p. 162). It is, indeed, probable that much of the pottery that has been recovered comes from the pots in which cremated remains were interred. The effect of ploughing on a cremation cemetery has been illustrated very clearly in the current excavation at Spong Hill in Norfolk, where cremation urns have been well preserved on the flanks of the hill but have been disturbed or destroyed on the hill-top. The same excavation also illustrates the uncertainty of our record of inhumations for the soil conditions there do not preserve human bones and the discovery of the burials has depended on most careful excavation to recognize the stains left in the soil by the coffins, or the discovery of the relatively few grave goods. Such burials could easily be destroyed by ploughing or remain undetected in an excavation.

Conclusions based on the presently understood distribution of either Romano-British settlements or pagan Saxon burials are, therefore, likely to be mistaken. There is a further, and more fundamental, difficulty. Some of these early names referred not to specific places but to districts. This meaning for *hām* is shown very clearly in the ninth-century translation of Bede's *History* in which the Latin word *civitas* is translated as *hām* while *tūn* is used for *villa*. An early ninth-century Kentish charter specifically describes Rainham and Faversham, both *hām* names, as *regiones* (S, 168). The name Waltham appears to have been used for large royal estates that were well placed for hunting and it is possible that the name *wīchām* originally referred not to a particular settlement but to a district that was dependent on a *vicus*. *Hām* was not the only name given to districts or large estates; even *-ingas* names could be used in this sense as is shown by an early eighth-century charter (S, 94) describing Wootton Wawen in Warwickshire as being in the region of the *Stoppingas*, and it has been suggested (Fellows Jensen, 1974) that names in singular *-ing* were also borne by large estates. Other early estate names include Ashbury and Blewbury in Berkshire and *Usmere*, now Ismere, in Worcestershire. These estates or districts were originally very large but, as they were reduced in size by grants or usurpations, their names have often come to be limited to particular places. Margaret Gelling (1976, p. 830) has pointed out that Blewbury was originally an estate of 100 hides, including the modern parishes of Aston Tirrold, Aston Upthorpe, North and South Moreton as well as Blewbury itself, to which the name is now limited. These large estates certainly contained many settlements but we rarely hear of their names. It is sometimes possible to show that names that are first recorded in the eleventh or later centuries were formed early in English history. A good example is the name *throp*, meaning an outlying or dependent settlement. It only occurs once in an early source, a charter that only survives in a thirteenth-century copy so that there can be no certainty that the name was in the original text. Few places with this name are mentioned in Domesday Book and they are generally small and unimportant. Nevertheless, their distribution throughout the southern Midlands and Wessex but not in Devon and Cornwall strongly suggests that the name was used in the seventh century but not in the eighth, when the English began to colonize Devon (Smith, 1956a, ii, pp. 205–12).

Many settlements are named after such natural features as rivers, streams, islands, fords, woods or hills, and there are good reasons for thinking that these represent a very early type of English place-name. In the upper Thames valley, which can be shown archaeologically to have been occupied by the English at an early date, names of this type are common, while other supposedly early English names, including those compounded with *hām* or *-ingas*, are relatively rare (Gelling, 1976, pp. 816–20). It is also significant that topographical names of this kind occur frequently in the earliest texts. Barrie Cox (1976) has shown that of the 224 place-names recorded in sources produced before the death of Bede, over half (119) were topographical while only a third (75) were habitation names, the rest being names of districts. The proportion of topographical names would be greatly increased by the inclusion of the forty-six river names in these sources. Most of these topographical names in fact refer to settlements or estates. This is sometimes shown by the use of a preposition, commonly *æt*, meaning at or by, or by a prepositional phrase, implying the existence of a farm, village or estate 'at the ford', 'by the river' or 'in the place called Redford'. Some of these prepositions have become parts of the names, thus Twyning in Gloucestershire is first mentioned in the early ninth century as *Bituinæum* meaning '[the place] between the streams', which was also the origin of the name Twineham in Hampshire (Ekwall, 1960, pp. xviii–xx). It is clear that habitation names alone give a very misleading impression of the extent of early English settlement. A large number of settlements, possibly the majority, had topographical names, and many others are only represented in early sources by the names of the estates or districts to which they belonged.

One large group of names that can certainly be dated are those that incorporate the distinctive words or personal names that were introduced into England by the Scandinavians and therefore cannot have been formed before the ninth century. The most common of these Scandinavian elements is *by*, which meant a farm or village and corresponds to the English *tūn*. There are well over 700 of these throughout northern and eastern England. Another common element is *thorp*, which may sometimes represent an earlier English *throp*, a name that also meant 'an outlying or dependent settlement'. It is, however, likely that most *thorp* names in the Danelaw and the north reflect Scandinavian influence. Many Scandinavian personal names have been incorporated in place-names, often combined with *by* or *thorp* but they are also found in Anglo-Scandinavian hybrids like Foston, Staxton and Muston in Yorkshire. There are over 100 names of this type in the Yorkshire Domesday and they are even more common in East Anglia.

These Scandinavian names, especially those in *by* and *thorp*, have generally been interpreted as new settlements formed by Scandinavian colonists, or by their descendants, in areas that had, by and large, not been occupied by the English. This interpretation agreed well with the 'expansionist theory' of English settlement. If, however, as argued here, this theory is wrong and there were no vast tracts of empty land in the ninth century, the interpretation of the Scandinavian place-names has to be reconsidered.

It is, in the first place, most unlikely that the Northumbrians would have left large areas of fertile land unoccupied. They were short of land, especially after they were limited to the area between the Forth and the Humber, and Bede himself complained of the lack of estates for the endowment of warriors needed for the kingdom's defence. The Yorkshire Wolds, according to the accepted interpretation of the evidence, were one of the main areas of new colonization in the tenth century, but they had been a particularly rich area in the Roman period and have yielded many pagan English graves and in Domesday Book they had assessments that were unusually high (Swanton, 1964; Fellows Jensen, 1972, pp. 222–4). It is, therefore, difficult to believe that this rich area was left empty between the sixth century and the ninth and that it then became one of the most prosperous regions of Northumbria. The shortage of water on the chalk Wolds may have hampered the development of large settlements but it seems more reasonable to accept that the resources of this potentially rich area were always exploited by the communities in the surrounding region and that, as in the woodland of the Weald and Arden, this exploitation was based on scattered, small, but permanent, settlements. In Lincolnshire there is more direct evidence of the previous occupation of areas with Scandinavian names. Field-walking in the area around Sleaford, west of the Car Dyke, which here defines the pre- and post-Roman shore line, has led to the discovery of occupation debris, particularly pottery, which must be dated to a period earlier than the Scandinavian invasions, in the vicinity of many villages with Scandinavian names: Asgarby, Aunsby, Dembleby, Dowsby, Hacconby, Keisby and Hanby.* The implication that such scatters of pottery are associated with settlements has been confirmed at Osbournby, where a house of the pagan English period has been excavated. Similar evidence of previous occupation has also been found on the site of deserted settlements that are now known only as field-names; Lusby and Hareby, for example, named on the Tithe Award map for Howell, close to Car Dyke, have both yielded a scatter of early English pottery, suggesting that these names refer to settlements that already existed when the Scandinavians came but have been abandoned since. Such evidence cannot, of course, prove that these settlements were occupied when the Scandinavians arrived but it does show that in Lincolnshire many places with Scandinavian names were already settled before the ninth century. Further north, in County Durham, one section of the fields of a place with an apparently Scandinavian name, Thorpe Bulmer, has been shown by pollen analysis to have been continuously cultivated from the Roman

* Information kindly supplied by Brian Simmons.

period until the eleventh century (Bartley *et al.* 1976). Some settlements were doubtless abandoned in the face of Scandinavian attacks, but lords were more likely to flee than their peasants and it is significant that the language of the Danelaw remained English. Modern studies of field-names have naturally concentrated on signs of Scandinavian influence but even in areas where that influence is most marked the majority of medieval field-names were English. These field-names and words adopted into the local dialects certainly prove that the Scandinavians worked the land, unlike the Normans who had little or no effect on the names of English fields or English agricultural vocabulary, but they do not prove that there was a massive displacement of the English population.

Hybrid Anglo-Scandinavian names, like Muston and Staxton, generally occur on good settlement sites and it has been suggested that they were English villages or farms which were taken over by, and renamed after, Scandinavians, a development that is closely paralleled outside the Danelaw by such names as Woolstone and Blackmanstone. The many Scandinavian names in *by* and *thorp* which have been previously interpreted as signs of colonization, are more likely to represent another stage of the same process, the main difference being that by the time these names were changed *by* had replaced *tūn* in local speech. The location of most *thorps* in marginal or peripheral areas is hardly surprising, for that is the implication of that element. The Scandinavian place-names in the Yorkshire Wolds, for example, are best understood not as new settlements but as well-established dependencies of distant estates around the Wolds, which were taken over by Scandinavians, possibly sometime after the initial conquest. Under their new lords some of these settlements ceased to be dependent on other estates, but even when some connection remained, and dues or services were owed, there can normally have been little doubt that new, Scandinavian lords had taken over and were regarding these places as their homes. It was from these men that later generations of owners traced their inheritance, and it is therefore natural that so many of the *by* and *thorp* names resemble the *tūn*-hybrids in having a Scandinavian personal name as the first element. This was not a habit imported by the Danish colonists from their homeland; place-names in *by* with a personal name as the first element are very rare in Denmark except in the southern parts of the country. In Yorkshire and the east Midlands, on the other hand, half the *by* names are of this type.

In all this there is much uncertainty. New surveys (whether on the ground or from the air), excavations and pollen analyses may well invalidate some of the assumptions on which current interpretations are based. It is, however, reasonable at this stage to suggest that in the seventh century the basic units of rural organization in England were large estates, sometimes called multiple, federal or discrete estates. These were held by kings and leading aristocrats, and they were also granted to churches. Some survived more or less intact until the eleventh century, and are described in Domesday Book, but many had by then been greatly reduced by grants and usurpations, while others had disappeared altogether and their existence is only revealed by earlier evidence. The pattern of settlements within these estates was not static. Some ideal sites have doubtless been occupied since Roman times, and still are, but, where local circumstances do not determine where people must live, or where climatic change has forced people to move, many settlements have shifted, perhaps several times. Some have been abandoned entirely but others have simply moved to a new location, possibly very close. Peter Wade-Martins (1975) has been able to trace some of these local changes in Norfolk with the help of occupation debris. In the parish of Longham, for example, pottery finds show that the area around the church was occupied during the eighth and ninth centuries, that during the twelfth century settlement spread around South Hall Green, about a mile south of the church, and that by the fourteenth century the original settlement has been more or less abandoned, except for the church, which remained in its original site. A similar process, in which the main centre of settlement shifted from the neighbourhood of the church and where village greens appear to have been formed in the eleventh and twelfth centuries has been detected in several other villages of central Norfolk.

One of the most important recent discoveries has been made on Church Down, about one mile south-east of the modern village of Chalton in Hampshire. Pottery and other occupation debris was recovered there from an area of about fourteen acres clearly indicating the existence of a village which is now being excavated. So far less than $\frac{1}{10}$ of the apparent area of the settlement has been uncovered and has revealed 30 rectangular timber buildings ranging in length from 3 to 28 metres. Some appear to be grouped together possibly to form individual farms, and there are traces of boundary fences. The few finds indicate that the site was occupied in the sixth and seventh centuries,

and the buildings that have been recovered so far seem to belong to
four periods, with some rebuilding and also some rearrangement. As no
trace of later occupation has been discovered so far, it appears that
the site was abandoned by the eighth century (Addyman and Leigh,
1973).

The excavation at Church Down shows that some of the English
lived in communities that can reasonably be described as villages. At
West Stow in Suffolk such a village has been completely excavated and
recent finds at Catholm by the Trent suggest the existence of a substantial settlement in the fifth and sixth centuries (West, 1969; Losco-
Bradley, 1974). Most pagan cemeteries, however, appear to have been
so small that they can hardly represent villages and many probably
served as the burial-grounds for single farms. It is true that few pagan
cemeteries have been completely excavated but that is no good reason to
assume that small cemeteries were the exception rather than the rule.
One very interesting group that has been investigated recently is at
Stretton-on-the-Fosse where the Fosse Way crosses the river Stour in
Warwickshire. Four cemeteries have been discovered so far, three are
closely associated with Roman buildings and contain small numbers of
graves, 12, 15 and 22 respectively, dating from the second century
to the end of the Roman period, and there is also a larger English
cemetery with 53 graves apparently belonging to two phases, 9 very
early irregular burials and a later group arranged more regularly in
rows, but no trace of an English settlement has yet been discovered.*

The archaeological evidence therefore suggests that early English
settlements ranged from separate individual farms to large, nucleated
settlements consisting of several houses and farms. Both types existed
in Britain before the English invasions. There were some British villages
but the most important rural nucleations were in fact villas, and many
later English villages appear to occupy the sites of villas; that at least is
the implication of the frequent association of medieval churches with
Roman sites that have often proved to be villas (p. 92). This is not to
suggest that there was necessarily any continuity of occupation. The
villa fields, even after they had been abandoned, would have provided
an ideal opportunity for the English to establish large nucleated settlements of the type they were familiar with in their continental homelands. Similarly, many of the separate English farms appear, as at
Stretton-on-the-Fosse, to be the successors of British farms, although

* I am indebted to William Ford for information about this site.

they may not occupy exactly the same sites and there may often have been some break in the continuity of occupation. The early history of such settlements is necessarily obscure. Archaeological traces of occupation are often slight and if villages have been continuously occupied, the early evidence will normally have been seriously disturbed if not destroyed. Some separate farms developed into villages but others have been abandoned, frequently before any record was made of their existence. Place-names, even if only recorded in later texts, may provide clues to the existence of some of the larger and more important settlements, but the names of separate farms are never recorded in early sources and if they were abandoned before the thirteenth century there is a good chance that their existence will remain unknown. The names of some abandoned settlements do appear to have survived as field-names; Lusby and Hareby in Howell are examples and William Ford (1976, p. 287) has drawn attention to some remarkable survivals in Warwickshire. A field called Ditchingworth, about half a mile north of the church of Brailes, has yielded signs of habitation from the first to the early fifth centuries, and another called Baldicote in Tredington has produced similar Romano-British material and in addition some English pottery and a single inhumation. If, as seems reasonable, these field-names refer to the deserted settlements that have left these traces, they are not only astonishing examples of the survival of names, they also show that the names *cot* and *worth* were used for small settlements at a very early date. Evidence of this kind shows that no interpretation of early English landscape can be based solely on the larger and more important settlements which tend to figure most prominently in our sources and in the archaeological record.

We know little enough about early settlements, but our knowledge of the field systems that were worked from these settlements is even less complete. The main problem is, of course, that in most areas the activity of successive generations has obliterated most, if not all, traces of earlier arrangements, leaving modern students to draw their conclusions from peripheral areas that have been left uncultivated for centuries and are consequently not likely to be representative of areas that have been more intensively used. The earliest detailed manorial surveys, from the fourteenth and later centuries, are not a satisfactory basis for a discussion of the field systems eight centuries before.

The early arrangements will have been subject to a great variety of changes, redivisions between kinsmen, or between lords and men, shifts of use from pasture to arable or back again in response to changing demand, and modifications caused by improved tools or different crops. In all this the physical circumstances could never be safely ignored. Soils and climate limit the uses to which any land can be put and the influence of social circumstances was no less significant. The rules of inheritance, mutual obligations between lords and men, relations between individuals and their neighbours in the community, relations between communities, especially in the exploitation of scarce resources, and the influence of towns all played their part in shaping the landscape. The resulting system of settlements and fields can never be understood apart from the men who lived in and cultivated them and it is these social aspects of English history that will be considered in the next chapter.

IV

Lords, kinsmen
and neighbours

Pre-Conquest law-codes show that English society was hierarchical and that two institutions were fundamental, the family and lordship. From the early seventh-century law-code of Æthelberht to the eleventh-century codes of Cnut, and even in such post-Conquest compilations as *Quadripartitus* and the *Laws of Henry I*, the same social framework is assumed. Between the seventh century and the eleventh there were, of course, many changes. The growing power of kings transformed southern English society and the church had some effect everywhere, but when the Normans conquered England, and for some time after that, the English were still hierarchically classified and many of them still depended on kinsmen and lords for the protection of their rights and their personal safety.

The law-codes and collections all assume the existence of both free and unfree people. The unfree were, by definition, under the lordship of someone for whom they had a value; if a slave were injured or killed compensation was due to his owner. Many freemen acknowledged lords who would similarly expect compensation if their men were injured or killed, but a freeman could also expect compensation for injury to be paid to him personally or, if he were killed, to his kinsmen. The alternative was a feud in which he would be aided, or avenged, by members of his family.

A freeman's value was expressed in terms of his wergeld, literally man-money, the sum with which a feud could be averted. It was, however, more than a man's price; it determined the scale of compensation due to him for injury, or for the breach of his peace, or injury to his servants. It also defined a man's status in society. The value of his oath in legal proceedings depended on his rank, and in seventh-century Kent a noble could clear himself of an accusation by his unsupported oath while a ceorl could only do so with three of his own class (Wi, 19; 20).

Written laws may not accurately represent the laws that men obeyed and that regulated society. They are often either out of date or reflect ideals. They also tend to impose a degree of systematization that is largely artificial. Some collections were deliberately archaic, others were private compilations, and even those issued by, or on behalf of, kings were sometimes intended to serve ideological or symbolic purposes as much as practical needs (Wormald, 1977b). The surviving codes are certainly incomplete. The English codes, for example, say nothing about inheritance and very little about the law of marriage. The conservative, even archaizing, tendencies of the compilers of law-codes may aid our understanding of primitive society; it is indeed this characteristic of the earliest Irish texts which makes them so valuable in opening a 'window on the Iron Age', but the same tendencies serve to conceal change, and to give a misleading impression of stability.

Literature can provide some independent evidence but here, too, there are difficulties. In imaginative literature many of the ideals may well be literary rather than real, and it has recently been suggested that the theme of the poem on *The Battle of Maldon*, the ideal of men fighting to the death beside their fallen lord, owes more to literary tradition than to any contemporary code of conduct (Woolf, 1976). Christian literature had its own ideals and we may reasonably doubt the relevance of some of these to Dark Age society. Not all the virtues approved by Bede would have been to the advantage of a seventh-century king: Aidán wept at the humility of Oswine and prophesied:

> I know that the king will not live long; for I never before saw a humble king. Therefore I think that he will very soon be snatched from this life; for this nation does not deserve to have such a ruler. (*HE*, iii. 14)

There is perhaps more hope of detecting contemporary values in the lives of saints, especially the passages that describe experiences before conversion. Correspondence, such as the letters of Boniface, or Bede's admonition to Archbishop Egbert of York, also reveals, almost incidentally, glimpses of society and its values. Charters are perhaps the most valuable complement to the laws, for they reveal the law, and society, in action. It was by charters that estates were granted, rights alienated and the resolution of disputes recorded. They allow us to see men buying, selling, leasing and stealing land, families attempting to recover their rights, and lords exercising theirs. There are unfortunately no reliable texts before the last quarter of the seventh century, and for large areas of the country we have none before the tenth century, but their evidence does give us some confidence in the laws. They show that although the laws may give an over-systematized impression, they do not misrepresent the fundamental character of English society in either the seventh century or the eleventh.

Additional illumination comes from the contemporary legal evidence from other parts of the British Isles and from the continent. There is also much to be gained from the work of social anthropologists who have studied modern societies that have simple technologies. It would, of course, be wrong to argue from analogy; the customs of the Nuer or the Dinka in the twentieth century are unlikely to be precisely paralleled in seventh-century England, but the observations of anthropologists are valuable in showing, for example, how the blood-feud actually works, and the mechanisms that maintain 'peace in the feud'.

One of the most important contributions made by social anthropologists to the study of Dark Age Britain has been to draw attention to the fundamental importance of gift-exchange. In many societies social relationships are expressed, or created, by gifts, which need not be material; and a gift can create an obligation to make a counter-gift. We still use gifts in this way. Christmas presents are in effect exchanges. If a present is not given in return, the exchange may end, even if the purpose is to win approval, or to gain some favour. The offering of a gift that cannot possibly be reciprocated is one way of humiliating someone. This discovery, given coherence by the French scholar Marcel Mauss (1969), has provided a key to the interpretation of many features in early Germanic and Celtic society. We can now recognize in the laws and literature, and in their languages, clear signs of this fundamental social reciprocity.

One of the best illustrations is provided by the custom of marriage.

The marriage itself, called *gift* in Old English (and in modern Scandinavian languages), is distinguished from the betrothal, *weddung* (from which the word wedding comes) (Charles-Edwards, 1976a, p. 181). The suitor first pays, or promises to pay, a gift or bride-price to the girl's father, or whoever has authority over and protects her. If the marriage does not take place the bride-price has to be returned with some, apparently heavy, penalty. On the first morning of the marriage the husband was supposed to make a further gift, *morgengifu*, 'morning-gift', in return for the gift of his wife's virginity. This morning-gift was, according to Æthelberht's laws, returnable to her kin if she did not bear a child. If she did have a child, itself a gift, her entitlement to part of her husband's property grew. According to the earliest laws, after a wife bore a living child she was entitled to half the husband's property if the husband died before her (the proportion was later increased). The implication that this was some return for the gift of a child is strengthened by another clause which provides for a wife leaving her husband. She could do this, take the children, and still be entitled to a share of the property. If the husband wished to keep the children – thus implying that his consent was needed for her to keep them – she was entitled to have the value of the children returned to her.

These arrangements, which agree well with those observed in other primitive societies and those revealed in other Germanic codes (especially the Edict of the Lombard Rothari), illustrate the reciprocal nature of these basic social customs. This principle of reciprocity permeated English society (p. 53). It is seen, for example, in the relations between a lord and his men; a young retainer would be given a place in the hall, with food and drink, and when he reached mature years, apparently 25, he would be given an estate appropriate to his rank and service. This relationship is seen most clearly in the households of great men but it existed at all levels of society. In Old English *hlaford*, 'lord', means 'loaf-giver'; he was the provider of food, and in Æthelberht's laws dependants were called 'loaf-eaters'.

A lord could expect to have the faithful service of his men, and when they died they were expected to render one final gift: their heriot, literally 'army-gear', varied with the status, not of the lord but of the man. As defined in the laws of Cnut it ranged from the heriot of an earl; 'eight horses, four saddled and four unsaddled, and four helmets and four coats of mail and eight spears and as many shields and four swords and 200 mancuses of gold [that is gold coins, each worth 30 pence]' (II Cn 70), to the £2 due from lesser men, which, according to Domesday Book, was owed on the death of the king's men in Lancashire (p. 176). One of the normal incidents of peasant tenure in later centuries was the requirement to pay heriot to the manorial lord.

Wergelds were expressed in terms of money. In Æthelberht's laws the wergeld of a ceorl, the ordinary freeman, was 100 shillings, while later in the century, in the Laws of the West Saxon king Ine, a ceorl's wergeld is defined as 200 shillings. This does not, however, reflect a difference in the value, and therefore in the status of such men in the two kingdoms. As Professor Philip Grierson has shown (1961a) the unit in Æthelberht's code was a gold shilling, a word that originally meant a cutting from a ring, and at that time referred to a Frankish gold *tremissis*, the only coin then current in England, which normally weighed 20 Troy grains, a grain being the weight of a barleycorn. In the Kentish laws, the shilling was divided into 20 sceattas, which must therefore have been units of account, not coins, each worth one grain of gold. By the end of the seventh century the short-lived English gold coinage had been replaced by one in silver, and the coins were pennies, theoretically of the same weight as the gold coins but worth much less. It is probable that ten silver pennies of fine silver would have been worth a shilling of fine gold (Lyon, 1976, pp. 177-8) but the West Saxon shilling consisted of only 5 pence, possibly because the gold shilling made in England in the middle years of the seventh century contained only half the gold of a good Frankish tremissis. This would make the value of the Kentish and West Saxon ceorls the same. It is possible that a wergeld of the seventh century has been preserved in the form of a hoard of gold coins found at Crondall in Hampshire in 1828. It consisted of 97 gold coins, three small pieces of gold with the same weight and one forgery and was deposited in about 670. Grierson (1961a, p. 349) has suggested that the number of pieces is 101 because the forgery was detected at the time and a pseudo-imperial coin, that had been used as an ornament, was added to make up the full amount. Unfortunately the neat agreement which can be demonstrated for the wergelds of the ceorls of Kent and Wessex apparently breaks down for the noble wergelds. In Ine's laws a noble was called a *gesith*, and his wergeld is stated to be 1200 shillings, that is six times the wergeld of a ceorl. The laws of Æthelberht do not state the wergeld of a Kentish noble, called an eorl, but later in the century the laws of Hlothhere and Eadric refer to a noble (*eorlcundne*) man with a (wer)geld of 300 shillings, three times that of a Kentish ceorl. This implies that Kentish nobles had a lower value, and status, than the West Saxon gesith. This seems most improbable. It is more likely that the 300-shilling eorl was the equivalent of either the *gesithcund* man without land or the *Wealh* or Briton who owned 5 hides of land and whose wergeld is stated by Ine to be 600 shillings, the exact equivalent of 300 Kentish shillings if the equation proposed for the ceorls is right (Chadwick, 1905, pp. 91–8). The Kentish law-codes, especially Æthelberht's, imply an elaborate social hierarchy. Three classes of semi-free *læt*'s are recognized and there are also three possible classes of slave-girls in a ceorl's household. A similar complexity among the nobility is implied by the clause which lays down the penalties for the breach of the *mund*, or peace, of widows. This can best be shown by comparing these penalties with the other penalties prescribed for the breach of the peace of the king, eorl and ceorl in Æthelberht's laws, and the wergelds in those laws and in Hlothhere and Eadric's.

	Breach of *Mund*	Wergeld	(Breach of) Widow's *mund*	
King	50 shillings		the highest class	50 shillings
			second class	20 shillings
eorl	12 shillings	300 shillings	third class	12 shillings
ceorl	6 shillings	100 shillings	fourth class	6 shillings

This comparison suggests that there was a noble class above the 300-shilling eorl. If so, the difference between the higher nobility of Kent and Wessex may be unreal. We cannot determine what that higher wergeld was, but 600 shillings is possible. Whether the 300 shilling eorl was in other ways the exact equivalent of the 600 shilling *wealh* with 5 hides of land is also unknown.

This brief discussion shows the complexity of the problems posed by the early law-codes. It also shows that Kentish society, and therefore that of Wessex, was far more complex than a simple division into noble, free, semi-free and slaves might suggest, and that the last two groups were not only elaborately classified, but were probably numerous.

The status of a child was determined by that of his father. It could be changed: freemen were enslaved and slaves made free, and kings could raise men by showing favour. It was, however, not enough to inherit or acquire status; that had to be maintained by worthy conduct and by wealth. Ine's laws provide for men of *gesith* rank with 20, 10 or 3 hides of land, and there was a notion, made explicit in the eleventh century but implicit throughout much of the period that the appropriate estate for a noble was 5 hides of land, just as the equivalent for a ceorl was 1 hide. The basic unit for purposes of assessment in the seventh century and afterwards was the land of one family; *terra unius familiae* is the formula used by Bede, and its vernacular equivalent was *hīd* or *hīwis*, referring to the nuclear family of man, wife and children (Charles-Edwards, 1972, pp. 4–8). There was naturally no standard size for a hide; what mattered was that it yielded enough to maintain a ceorl's family with their servants and dependants, for Æthelberht's laws show that these were a normal element in a ceorl's household.

The man, his family, his land and status were all protected by his kin, the natural group from which to expect support. When St Cuthbert was once in Teviotdale, his young companion said that he 'knew no kindred there and did not expect any kindness from strangers of other kindreds' (*Life of Cuthbert*, ii. 5). A kin might be powerful enough to protect evil men, a problem that appears to have been acute in the early tenth century (cf. III As 6; IV As 3; VI As 8.2). The kin appear most dramatically when pursuing a feud. Many clauses in the law-codes are about the regulation of feuds and the procedures to facilitate the payment of wergeld, thus reducing the threat of violence.

As now the size of a family varied with circumstances. For purposes of holding land and making renders to the king it consisted of the nuclear family, extending perhaps to fifth cousins if a feud was embarked upon, or compensation paid. There was also an intermediate group, of unknown size, which was entitled to the payment that had to be made immediately in order to stop violence breaking out in the heat of the insult. The payment was called *healsfang*, and meant 'grasp of the neck'. Kinsmen also shared the inheritance of land. The rules are never clearly or fully stated, and were probably not uniform. There are reasons for thinking that in seventh-century Northumbria a man's children divided his land, the eldest taking the *frumstōl*, or main residence, but the laws of Cnut provide that if a man dies without making a will 'the property is to be very justly divided among the wife, the children and the close kinsmen, each in the proportion which belongs to him' (II Cn 70). Inheritance of this kind does not necessarily increase the number of adult males but it could and sometimes did lead to such minute subdivision that the shares were too small for individuals. With such a close connection between status and landed wealth, and the family interest in maintaining both, it is not surprising that there were great restraints on the alienation of land. It may indeed not have been possible to alienate ↗ land before the seventh century unless it had been acquired by conquest. Kings and other lords could grant land for life, as a reward for service and a means of ensuring continued loyalty, but the land, in theory, remained the lord's. Several legal disputes mentioned in the charters had their origin in the alienation of land away from a kin (e.g. *EHD*, 77).

Land was not only inalienable, it was also subject to a variety of obligations to render services and dues to the king's *tūn*. When churches had to be endowed, royal charters were needed not only to break the traditional restraint on alienation but also to transfer the right to those dues. In one sense a grant to a monastery was made to a new kin, the family of the abbey, and that 'religious' family was occasionally closely related to the 'secular' family that had held it before. By the ninth century, grants of this kind were being made to laymen without any avowed religious purpose, by means of charters, called books. The resulting book-land was privileged in various ways, not least in its freedom from the traditional restraints on alienation.

It is in Northumbria that we can hope to gain the best impression of the character of early English society for, in the eleventh century, Northumbria had been largely unaffected by the growth of royal power that was transforming England south of the Humber. Unfortunately, Domesday Book does not extend north of the Tees, and Yorkshire, although described in detail, had been brutally treated by William. The Domesday description of the lands between the Ribble and the Mersey is some compensation. The area was divided into six hundreds. One of these hundreds, Newton, appears to have been a new development, but the others were ancient 'shires' each associated with a royal *tūn*. The hundred of West Derby, for example, consisted of 44 holdings called manors, and Domesday Book notes their names, their assessments for taxation and their values. It also gives the names of all the men who were sole tenants, some of whom held more than one manor. Joint tenants, of whom there were 37, are simply recorded as, for example, 'five thegns held Sefton', or 'four radmen held Childwall'. It records that the king used to receive £26. 2s from those manors, and that some had been granted exemption, and it continues:

All these thegns had by custom to render 2 ores of pence for each carucate of land, and by custom used to make the king's houses and the things which appertained thereto as the villeins did, and the fisheries and the enclosures in the wood, and the deer hays; and he who went not to these tasks when he ought paid a fine of 2 shillings and afterwards came to the work and laboured until it was completed.

Each one of them sent his reapers one day in August to cut the king's crops. If not he paid a fine of 2 shillings.

If any free man committed theft, or *forestel*, or *heinfara*, or broke the king's peace, he paid a fine of 40 shillings.

If any committed bloodshed, or rape, or if he remained away from the 'shiremoot' without reasonable excuse, he paid a fine of 10 shillings. If he remained away from the hundred or went not to a plea when the reeve ordered, he paid a fine of 5 shillings.

If the reeve ordered anyone to go upon his service and he went not, he paid a fine of 4 shillings.

If anyone wished to withdraw from the king's land, he gave 40 shillings and went whither he wished.

If anyone wished to have the land of his deceased father, he paid a relief of 40 shillings; he who would not, the king had both the land and all the goods of the deceased father. (DB, i. 269b)

It gives some other specific exemptions and ends with the names of the men who held this land at the time of the survey and a brief description of their resources.

Estates, or communities of this kind, once existed in all parts of Britain south of the Mounth. They underlay the complex pattern of settlements and lordships that we can begin to study in detail only after the Norman Conquest. In many places traces of the former structure have fortunately survived, such as the radmen of the Welsh Border counties, the sokemen of Lincolnshire and the *censarii*, 'rent-payers', of Derbyshire and Staffordshire, whose duties correspond closely to those of the *geneat*, the 'companion' or 'retainer', as described in the eleventh-century treatise known as *Rectitudines Singularum Persona-narum* (Douglas and Greenaway, 1953, no. 172). It was with the help of such men that the king's reeve administered the estate, collected the dues and, when the king came, provided him with the services and entertainment that he demanded.

Northumbria was also the scene of one of the most famous feuds of English history. The murder of Earl Uhtred by a noble called Thurbrand began a chain of killings which ended in 1073 when Uhtred's great-grandson, Earl Waltheof, killed many of Thurbrand's descendants at Settrington, not far from York (Stenton, 1971, pp. 417–18). The feud might well have continued but Waltheof was himself executed by William in 1076. There are other signs of the continuing importance of kinship in the north. The writ of Gospatrick, lord of Allerdale and Dalston in Cumbria, shortly before the Norman Conquest, was addressed not only to his retainers and to the freemen and drengs, but also to his kindred (S, 1243).

This writ is a reminder that kinship and strong lordship were not incompatible. The more powerful a kin, the more effective it could be in protecting the interests of its members. In so far they were free to do so, men frequently chose their lords, or retainers, from among their own kinsmen. The fact that kinship and the feud declined in southern England was due not to the rise of lordship, but to the growth of royal authority. Tenth-century kings did not prohibit the feud. It was still recognized as a normal and proper procedure in the middle of the tenth century when Edmund attempted to regulate its conduct (II Edm), an extension of Alfred's earlier attempt to limit violence (Alf 42). Nevertheless, the greater responsibilities imposed on royal agents, reeves and ealdormen, in the regulation of the feud and in much else, and their success in combating cattle-thefts must have reduced the occasions for the feud, and hampered the freedom of kinsmen to pursue it.

Kings also emphasized the importance of communal action. At one level this was seen in the responsibility to repair and man fortifications around shire towns, but they also had great success in organizing groups of neighbours to act as hundreds or tithings (p. 198). Communal action was not new. Joint cultivation is well evidenced in both England and Ireland in the seventh century. What the English kings did was to institutionalize local communities in their own service.

The description of English society in Domesday Book is in some respects misleading. Some of the terminology employed by William's surveyors was new; they introduced words like manor and villein, and by using them concealed a great variety of English terms. Even more serious is the suspicion that in some areas it omits large numbers of people, including the richest, most independent, of the peasantry.

Domesday Book is, therefore, an unsatisfactory basis for the kind of detailed discussion of English social structure that its apparent comprehensiveness encourages. It is, naturally, most reliable in those matters that relate directly to its purpose, an enquiry into the king's rights and the value of his tenants' lands (p. 138). Its information about subtenants is manifestly incomplete, but as an account of the main landowners in 1086, and of their predecessors, it may be trusted. The landowners before the Conquest were very varied and ranged from a few great lords, generally the earls or their close relatives, to landowners whose holdings appear to be absurdly small. Any discussion of the pre-Conquest landowners is hampered by problems of identification. We cannot know how many men are represented by one name, for only a few of them are more precisely identified by being described as Alnod Cild, or Baldwin son of Herluin. Despite all the difficulties it is possible to recognize that on the eve of the Conquest, in most counties, English society was dominated by a small group of leading local landowners and that there was a much larger group who had only one or two small estates. In the Danelaw many of these men had Scandinavian names, but the Scandinavian settlers do not seem to have had a significant effect on English society. By taking over English estates, and treating them as their own, they certainly weakened the structure of many old 'shires' but English lords were doing the same elsewhere. By the late tenth century they all, English and Scandinavian alike, owed service to the king, and their lands were assessed for taxation. It is possible that the Scandinavian conquests increased the free element in society but that is doubtful. Domesday Book does record a higher proportion of freemen and sokemen in most Danelaw counties, but its omission of the *censarii* of Burton Abbey shows how misleading it can be (p. 149). More important, the obligations of these freemen and sokemen as revealed by later evidence are so similar to the obligations recorded elsewhere for drengs, thegns, radmen and *geneats* that it is difficult to believe that the Vikings did more than affect the language, and take control of kingdoms, king's *tūn* and some of the estates that were tributary to those *tūn*. The main agent of change were not Viking invaders, or acquisitive lords, but kings who, with their agents, brought England increasingly under their control.

V

Kingship and government

There were many and great changes in the character and resources of English kingship between the seventh century and the eleventh. The growth in the size of the kingdoms and their eventual absorption into one English kingdom made it necessary for kings and their agents to devise new machinery of government, not least to collect and dispose of such royal dues as food renders and to organize military forces for defensive as well as offensive purposes. There were also fundamental changes in royal functions. At first English kings did not issue coins; they had a limited role in legal disputes and perhaps even in the declaration of the law; and their sacrality, as kings, in and before the seventh century may be doubted. The four centuries between the conversion of the English and the Norman Conquest witnessed a significant development of royal authority in these and many other respects. One source of change was the example of Frankia which was a major influence throughout the period, not least in providing a model for the government of a large area, and the English learned much from their Frankish neighbours about both the theory and the practice of kingship. This Frankish influence reinforced some elements in royal authority which can be traced back to the period when Britain was under Roman rule. The most fundamental changes were, however, a consequence of the conversion of the English to Christianity: by the eleventh century the royal office in England, as in most other parts of Europe, had been deeply and permanently affected by the teaching of the Christian church.

Before English kingship was influenced by either Frankish example or Christian teaching, one of the main functions of kings was to be war-leaders; they were *duces* as much as *reges*. The English kingdoms of the seventh century appear, in fact, to have been created by the leaders who were particularly successful in the second half of the sixth century, and in forming these kingdoms they also established royal dynasties; it was from these men that later rulers traced their descent (p. 86). Their armies, or war-bands, were fundamentally aristocratic. Peasants might accompany the warriors to bring supplies and perform other services, but unless their own homes were threatened, they did not normally fight (but see Charles-Edwards, 1976a, p. 182). The different roles of the different classes is shown very clearly in a story Bede tells about Imma, a young member of King Ælfwine's army, which had been defeated at the Battle of the Trent. He was left for dead but recovered and while he was looking for his friends

> he was found and captured by men of the enemy army and taken to their lord, who was a *comes* of King Æthelred. On being asked who he was he was afraid to admit that he was a warrior (*miles*); but he answered instead that he was a poor peasant (*rusticus*) and married; and he declared that he had come to the army in company with other peasants to bring food to the soldiers (*milites*). The *comes* took him and had his wounds attended to. But when Imma began to get better, he ordered him to be bound at night to prevent his escape. However it proved impossible to bind him, for no sooner had those who chained him gone, than his fetters were loosed. (*HE*, iv. 22)

The reason for this miracle was, Bede explains, that Imma's brother, Tunna, was a priest and abbot who, thinking that Imma was dead, 'took care to offer many masses for the absolution of his soul'. Imma denied any knowledge of magical arts but, having realized what was happening, explained it to his captor. Bede continues:

> When he had been a prisoner with the *comes* for some time, those who watched him closely realized by his appearance, his bearing, and his speech that he was not of common stock as he had said but of noble family (*non erat de paupere uulgo, ut dixerat, sed de nobilibus*). Then the *comes* called him aside and asked him very earnestly to declare his origin, promising that no harm should come to him, provided that he told him plainly who he was. The prisoner did so, revealing that he had been one of the king's thegns (*ministri*). The *comes* answered, 'I realized by every one of your answers that you

were not a peasant, and now you ought to die because all my brothers and kinsmen were killed in battle; but I will not kill you for I do
not intend to break my promise.'

The core of a royal army was the king's own retinue, which included
young nobles like Imma. It might be enlarged on special occasions but
it can never have been a vast assembly in the seventh century – the main
chamber of Edwin's hall at Yeavering was only about 60 feet long. On
campaigns the army would be reinforced by subordinate kings, by
allies and by *comites*, like Imma's captor, with their own retinues of
'brothers and kinsmen', as well as others. Penda's army at *Winwæd*
consisted of 'thirty legions of soldiers experienced in war' commanded
by royal leaders, *duces reges* (*HE*, iii. 24).

Kings lived in royal *villas* or *vici* which were presumably always
fenced, and might in English be called the king's *tūn*, while some were
certainly fortified making such descriptions as *burh* or *ceaster* appropriate. At Yeavering a fort was discovered near the royal *tūn* and the
defences of royal palaces figure prominently in early literature, notably
Beowulf. In their households kings had servants of various kinds: the
laws of Æthelberht mention his smiths, messengers and women-ser-
vants of different grades, but their close companions were nobles, men
like Lilla, Edwin's most devoted thegn (*minister amicissimus*), who
sacrificed his own life to save his king's. The food to sustain the royal
household came from the royal estates, but kings could also expect a
supply of provisions from all estates, what was later called the royal
feorm, the word from which the Modern English word 'farm' comes.
Ine's laws show how substantial royal *feorm* could be (p. 144). It must
have been delivered in season to local centres, king's *tūn*, and either con-
sumed there during a royal visit or sent on to wherever the king was
staying. The king could also expect many different services for himself
and his agents. No early text lists these systematically but some impression of the variety of such obligations is given by a charter of
Ceolwulf of Mercia freeing a Kentish estate:

> from all servitude in secular affairs, from entertainment of king,
> bishop, ealdorman, or of reeves, tax-gatherers, keepers of dogs, or
> horses, or hawks; from the feeding and support of all those who are
> called *fæstingmen* (probably men who were entitled to lodging when
> on royal business); from all labours, services, charges or burdens.
> (S, 186; *EHD*, 83)

The status, functions and resources of early English kings were very similar to those of their contemporaries in Ireland (pp. 70–2). There were, of course, some differences. English kingdoms were then already much larger than Irish, the evidence for the sacrality of English kings is not so clear as for the Irish and, most significantly, English kings appear to have acquired some rights and resources that derived from the time Britain was under Roman rule. Their ability to give Christian missionaries sites for their churches in former Roman cities, *castra* or *vici*, strongly suggests that such places were under royal control (p. 73); and the later royal right to toll at both coastal markets and inland salt-springs, all called *wic* in English, is likely to have been another inheritance from Rome. The markets over which kings had such rights in the eighth century were probably only those visited by strangers from other kingdoms or from overseas. There were certainly other local markets but these do not seem to have been brought under royal control until rather later (p. 222). The recognition of some roads as royal or public is probably another feature deriving from the Roman past. At the end of the eleventh century there was a tradition that the four great roads, Watling and Ermine Streets, the Foss and Icknield Ways, were all special in that travellers on them were protected by the king's peace (Stenton, 1970, p. 236). These late texts certainly give too limited an impression of the extent of royal rights over roads. In the Yorkshire Domesday, for example, the king is reported as having 'three ways by land and a fourth by water. In these every forfeiture is the king's and the earl's wherever the ways lead, be it through the land of the king, or of the archbishop, or of the earl' (DB, i. 298b). Many roads throughout England were considered to be the king's. On the first folio of Domesday Book the account of royal rights in East Kent begins:

> If anyone makes a fence or a ditch in the making of which the king's public way is narrowed, or lets fall within the road a tree standing outside the road and takes therefrom a branch or twig, for each offence of this sort he shall pay 100 shillings as amercement to the king.

These eleventh-century royal rights were certainly very old, for Bede refers to 'public roads' in Edwin's reign (p. 28).

Such Roman influences were reinforced by contact with the Franks under whom Gaul remained far more Romanized than Britain. In the seventh and eighth centuries this Frankish influence is seen most clearly in the coinage. The first coins struck by the English were gold shillings, modelled on Frankish *tremisses*, but by the end of the seventh century, although the size and weight of the English coins was virtually unchanged, they were made of silver not gold, and were called pennies. In this change of metal the English followed Frankish example as they did at the end of the eighth century when, somewhat belatedly following the lead of Pippin in 755, they began to produce thinner coins, larger in diameter. These new pennies included the king's name as the earliest coins normally did not, a change that may reflect a growing royal control of coin production.

As already explained (pp. 48–9), the seventh-century English kingdoms were themselves composed of several smaller kingdoms. This is seen most clearly in Wessex because it was not until the ninth century that one of its constituent kingdoms, or rather one of its royal families, gained sufficient mastery to be able to hold the West Saxon kingship for more than two generations, a lack of continuity that has to some extent been obscured by the genealogical convention that West Saxon kings descended from Cerdic or Cynric. Other kingdoms which appear more stable and united than Wessex similarly comprised several kingdoms or subkingdoms. It was natural for these rulers to wish to extend their hegemonies, for by so doing they not only strengthened their own authority but also increased the likelihood that some close relative would be the next king. Such limited successions were, however, never more than a probability, for claimants from other branches of the royal family, or even from the royal families of the constituent subkingdoms, were sometimes successful. In Northumbria the apparent chaos of the late eighth and ninth centuries may have been caused by conflicts between rivals coming not simply from different branches of the royal family, by then very large, but from different Northumbrian kingdoms. Offa made determined efforts to secure the succession of his son Ecgfrith, but he survived only 141 days in 796 and, as Alcuin wrote shortly afterwards,

> truly, I think, that most noble young man has not died for his own sins; but the vengeance for the blood shed by the father has reached the son. For you know very well how much blood his father shed to secure the kingdom on his son. This was not a strengthening of his kingdom, but its ruin. (*EHD*, 202)

After Ecgfrith the Mercian kingdom passed to Cenwulf (796–821), a very distant kinsman. In other words, at the very time the West Saxon kingship was acquired by the family which was to retain it until the eleventh century, the royal succession in Mercia became far less stable. The dynastic disputes and undoubted violence did not, however, mean that rulers, once acknowledged, were not fully kings. That the recognition of a king involved more than lip-service is shown by a Mercian king-list which includes the name of the West Saxon Egbert who briefly displaced Wiglaf; the latter's resumed reign was, to judge by his charters, dated from the time he recovered the Mercian throne. This implies a degree of acceptance denied to Beornwulf who was treated as a usurper and omitted from the list of Mercian kings (Dumville, 1977b, p. 98).

English kingship was certainly much affected by the experience of overlordship. There must have been an accumulation of experience in the control of subkings and the collection of tribute; administrative improvements may have contributed to the tendency for overlordships to last longer after the mid-seventh century. Rulers could also profit from the mistakes or unpopularity of their predecessors from rival kingdoms. The hostility of the monks of Bardney towards Oswald must have helped the Mercian kings who ruled Lindsey after him, just as Egbert of Wessex was able to take advantage of Kentish hatred of the Mercians (pp. 30, 104).

English kingship was also deeply influenced by the church. In the first place the missionaries, as strangers, needed protection and this was best provided by kings who, in return, gained great benefits. Christian influence on English kingship is most clearly and dramatically seen in the ceremonies devised by churchmen for the inauguration of a king, and we are fortunate to have the full order of service used at Bath on Whitsunday in 973 for the coronation of Edgar, a ceremony also described in the *Life*, written shortly afterwards, of one of the leading participants, Oswald, archbishop of York (Legg, 1901, pp. 14–29; *Life of Oswald*, pp. 436–8). These texts show that the king, who was already wearing his crown, was led into the church by two bishops to the anthem 'Let thy hand be strengthened and thy right hand exalted', and he then prostrated himself before the altar during the singing of the *Te Deum*. It was at this stage that the archbishop of Canterbury, Dunstan, is said to have wept at the king's humility. The king then rose and made a threefold promise, 'chosen by the bishops and the people':

that the church of God and the whole Christian people may by my will preserve true peace for all time; second, that I shall forbid to all ranks thefts and all injustices; third, that I shall ordain fairness and mercy in all judgements, so that the gentle and merciful God who lives, may grant to me and to you his mercy.

Then, after prayers, the consecration, the central act of the coronation (itself called *consecratio*), took place.

Almighty eternal God, creator and governor of heaven and earth . . . king of kings and lord of lords . . . multiply the gifts of your blessings on this your servant——, whom we choose, with humble devotion, to rule the Angles and Saxons . . . anoint him with the oil of the grace of the Holy Spirit. . . .

The significance of this act was underlined by the anthem that accompanied it ('Zadok the priest and Nathan the prophet anointed Solomon king, and the people rejoiced and said "May the king live for ever" '); and the prayer that followed began:

Christ anoint this king to his reign, as you have anointed priests, kings, prophets and martyrs.

The king was then invested with the symbols of kingship; the ring, 'the seal of the Holy faith, strength of your kingdom and the increase of your power'; the sword, 'with which by the power of the Holy Spirit may you be able to withstand and drive out all your enemies and all the adversaries of the Holy Church of God, and to protect the kingdom entrusted to you'; the crown, 'that you, by our ministry, having a right faith and manifold fruit of good works, may obtain the crown of an everlasting kingdom through the gift of him whose kingdom endures for ever'; the sceptre, 'the sign of the kingly power'; and the rod or staff 'of virtue and equity'. The king was then blessed and the archbishop of Canterbury made a declaration beginning *Sta et retine*:

Stand and hold fast from now on to the status that until now you have held by hereditary right and the succession of your ancestors, now handed over to you by the authority of God almighty and by the present act of ours, that is, all the bishops and other servants of God. And just as you see the clergy closer to the holy altars, so remember to give them greater honour in suitable places, so that the mediator between God and men may establish you on this royal throne as mediator between clergy and people.

The service was then completed by prayers, the consecration of the queen, and mass; it was followed by a banquet.

This order of service, which Janet Nelson (1978) has shown was a combination of earlier English and West Frankish rituals, has been the basis of all English coronations since, including the most recent in 1953 when the anthem 'Zadok the priest' still accompanied the anointing, but was sung to the music of Handel. Some changes have, of course, been made, the greatest being in the seventeenth century, but the coronation of Charles I in 1625 followed the order of 973 very closely indeed, and many of the prayers as well as the final declaration of the status of the king were fairly direct translations of the Latin used in the tenth century (Legg, 1901). The prayers were drawn mainly from the Old Testament and one scholar has remarked that they are filled with a wealth of Old Testament illustration that would not have disgraced one of Scott's Covenanters. The dependence on the Old Testament, and in particular on the Books of Kings, is not surprising for that part of the Bible describes a society that was in many respects similar to the barbarian world of the Franks, the English and their neighbours, a violent world in which powerful spiritual forces were manifestly at work, a world in which the success of kings, as they led their armies in search of glory and gain, depended on their obedience to the will of God. Many Dark Age kings were directly compared with David: Charlemagne was called David at court, and in the seventh century Eddius described Ecgfrith of Northumbria as 'strong like David in crushing his enemies' (c. 20).

The central and, in the eyes of the church, most important element in the coronation ceremony was the anointing, coming as it did after the promises and before the king was invested with the symbols of kingship. Unction was deliberately introduced into the king-making of the Franks in 751 when the Carolingian Pippin became king in place of the old Merovingian dynasty, descendants of the founders of the Frankish kingdom in Gaul. That family had by the eighth century lost its power but its divinely ordained right to the kingship was respected by many Franks and when, with the explicit approval of the pope, it was accepted that Pippin, son of Charles Martel, who held the real power, should also have the name of king, his elevation to the new status was marked by anointing, first in 751 by St Boniface and again in 754 by the pope himself. This act may have been modelled on the Old Testament example of Samuel's anointing first of Saul and then, when Saul had through disobedience lost God's favour, of David. Unction was therefore frequently used in Frankish king-making, but what appears to have been important to the Franks in the eighth century was not the act itself so much as the fact that it was performed by the successor of St Peter, or his agent, and in 781 Charlemagne took his two sons to Rome to be anointed by the pope. Six years later Offa of Mercia may have been influenced by this example when he had his son Ecgfrith anointed as his designated successor. In the ninth century the *Chronicle* reports simply that kings succeeded. The first king, after Ecgfrith, said to have been consecrated was Athelstan in 925; and after him only two other tenth-century kings, Edgar in 973 and his son Æthelred in 978, were, according to that source, consecrated as kings, the word used, *gehalgod*, being otherwise reserved for the consecration of bishops. Perhaps little weight should be placed on the chronicler's choice of words for there is good charter evidence that Eadred was consecrated 'by pontifical authority' at Kingston despite the *Chronicle's* simple statement that he 'succeeded to the kingdom' in 946, and there is similar charter evidence for the consecration of Ceolwulf of Mercia in 822 (Nelson, 1977, p. 66n; S, 186; *EHD*, 83). Janet Nelson (1978) has shown that the coronation ritual of 973 was not an innovation but had been used from early in the century, and was based on an earlier *ordo*, including anointing, that is preserved in the Leofric Missal, and was composed no later than the middle of the ninth century. The language of the *Chronicle* does, however, suggest that the symbolic act of anointing was not initially invested with quite the same importance as it was later to acquire. Anointing did not, in fact, much affect the position of claims of kings at first; churchmen had long taught that they were chosen by God and ruled by his grace, but during the ninth century the importance of royal unction was increasingly emphasized by Frankish churchmen to the point of asserting that it was unction that made the king. This was a very large claim and it is well to remember that, although churchmen were in this and other ways transforming the ideology and forms of kingship, its roots were old and pagan.

Janet Nelson (1977, p. 66) has drawn attention to evidence which strongly suggests that all tenth-century English kings, including Edgar, were consecrated in a ceremony which included anointing as soon as possible after their election, but there are nevertheless indications, amounting in Edgar's case to certainty, that they dated their reigns from their election, not their consecration. Their power and authority were reinforced by, not completely dependent on, the 'agency of God's bishops and other servants'.

Those bishops were, however, an important element in royal courts. They always have a place in charter witness-lists and the attendance of the bishop or bishops of a kingdom at meetings of a royal court devoted to secular business was one way a king's authority was manifested. The attendance of metropolitans was obviously even more significant. The archbishop of York would of course be expected to attend the court of the Northumbrian king, and the archbishop of Canterbury would similarly attend the Kentish court, but the presence of the southern archbishop at the court of kings of Mercia or Wessex revealed that ruler's power. It was this that made Archbishop Iænberht's hostility to Offa so damaging to the Mercian king, and caused him to make great efforts to create a third archbishopric.

The church contributed to the development of English kingship in other and very fundamental ways. Its need for a permanent endowment meant that traditional restraints on the alienation of land had to be broken, and it was only kings who could do this. It was by royal charters that permanent rights could be conferred, and the claims of kinsmen defeated. No king could make such grants by his own unsupported authority; he had to have the consent of at least his leading lay nobles, but the nobles could not do it themselves. If a layman wished to found or even to make a benefaction to a monastery, he could do so only with the king's consent, a very significant enlargement of royal authority which in time enabled kings to make similar grants to laymen for no religious purpose.

Another change of great moment effected by the church was to cause English kings to write down their laws. This may have been in part to provide a place for the church and churchmen in customary procedures and the first clauses of the earliest English law-code, produced after Æthelberht's conversion, are concerned with the compensation due to the church and clergy for stolen property or breach of the peace of the church, but most clauses in Æthelberht's laws have nothing to do with the church and there must have been some other reason for writing them down. The clue is provided by Bede who says that Æthelberht, with the advice of his councillors, established a code of laws *iuxta exemplum Romanum* meaning either 'after the manner of the Romans' or, as has recently been suggested, 'following Roman patterns or copies' (Wallace-Hadrill, 1971, p. 37). In either case Bede meant that

Æthelberht was following the example of barbarian rulers who, having settled within the Roman Empire, produced codes of laws. Those codes are Roman not only in being written in Latin but also because they include many provisions, especially concerning the law of property, which derive from late Roman legal practice in the western provinces of the Empire. The laws of Æthelberht are very different for they are Germanic in both language and substance, being written in English and consisting largely of an elaborate tariff of compensations for injuries of various kinds, but they do have parallels in other barbarian codes, notably early seventh-century laws produced under Frankish stimulus, for example, the Alamannic and Bavarian laws and Rothari's *Edict*. Bede said that Æthelberht's laws were still observed in his day, a century later, and there is no need to doubt that they were a statement of law that was current, if possibly archaic; they cannot, however, have been a full statement. They are very limited in scope and omit many topics for which there must have been provision in the contemporary law of Kent. Their significance is rather that they were, in the words of the heading in the surviving manuscript, 'the decrees which King Æthelberht established in the lifetime of Augustine'. This heading may well be a later addition but it declares an important truth, that these laws were established by King Æthelberht, and later codes of law are similarly regarded as the work of kings. We have no means of telling what changes Æthelberht made when his laws were written down, or indeed if he made any apart from the provision made for the church, but it was certainly possible for laws to be altered. The notion that law is eternal and unchanging is perhaps the greatest of all legal fictions. New situations demand new remedies and the law-codes are full of new laws and modifications of old ones. Alfred prefaced his code with the explanation that, having collected earlier laws

> and ordered to be written many of them which our forefathers observed, those which I liked; and many of those which I did not like, I rejected with the advice of my councillors, and ordered them to be differently observed. For I dared not presume to set in writing at all many of my own, because it was unknown to me what would please those who should come after us.

Consultation was certainly needed; Bede reports how Æthelberht took the advice of his councillors; and the laws of Ine, king of Wessex, Bede's contemporary, emphasize the role of his councillors, lay and clerical. As long as law was preserved by oral tradition it could easily appear to be unchanging, even to those who declared it; the novelty of any change might never be realized, or be quickly forgotten. Written law, on the other hand, despite its apparent permanence, made any changes obvious, and as written laws were peculiarly associated with the name of the king in whose name they were produced his part in changing them was made manifest. His councillors were certainly important, as they must always have been, but written law both enhanced his prestige and emphasized his role in declaring as well as changing the law.

Christianity not only influenced the character of kings as law-givers, it also affected the laws themselves. This is seen most clearly in the provision made for the protection or support of the church; the first clause of Æthelberht's code, setting high values on the property of churchmen and prescribing the same compensation for breach of the peace of the church as for breach of the king's peace, are followed in many later law-codes by clauses conferring special privileges on churches and churchmen. Christianity took longer to influence the substance of secular law but already by the end of the seventh century such matters as Sunday observance and marriage were dealt with in West Saxon and Kentish law. By the eleventh century the laws of Cnut include a great variety of regulations affecting such matters as the conduct of priests, the payment of church dues and tithes, Sunday trading, fasting, confession and the prohibited degrees of marriage, and there is an injunction on all Christians to learn the *Pater Noster* and the Creed. The merciful influence of Christianity is well shown by the prohibition of the death penalty for Christians for trivial offences:

> on the contrary, merciful punishments shall be determined upon for the public good, and the handiwork of God and the purchase which he made at a great price shall not be destroyed for trivial offences. (V Atr 3)

The same concern 'that the souls which Christ bought with his own life be not destroyed' (V Atr 2) led to the prohibition of the sale of Christian slaves abroad and Christianity almost certainly contributed to that most fundamental change in English law, the gradual limitation of freedom to pursue the feud.

One of the most important and obvious ways in which the church affected kingship in England as elsewhere was by providing a body of men who, dependent on kings for their support and protection, gave their services, practical and spiritual, in return. The aid of men who were literate was clearly of great value in practical affairs and soon after the conversion churchmen were prominent among royal councillors. They could help in many ways – drafting letters, laws, charters – and were able to draw on the experience of a wider world. By the time of Alfred, if not before, bishops were involved in settling disputes about land, and by the end of the tenth century they, together with the king's other main agents, the ealdormen, were to be present at borough and shire courts to direct the observance of ecclesiastical and secular law, *Godes riht ge worldriht* (III Edg 5).

Contemporaries, from the seventh century to the eleventh, would have judged that such practical support counted for little beside the spiritual benefits gained by kings, in particular the offering up of prayers. The power of prayer is dramatically illustrated in the life of St Guthlac, who was visited by Æthelbald, when he was being hounded by his distant kinsman Ceolred, king of Mercia, who doubtless wished to exclude rival claimants. Guthlac reassured Æthelbald:

> O my child, I am not without knowledge of your hardships, I am not ignorant of the miseries that have been yours from the beginning of your life. Pitying your distress therefore I have prayed the Lord to help you in his compassion, and he has heard me; and he has given you domination over your people, and he has set you as a ruler of nations, and will subdue the necks of your enemies under your heel. ... Not as pillage or as spoil will a kingdom be given to you, but you will be given it from the hand of the Lord. (c. 49)

That prophecy was fulfilled in 716 when Æthelbald 'succeeded to the kingdom in Mercia'. The literature of the period is full of examples of the efficacy of prayer and it is not to be wondered at that kings, and claimants, were ready to make lavish gifts to ensure the continuance of such spiritual support by holy men. Æthelbald richly adorned Guthlac's tomb, but a more common procedure was for kings to grant privileges and endowments to communities of monks or nuns for the sake of their souls, for the remission of their sins and in the hope of reward in eternity. This much is made explicit by the charters of donation which, although they were drawn up by interested ecclesiastics, can hardly have seriously misrepresented the thoughts and hopes of the grantors.

The charters normally do not define what prayers were expected, but there is a precious glimpse of what was involved in a late ninth-century charter of Æthelred, ruler of Mercia, and Æthelflæd his wife, granting privileges to the cathedral church of St Peter at Worcester,

> that things may be more honourably maintained in that foundation and also that they may more easily help the community to some extent; and that their memory may be the more firmly observed in that place for ever, as long as obedience to God shall continue in that minster.

The way in which their memory was to be preserved is described in uncommon detail:

> And Bishop Wærferth and the community have appointed these divine offices before that which is done daily, both during their life and after their death; i.e. at every matins and at every vespers and at every tierce, the psalm *De Profundis* as long as they live, and after their death *Laudate Dominum*; and every Saturday in St Peter's church thirty psalms and a mass for them, both for them living and also departed. (S, 223; *EHD*, 99)

It was for such unceasing prayer that rulers looked to the church. King Athelstan ordered that every Friday at every minster all the servants of God were to sing fifty psalms 'for the king and all who desire what he desires, and for the others as they may deserve' (V As 3), and later that century Edgar vigorously supported reformed monasticism, for he believed that the prayers offered by reformed communities would be of greater value than those from the others (S, 745).

Success in this world could not, of course, be guaranteed, but failure could always be explained as the result of disobedience to God's will. The demands on kings were such that they were all at some time disobedient. Eddius thought that the defeat and death of Ecgfrith at *Nechtansmere* in 685 were a consequence of his abandonment of Bishop Wilfrid. The English missionary St Boniface believed that Osred of Northumbria and Ceolred of Mercia, both of whom died in 716, had violated the privileges of churches and had consequently met their just deserts. In an important letter to Ceolred's successor, Æthelbald, he emphasized their fate as a dreadful warning:

> And lingering in these sins, that is in debauchery and adultery with nuns and violation of monasteries, condemned by the just judgement of God, thrown down from the regal summit of this life and over-

taken by an early and terrible death, they were deprived of the light
eternal and plunged into the depths of hell and abyss of Tartarus.
(*EHD*, 177)

Prominent among the offences of Ceolred and Osred was 'debauchery
and adultery with nuns' and Æthelbald was himself accused of the same
crime. Boniface was also moved to complain to Æthelbald about his
own behaviour. He did not criticize him for failing to take a lawful
wife for 'if you had willed to do this for the sake of chastity and ab-
stinence or had refrained from women from the fear and love of God
. . . we should rejoice, for that is not worthy of blame but rather of
praise, but,' he continues,

> if, as many say – but which God forbid – you have neither taken a
> lawful spouse nor observed chastity for God's sake but, moved by
> desire, have defiled your good name before God and man by the
> crime of adulterous lust, then we are greatly grieved because this is a
> sin in the sight of God and is the ruin of your fair fame among men.
> And now, what is worse, our informants say that these atrocious
> crimes are committed in convents with holy nuns and virgins con-
> secrated to God and this, beyond all doubt, doubles the offence.
> (*EHD*, 177)

Some fifty years later Alcuin urged a Mercian noble 'to admonish his
king to hold himself in Godliness, avoiding adulteries; and not des-
pise his former wife in order to commit adultery with women of the
nobility' and he expressed the fear that Eardwulf (king of Northumbria) must quickly lose the kingdom on account of the insult he did to
God dismissing his own wife, and publicly taking a concubine' (*EHD*,
202). The Christian teaching on marriage was clear and its implications
for royal succession were bluntly stated by the Legatine Synod of 786:

> We decreed that in the ordination of kings no one shall permit the
> assent of evil men to prevail, but kings are to be lawfully chosen by
> the priests and elders of the people, and are not to be those begotten
> in adultery or incest; for just as in our times according to the canons
> a bastard cannot attain to the priesthood, so neither can he who was
> not born of a legitimate marriage be the Lord's anointed and king of
> the whole kingdom and inheritor of the land. (*EHD*, 191)

It is clear that even by the end of the eighth century Christian teaching
on marriage had not greatly affected the marital habits of at least some

English kings; Æthelbald had failed to take a lawful wife, Eardwulf had dismissed his, and both were suspected of taking concubines. Such conduct is not, however, particularly surprising; even Charlemagne had concubines, and nuns had the great advantage of being of noble birth and unable to give birth to legitimate heirs.

However ineffective Christianity was in changing some of the habits of kings, there was no doubt of its value to them. This was demonstrated in many ways, including the failure of pagan reactions. There were certainly powerful interests opposed to many royal conversions, there were pagan revolts and some cases of apostasy, but these pagan reactions did not last long; as Professor Wallace-Hadrill (1971, p. 44) has said, 'paganism had nothing to offer a seventh-century king: only the solace of what was old'. The Christian church, in contrast, offered a new and powerful mythology with Christ as the King of Kings, Lord of Lords; it also brought the English a rich literature, filled with kings both good and bad. The English themselves made important contributions to that literature, most notably Bede's *Ecclesiastical History*, which is in part a demonstration of Christian virtues as exemplified by English kings. Almost two centuries later an English king, Alfred, revealed his views on kingship in his translation of Gregory's *Pastoral Care* and of Boethius. The sources used by Bede and Alfred are a reminder that the conversion not only brought English kings into communion with the kings of Europe, it also brought the English into contact with the thinking of a wider world in which old ideas about kingship, inherited from a pagan and Hebrew past, were being modified. Important developments were taking place in Frankia and it is significant that the English coronation service used in the tenth century, which so completely symbolizes the Christian remoulding of barbarian kingship, is in part based on the order of service developed a century before for Frankish kings.

Kings also gained much from the protection they gave to merchants and to markets. This is discussed in the next chapter (pp. 225–31); here it is only necessary to make the point that this royal protection appears initially to have been limited to foreign merchants and to the markets they visited either on the coast or at inland salt-producing centres. When markets were attacked by Vikings, it was the responsibility of kings to provide defences. The Mercians did this first (p. 109) but it was the West Saxons, above all Alfred, who developed and refined a system of fortified *burhs* that sheltered markets and also served as centres of royal administration. These *burhs* were regulated by royal reeves, occupied by tenants of the king who owed him a variety of rents and services, and it was in the *burhs* that the royal coinage was produced. They were also centres for the collection of the dues and services owed to the king from large districts known as shires. Some shires had more than one *burh* – Dorset had four: Dorchester, Bridport, Wareham and Shaftesbury – but most had only one, which in many cases gave its name to the shire.

The collection of royal dues was ultimately the responsibility of the king's main agents, the men called in the tenth century ealdormen and in the eleventh, under Scandinavian influence, earls. It was their responsibility to lead the military forces of the shire and in Latin texts they are termed *duces*. They were aided by various other royal agents called reeves (from the Old English word *gerefa*) but it was the ealdorman who, sometimes with the bishop, presided over the court of the shire, a meeting of the local landowners which, according to a law of Edgar (III.5.1), occurred twice a year. We hear only incidentally about the proceedings of these courts but it is clear that one of their main functions was to provide an opportunity to make important announcements. These were mostly of local interest; a gift of land, a bequest and even the disinheritance of a son were all announced in shire-courts. They were, therefore, ideal opportunities for ealdormen to proclaim royal ordinances and for royal grants or appointments to be published. It was, for example, to the shire-court of Oxford that Edward the Confessor announced his grant of an estate at Taynton to the church of St Denis at Paris, and he similarly notified the shire of Somerset that he had appointed Giso as bishop of Wells. It was in the shire-court that land-grants, exchanges and bequests were made or announced, and these meetings were therefore suitable occasions for the resolution of any disputes which might arise. The ealdorman's function was, however, to preside, to ensure that justice was done; the procedures themselves were determined by local custom. A century after the Norman Conquest a legal writer describing the royal law of England omitted to describe the legal processes in shire-courts,

partly because of the different customs observed from county to county, and partly because the brevity of my plan does not require it, for I am considering only the custom and law of the chief court of the lord king. (Glanville, xii. 23; cf. xiv. 8)

The king's power to interfere in and regulate local affairs was certainly growing in the tenth and eleventh centuries but the astonishing persistence of local customs and procedures shows what a limited role even the most effective kings had.

Edgar made a determined effort to impose a uniform procedure against theft which was to apply to all the nation,

> whether Englishmen, Danes or Britons, in every province of my dominion to the end that poor man and rich may possess what they rightly acquire, and a thief may not know where to dispose of stolen goods (IV Edg, 2. 2)

but he had to recognize that otherwise secular rights were matters to be determined locally 'according to as good laws as they can best decide on'.

Most royal dues, including such military obligations as service in the army or contributions to fortifications, were based on assessments that were in the eleventh century expressed in terms of hides, carucates or sulungs. Most of England appears originally to have been assessed in hides, but by the time of Domesday Book these had been replaced in large areas of eastern England by carucates. These have been interpreted as a sign of Scandinavian influence, but the absence of similar units in Scandinavia at that time, the occurrence of a similar unit – called the ploughgate – in parts of Scotland far removed from Scandinavian influence, and evidence that, in the early eleventh century, hides were still being used in areas that were carucated by the time of Domesday Book, show that Sir Frank Stenton (1910, pp. 88–9) was right to argue that the change occurred in the eleventh century. It appears in fact to be a new system of assessment introduced by the English themselves, possibly in response to the need to raise large sums of cash by taxation to pay tribute to the Vikings. The interest shown by the compilers of Domesday Book in ploughlands in all parts of the country, including areas assessed in hides, may indicate that the government was considering the extension of this system. In the event, the change from hides to carucates as a general basis of assessment was postponed until the end of the twelfth century (Mitchell, 1951, pp. 14–15).

The assessments of shires, or parts of shires, could be and were changed from time to time, and there are some indications that in the eleventh century they were largely determined by the size of the *burh* or *burhs* that had to be maintained and manned (pp. 226–9). Changes in the assessment did not, however, affect the extent of a shire and the boundaries of some appear to be very ancient indeed. Kent and Sussex were based on former kingdoms and the shires of Wessex may well have been similarly based on the various kingdoms of the West Saxons. Norfolk and Suffolk represent an early division of the East Anglian kingdom, and there are reasons for thinking that Yorkshire has much the same extent as Deira. Such neat coincidences are not so clear in Mercia. The kingdom of the Hwicce, represented by the medieval diocese of Worcester, was disregarded when the shire of Warwick was created, although the bishop's lands were still considered to be in Worcestershire and remained until modern times as detached islands in Warwickshire. Similarly Shropshire cuts across the northern boundary of the *Magonsæte* (figure 11, p. 247). There is no means of determining when these rearrangements were made; one strong possibility is that they were the work of Æthelred and Æthelflæd following their construction of fortifications at Worcester and elsewhere. It has also been argued that the East Midland shires of Nottingham, Derby and Leicester were artificially created, possibly by Edward the Elder, on the basis of territories seized from the Viking armies in those places, and that the anomalous shire of Rutland was a creation of the eleventh century. Very good arguments have, however, been advanced by Charles Phythian-Adams (1977b) for thinking that Rutland is a much older unit and, as he has pointed out, the location of Roman settlements at points where Roman roads cross the boundary of Leicestershire suggests that that shire represents a territorial divi ion that was very old indeed (pp. 62–3). It is, therefore, possible that in the Midlands as elsewhere the tenth-century kings developed this system of shires and *burhs* on the basis of units which already existed.

The same is also true in general of the subdivisions of the shires, known as hundreds or, in Danish areas, wapentakes. These sometimes contained approximately a hundred hides or carucates, although the hundred was sometimes the older long hundred of 120, but such regularity was not universal and south of the Thames relatively few hundreds contained that number of hides. In 1086 the Wiltshire hundreds varied from 11 to 195 hides. In the eleventh century these local units had a key role in the collection of taxes, and we are fortunate to have some records of a tax collected in parts of Wessex in 1086 which show what exemptions were granted and how thoroughly the collectors worked to gather a tax levied at the very heavy rate of 72 pence from every hide.

Hundreds and wapentakes had another, possibly even more significant, role in the development of royal government, for it was through these local units that the tenth-century English kings asserted their authority throughout England south of the Humber. They did this principally by emphasizing the function of the local community in the preservation of peace and the prevention of theft.

In the middle of the tenth century a royal ordinance required that hundreds were to meet every four weeks 'and each man is to do justice to another', with the implication that this just dealing was to take place at the monthly meeting (*EHD*, 39). It was also ordered that the men of the hundred, under their leaders, were to pursue thieves, and that strange cattle should not be kept without the knowledge of 'the man in charge of the hundred or the man over the tithing'. This rule was later elaborated by Edgar in his fourth code, which ruled that anyone setting out to make a purchase must first tell his neighbours of his intention and that when he returns he must report 'in whose witness he bought the goods'. Unexpected purchases made on a journey had to be announced on his return home 'and if it is livestock, he is to bring it to the common pasture with the witness of the village (*tūnscip*)'. Then followed the draconian rule that, if the villagers found that he had not done so, within five days they had to inform the man in charge of the hundred and so free themselves and their herdsmen from any penalty, but if they did not 'each herdsman is to be flogged'. The cattle were forfeited, even if acquired legally, 'because he would not announce it to his neighbours'. The confiscated cattle were to be divided between the lord of the estate and the hundred, an incentive to encourage villagers to report offences. These rules were explicitly said to apply to every province of the king's dominion and to apply to all, whether Englishmen, Danes or Britons.

Each member of a hundred over the age of twelve was also expected to belong to a tithing, a group of ten or twelve men who were mutually responsible for their good behaviour and, if necessary, for accusing, arresting and producing any of their number found guilty of a crime. This arrangement is first explicitly described in the laws of Cnut (II Cn 20), but the reference in the mid-tenth century to 'the man over the tithing' shows that these groups already existed at that time. Post-Conquest evidence reveals in more detail how this system, then called frankpledge, worked, and that the sheriff checked each hundred twice a year to ensure that all men were in tithings. The system has been neatly described as one of 'compulsory collective bail, fixed for individuals, not after their arrest for a crime, but as a safeguard in anticipation of it' (Morris, 1910, p. 2). This later evidence shows that the system of frankpledge did not extend north of the Humber nor is it found in the marcher counties of Cheshire, Shropshire and Hereford (Stewart-Brown, 1936). This demonstrates that Edgar's attempt to impose it throughout all his dominions was not completely successful. In the areas without tithings their place was taken after the Conquest by Serjeants of the Peace.

Both English and British society had long been familiar with the principle of sureties or pledges for the performance of legal actions, and the laws of Ine show that in the seventh century it was normal for men either to have such sureties or to have a lord who served the same function. What was novel about England south of the Humber in the eleventh century was the emphasis on communal responsibility. The tenth-century legislation may have been influenced in this, as in much else, by Frankish example, but the success of the English kings in imposing such a system of collective responsibility over the greater part of their kingdom was indeed a remarkable achievement. It was a manifestation of royal authority in the most humble levels of society, and made the hundred men, and even the chief men of tithings, agents of the king in his work of maintaining a general peace.

The fact that many of the hundreds north of the Thames were assessed at close to a hundred hides, or carucates, suggests that these assessments were relatively new, and the occurrence of double or half hundreds confirms the impression that the hundredal assessments had been imposed on earlier units. Miss Cam (1932) was able to show systematically that, when rights over hundreds, including the right to profits of justice, were in private hands in the twelfth and thirteenth centuries, they were, in many parts of England, attached to particular manors, which sometimes gave their names to the hundreds, much as some shires were named after their *burhs*. Thus in Buckinghamshire the hundred of Aylesbury was named after that place. Many of the hundredal manors in private hands can be shown once to have been royal. Of the sixty royal *tūn* mentioned in the will of King Alfred, twenty-nine gave their names to hundreds, and the same is true of ten of the twelve *tūn* named in King Eadred's will. Miss Cam was able, on the basis of this and similar evidence, to elaborate a suggestion, made earlier by Chadwick, that hundreds were originally districts, or estates, that were dependent on king's *tūn*, and that were once administered by a king's reeve. In these districts or estates we can recognize the so-called multiple estates that are found in many parts of Britain. The dues and services owed by the inhabitants of these estates had always been rendered at the king's *tūn*, and they continued to be due even when, as often happened, kings granted the estates to churches or later to laymen. The eleventh-century taxation is little more than an extension of this ancient obligation, but one which kings took care to retain in their own hands. This taxation system extended into parts of England which were never organized in tithings, and the superimposition of hundreds or wapentakes for fiscal purposes can be seen in many parts of the north, for example in the ancient shire of Richmond which appears to have been treated as five wapentakes in the twelfth century (Cam, 1933).

South of the Humber many of these ancient 'shires' were similarly subdivided into hundreds, but some survived as lathes in Kent, rapes in Sussex, sokes in eastern England, or simply as multiple hundreds. In Oxfordshire, for example, there were seven groups of hundreds, the largest being the four-and-a-half hundreds of Benson. Each of these groups was associated with a manor that was royal in Domesday Book. In addition three hundreds, Dorchester, Thame and Banbury, were held at the Conquest by the bishops of Dorchester. As Thame was a Mercian royal vill in the seventh century (S, 1165; *EHD*, 54) it had been granted to the bishop since then, with the result that the bishop acquired the former royal right to the dues and services which had anciently been rendered there, from, in the words of later texts, the estate that 'lay to' that king's *tūn*.

These dues were sometimes described in Domesday Book as a 'night's farm,' *firma unius noctis*, implying that they were originally what was needed to support the royal household for a day. In Domesday Book these farms are expressed in money-payments and on the eve of the Conquest a 'night's farm' amounted to about £80. The conversion of produce into cash in this way would only have been possible if there were markets in which it could be sold, and it has been suggested that some markets grew up near royal vills for that purpose (Phythian-Adams, 1977a).

There is nothing improbable in such large sums of cash at that time.

English kings of the tenth and eleventh centuries devoted great attention to the control and manipulation of the coinage, and large quantities of coin were produced. Their success in regulating the currency
and their ability to raise very large sums of cash by taxation are two of
the most remarkable features of English royal authority in the century
before the Norman Conquest.

The full development of that authority is well displayed in Domesday
Book, which gives a detailed, if unsystematic, account of royal
rights in the shires of England in the mid-eleventh century. In Wiltshire the king had '£10 for a falcon and 20 shillings for a sumpter horse',
while in Berkshire a dying thegn or knight (*miles*) sent all his weapons to
the king together with two horses, one saddled and one not, and if he
had hounds or falcons these were also offered to the king. Escort duties
are defined: in Shropshire twenty-four horses accompanied the king
from Shrewsbury to the boundary of the shire. Obligations to guard
the king, and to assist him when hunting, are described, and tariffs are
given for breaches of the king's peace and for a great variety of offences.
The entitlement of the earls to a third of most royal revenues from their
shires, known as the earl's third penny, is frequently noted, underlining
their role as agents of the king. In all this there is much that appears
archaic, but there is also much that was new. References to mints furnish glimpses of the sophistication of the coinage and everywhere there
are the assessments on the basis of which *burhs* were built, maintained
and manned, warriors recruited and taxes gathered. Domesday Book
can tell us much about the working of the government for, in attempting to supply the king with the information he wanted about the value
of his men's estates, his agents used assessment lists, and it was in shire-
courts that disputed claims were stated, if not resolved. And the whole
enquiry was completed in a year, an achievement that says much for the
efficiency of the government which William acquired when he conquered England.

Pre-Conquest English kings were, however, unable to assert their
authority in Northumbria as effectively as they did in the south. Edgar
failed to institute hundreds and tithings in Northumbria and English
kings were not able to establish a network of *burhs* there to serve as
centres of royal influence. In 1066 there was only one *burh* and one
mint in the north. York may have been the second largest city in
England, perhaps in Europe, at the time, but there was no other royal
burh north of the Humber. In the absence of an effective royal power of

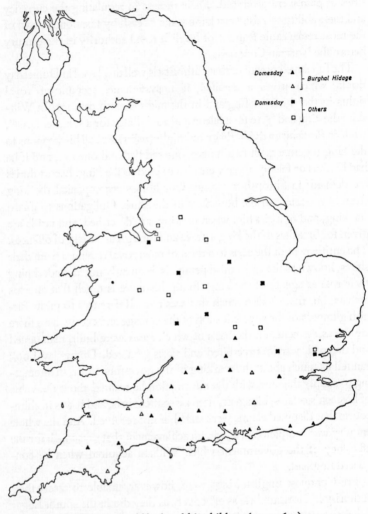

Domesday ▲ ⎱ Burghal Hidage
Domesday △ ⎰

Domesday ■ ⎱ Others
Domesday □ ⎰

Figure 9   Burhs built by Alfred and his children (pp. 226–9)
Cf. Hill (1969) and *Chronicle.*

the kind that was being created in the south, Northumbrian society remained archaic. Disputes were resolved in traditional ways, kinsmen and lords were more important than the king and his agents, buying and selling took place in fairs and markets, not in royal *ports*, and, although there were many religious communities in Northumbria, they too were old-fashioned; the monastic reformation wrought in the south by royal power did not penetrate so far north. It is, therefore, in Northumbria that we can gain some idea of what English society, and royal authority, were like before the West Saxon kings transformed both. It is in the contrast between north and south that we can perhaps gain the best measure of the achievement of Alfred and his successors, an achievement that had, as one of its most significant consequences, the creation of a network of royal *burhs*.

VI

Towns and trade

1 *Towns in Domesday Book*

England was, on the eve of the Norman Conquest, one of the most highly urbanized parts of Europe with at least 10 per cent of its population living in towns, a proportion that was not reached in many other areas until modern times. Some of these English towns were, by the standards of the time, very large and in 1065 at least five, London, York, Norwich, Lincoln and Winchester, had over 1000 tenements, implying populations of at least 5000 and probably more. At the other end of the scale were such tiny boroughs as Langport and Axbridge in Somerset, each with fewer than 35 burgesses in 1086. Between these extremes there were certainly 26 with more than 1000 inhabitants, a group that includes most of the towns from which the shires north of the Thames take their names, but excludes some important places like Bristol and Worcester that were probably as large but about which it is difficult to make estimates because of the irregularity of their treatment in Domesday Book.

There was no single specialized word to describe eleventh-century English towns: in Domesday Book 14 are called *civitates*, 'cities', and many others are called *burgi*, 'boroughs', but undoubted towns like Dover and Bedford were described as vills, a term commonly used for rural settlements, and some others were simply manors. There was a similar variety in English, including *tūn* and *burh* from which town and borough come, as well as the significant word *port* which, in the tenth and eleventh centuries, implied the existence of a market. A market was indeed one of the most important features of a town, for it was by producing for or selling in markets that many townsmen earned their living, but a market did not automatically create a town and in Domesday Book there are over 30 non-urban markets including some, like Hoxne and Clare in Suffolk, which certainly existed before the Conquest (Darby, 1977, pp. 369–71).

The towns of eleventh-century England were in fact places subject to special laws or customs more appropriate for an urban community living by trade than those normally current in rural society – in the words of a contemporary, borough-right in contrast to land-right (*Episc. c. 6*). Only the king could confer or recognize such a distinctive legal status and, although there are no pre-Conquest charters granting or defining urban privileges, the dependence of urban communities on the king is shown by the importance of the king's reeve in urban affairs as well as by the two most common and distinctive features of eleventh-century towns: the division of revenues between the king and his main agent, the earl, who received a third share, and the existence of tenements normally held by men called burgesses on privileged terms that included the payment of a special rent called *landgable* to the king.

In Domesday Book the most common terms for an urban tenement were *masura* or *mansio* meaning a messuage, for which the English word was *haga* that later became *haw* and is closely related to the modern word 'hedge'. There was, of course, nothing peculiarly urban about a hedged enclosure, what distinguished town *haws* or messuages was the relatively free terms on which they were held, for they could be bought, sold, bequeathed and even mortgaged and they rendered money instead of the servile obligations that were commonly exacted from rural tenements. The basic money render was *landgable*, a term which shows that it was a payment or rent, in English *gafol*, paid in respect of an area of land, the messuage or *haw*. The amount varied: at Malmesbury there were 51 messuages each rendering 10 pence *de gablo* and at Lincoln the *landgable* on most messuages was one penny. The rate sometimes varied within a town, especially in old-established ones, sometimes because tenements were different sizes, or some had been favourably treated, or because they were laid out at different times. At Hereford each complete messuage (*integra masura*) within the walls paid 7½ pence, more than twice the sum owing from messuages outside the walls, and at Southampton there were three rates, fifty paid 6 pence, twenty-seven 8 pence and two 12 pence. The emphasis at Hereford on whole messuages is a reminder that they could be subdivided and several houses could be built on one plot. This seems to have happened at Chichester where in 1065 there were 97½ *haws* and 3 crofts on which there were, by 1086, '60 houses more than there had been earlier'. Subdivision of this kind probably explains why at Guildford there were 175 men living on 75 *haws*. On the other hand some tenements were uninhabited and at Huntingdon, where 256 burgesses held the 240 messuages that paid *landgable*, it is clear that many messuages had more than one burgess and that over a hundred were uninhabited but nevertheless paid the full customary dues, as did the 25 waste or uninhabited messuages at Malmesbury. *Landgable* was therefore normally due from urban tenements whether or not houses had been built on them and the total amount paid was determined by the number of tenements, not by the uses to which they had been put; at Cambridge the total due in 1485, then called *hawgable*, was little different from the *landgable* of 1086, despite the great changes that had taken place in those four centuries (Tait, 1936, p. 91). The sums owed as *landgable* were probably determined when the streets and tenements of a town were planned, or reorganized, and this payment to the king was a recognition of his responsibility for organizing or creating the town.

Domesday Book shows that in many towns normal tenements owed other customary payments as well as *landgable*. They are rarely specified in detail but the penny poll tax that sometimes occurs after the Conquest may have been an old payment. There are some references to specific payments such as the 10 pence owing from the women of Hereford who brewed either inside or outside the city, and similar payments are reported from smiths and bakers. Tolls and the profits of justice were important, but obviously variable, sources of revenue. They were collected either by the king's reeve or by a farmer, that is someone who undertook to pay a fixed sum for the privilege. At Huntingdon, for example, the total yield of the town in 1065 was £45, made up of the three fixed payments, £10 *landgable*, £3 for the mill and £2 from the moneyers, the remaining £30, described as the farm of the borough, was an agreed sum, which Domesday implies could be altered, to cover the rents from fisheries and the borough lands as well as tolls and the profits of justice.

The account of some towns in Domesday Book illustrates what profits of justice could mean. At Chester the penalty for shedding blood on weekdays was 10 shillings and twice as much on Sundays, Holy days and the twelve days of Christmas; 4 shillings was the penalty, imposed on women as well as men, for making false measures or for brewing bad beer. Breach of the king's peace was far more serious and in many towns the penalty was 100 shillings, while if the breach was caused by killing, the man responsible could be outlawed and all his land and property forfeited to the king. Other offences ranged from adultery, for which the penalty at Lewes was 100 pence, to interference with the free passage of the river Trent or the king's highway which at Nottingham carried a penalty of £8. One of the main hazards of town life, fire, could also result in a penalty as well as compensation and at Shrewsbury 'if the house of any burgess were burnt by accident or misfortune or by negligence he paid 40 shillings to the king as penalty and 2 shillings to each of his two nearest neighbours'. Domesday Book pays less attention to tolls than to legal penalties, but at Lewes the reeve collected a penny from both the buyer and seller of a horse, the rate for oxen being a halfpenny and for men 4 pence. The most detailed mention of toll is in the Domesday account of Chester and even there the emphasis is on possible penalties:

> If without the licence of the king ships arrived at or departed from the port of the city, the king and the earl had 40 shillings from each man who was on the ships. If against the peace of the king and in spite of his prohibition, a ship arrived, the king and the earl had both the ship and the men and all that was in it. But if it came with the peace and licence of the king, those who were in it quietly sold what they had: but when it departed, the king and the earl had 4 pence from each last (*lesth*). If those who had marten pelts were ordered by the king's reeve to sell none till he had first seen and examined them, he who did not observe this paid a penalty of 40 shillings. (DB, i. 262b)

The king shared almost all his urban revenues with the earl, who normally took a third of them, which was also the proportion of the profits of justice in the shire allocated to him, both payments being made because he was the king's main agent in local government. Where borough-revenues were farmed the earl's part was fixed – his share of the farm of Huntingdon was £10 – but if not he might have to appoint an agent to look after his interests, as he must have done at Chester. The earl did not, however, share all borough-revenues and at Colchester a payment of 6 pence from each house for the support of the king's soldiers or for expeditions by land or sea, is explicitly stated not to belong to the farm, and it is probable that the payments for military service which are a prominent feature of the Domesday account of many towns were similarly rendered to the king alone.

Burgesses were not simply men who lived in towns; urban populations included men of higher rank and greater importance, like the lawmen of Stamford, as well as poor cottagers, and Domesday Book sometimes lists a miscellaneous population as at Stafford where there were 13 canons, 13 villeins, 8 bordars and 4 serfs in addition to the 36 burgesses, or at Nottingham where 19 villeins are mentioned alongside 173 burgesses. What distinguished a burgess was his tenure of one or more urban tenements for which he paid *landgable* and rendered other customary dues and services, gaining in return special privileges which might be as extensive as the freedom from toll throughout England enjoyed by the burgesses of Dover or more limited as at Torksey where the men who held messuages were freed from custom or toll when entering or leaving the town. Urban tenements were heritable and at Lincoln the owner's family had claims which could be defeated only by royal grant. On the death of a burgess the king's lordship over him was acknowledged by the payment of a heriot, often specified as 10 shillings, but sometimes, if the burgess had a horse, it consisted of both horse and arms, reminiscent of the heriot of a thegn as defined in the laws of Cnut. Tenements could be sold and at Torksey that freedom appears to have been unrestrained so that 'any burgess who wished to depart elsewhere and sell his house could do so without the licence and knowledge of the reeve if he wished', but at Lincoln the burgesses asserted that 'no one was at liberty to give his property to any person outside the city and not of his family, without the king's grant'. At Hereford a burgess could sell only with the permission of the reeve who took a third of the selling price. It is possible that inherited tenements were subject to limitations designed to protect the interests of the family, while tenements that had been purchased could be disposed of more freely. Most remarkable of all was the freedom to mortgage urban tenements, revealed in Domesday Book when mortgagors are accused of withholding the customary dues, as happened at Exeter.

Burgesses were not a uniform group, for some were wealthier or more privileged than their fellows. At Shrewsbury the responsibility for guarding the king fell on the men of higher status and it was the better class burgesses with horses who had the duty of protecting the king when he went hunting. Some burgesses were exempted from pay-

ing customary dues and at Southampton Domesday lists a small
group of men whose land was 'quit by the king himself in the days of
King Edward', implying that Edward relieved them of customary
payments – a privilege that occurs elsewhere, for example at Warwick
where 19 burgesses held 19 tenements 'with rights of jurisdiction (sake
and soke) and all customs'. Failure to pay customary dues, especially
landgable, could lead to loss of status. At Hereford one of the reeve's
responsibilities was to ensure that the king lost no service through the
abandonment of holdings by men who were too poor to render the
services due. The Conquest itself had a disastrous effect on many burgesses and at Ipswich the 538 burgesses of 1065 had been reduced
thirty years later to 110 who rendered customs and a further 100 poor
burgesses who could only contribute a penny poll-tax to the geld. The
situation at Norwich was neatly described by Tait (1936, p. 69) when he
wrote that 'the 480 bordars [cottagers] of Norwich who first appear in
1086, contrasted with the burgesses as paying no custom owing to
poverty, were clearly former burgesses impoverished by the rebellion,
fire, taxation and official extortion which had almost halved the burgess
body in twenty years'. Domesday mentions similar groups of men in
several towns; at Malmesbury there were 9 cottagers (*coscez*) who paid
geld and at Huntingdon there were 100 bordars who helped the burgesses pay geld. They are mentioned because they still contributed
to the tax levied on their towns although they no longer ranked as
burgesses, presumably because they no longer paid the customary
dues.

Burgesses were normally free of servile obligations but were expected to provide services that were appropriate for free men, like the
duty of guarding the king at Shrewsbury, or the Hereford obligation
of sending a man from every house to cordon the wood when the king
was hunting, while men who did not have whole tenements had to find
guards for the hall when the king was in the city. Burgesses might also
be expected to provide facilities for the king's agents, as at Dover
where the burgesses had to provide a steersman and one other crew-
man when the king's messengers needed transport, or at Torksey
where the men were required to conduct royal agents as far as York
with ships and other 'instruments of navigation'. Military service is
commonly mentioned in Domesday Book and ranged from the obligation of Dover to supply the king once a year with 20 ships each with a
crew of 21 men for 15 days to the kind of service described at Warwick:

The custom of Warwick was that when the king went on an expedition by land 10 burgesses of Warwick went for all. Anyone who was warned and failed to go paid a penalty of 100 shillings to the king. But if the king went by sea against his enemies they sent him either 4 boatswains (*batsueins*) or 4 pounds of pennies. (DB, i. 238)

Oxford sent '20 burgesses for all or gave the king £20 that all might be free'; Leicester sent 12 men to expeditions by land but if it was by sea they sent 4 horses to London to carry arms or any other necessities. It is possible that the military obligation levied on towns was related to their assessment for the geld, expressed in hides, and that one man was due for each five hides. Towns were specially assessed for the geld and it appears to have been levied every year at the rate of 16 pence or one *ora* from each hide. The Norman conquerors continued to demand the full payment even from towns whose burgess population was greatly reduced. The English burgesses at Shrewsbury complained in 1086 that it was 'hard on them that they now pay the same geld as they did in the time of King Edward' although 183 of the 200 tenements no longer paid geld because they were held by Frenchmen, occupied by the castle or the abbey, or were simply uninhabited. Even the poor burgesses of Ipswich and the cottagers at Huntingdon or Malmesbury were expected to contribute to the geld, if no more than a penny a head.

The king not only benefited directly from the money paid as *landgable*, tolls, judicial penalties and geld, he also was an important landowner in most towns. At Warwick 113 of the 244 tenements belonged to the royal demesne and although nothing is said about additional rents paid by these houses it is clear that the rents of the other houses contributed to the revenues of their owners as well as rendering *landgable* to the king. Domesday Book explains that the 112 baronial tenements at Warwick 'pertained to the estates which the said barons held outside the borough and are valued with them' and some are duly noted in the descriptions of rural estates, like the two tenements noted in the main description of Warwick as belonging to William fitz Corbucion which appear in the accounts of two of his estates, Bearley and Wolverley, as houses valued at 8 pence each. In all parts of the country rural estates included among their appurtenances tenements in a nearby town. The Kentish Domesday, for example, reports no fewer than 260 burgesses or tenements in Canterbury on the eve of the Conquest which were associated with 18 estates, while 12 estates in west Kent had more than

115 tenements or burgesses at Rochester. Such arrangements were very old; as early as 786 Offa granted a substantial estate at Ickham, Palmstead and Ruckinge in Kent together with a property in Canterbury called *Curringtun* (S, 125) and in 811 a grant of land at Rainham and Faversham included 2 *haws* in Canterbury with appurtenant meadows on the bank of the river Stour (S, 168). Town properties of this kind could be used as refuges in case of attack – in 804 the nunnery of Lyminge was given land in Canterbury for that purpose (S, 160) – but they were normally a convenient urban base useful when attending market or court, and are reported in Domesday Book as sources of rent.

In the confusion after the Conquest, many of William's followers acquired urban properties and some refused to pay the customary dues. The complaint of the English burgesses at Shrewsbury shows that the invaders there considered themselves exempt from the payment of geld, and even at Winchester an enquiry undertaken by Henry I revealed that many of the dues that had been customary before the Conquest were being withheld. It is, therefore, not surprising that Domesday should so often emphasize the king's losses; at Dover the only tenements mentioned were the 29 from which the king 'had lost his custom', and at Gloucester similarly we are told only of 16 on the site of the castle, 14 that were waste, or uninhabited, and 23 which had been withdrawn from the royal demesne and no longer paid customary dues. At Chester a Norman, Robert of Rhuddlan, claimed that some land in the city did not pay customary dues because it was attached to a rural estate, but Domesday reports the decision of the county court that it had always been in the custom of the king and earl like the land of the other burgesses. The king could, of course, grant exemption from customary dues as a privilege, as Edward did at Southampton, but before the Conquest it was normal for all tenements, whether they belonged to the king or to a local landowner, to render the customary dues that were the distinctive feature of urban property. It was, however, possible for the king to grant away a large part of his interest in a town. Edward the Confessor gave his annual revenue from the borough of Sandwich to the archbishop of Canterbury and his cathedral community, and thereafter the town was treated as the archbishop's, not the king's, although it continued to render naval services to the king (DB, i. 3). The same king granted his share (two thirds) of Fordwich to St Augustine's abbey at Canterbury, the earl's third being granted to the abbey after the Conquest (DB, i. 12). The earliest borough to be completely alienated by the king was Taunton. This great estate, with very extensive royal privileges, had long been held by the bishops of Winchester when the grant was renewed by King Edgar, and it included the borough which was a mint town from Æthelred's reign (S, 806).

The reeves who looked after the king's interests in towns were men of great importance. They had a wide range of duties, including responsibility for supervising the mint and the market and ensuring that transactions were properly witnessed, they collected tolls and other dues, including penalties for breach of the king's peace and other offences; they also had to arrange for such proceedings as the ordeal. They appear to have been appointed by and to have been responsible to the king himself, and when one of Æthelred's ealdormen had cause to complain about the actions of the reeves of Buckingham and Oxford he had to make his complaint directly to the king. One of the reeve's main functions was to ensure the smooth running of the borough-court, an assembly developed in the tenth century to regulate the affairs of urban communities, ranging from such planning matters as preserving the correct distance between houses – in ninth-century Canterbury it was two feet – to controlling weights and measures and settling disputes that arose in the course of trading. The laws or regulations within towns certainly varied, being known and declared by the burgesses themselves, or their leaders. Kings tried to impose some uniformity, as for example in the laws about the witnessing of transactions, and Cnut ruled that 'one and the same law is to be valid in boroughs as regards exculpation'. It was no doubt left to the king's reeves to implement such decisions, and in time they may have encouraged some standardization of penalties and procedures, but Domesday Book and later evidence shows that there was more variety than uniformity in the laws of English towns. The assemblies in which the laws were made and enforced originally met in the open air, like their rural counterparts, and the twelfth-century meeting-places, like the churchyard of St Martin in Oxford, had probably been used for many years. London continued to have a general assembly, called the *folkmoot*, which met out of doors, but by the end of the tenth century the court known as the *husting* had already been established, apparently with a particular responsibility for weights and measures (S, 1465). The name shows that it met indoors, for it is compounded of the word 'house' with a Scandinavian word for an assembly or court, *thing*.

The burgesses of pre-Conquest English towns certainly had a real sense of community. They acted together in assemblies; at Cambridge sales of land were witnessed by the whole city and it was the Cambridge burgesses who proudly asserted the claim that anyone buying land there need find no surety. Some ten years before the Conquest, the arrangements made for the endowment of the monastery at Stow near Lincoln were witnessed by, among others, 'all the citizens of Lincoln and all who attend the yearly market at Stow' (S, 1478). Burgesses can be seen acting in a corporate capacity in Domesday Book, for example at Huntingdon where the abbot of Thorney pledged the church of St Mary, in Huntingdon, to the burgesses, apparently as a group, and at Canterbury the burgesses held 45 tenements outside the city from which they received *landgable* and other customs by royal gift. Canterbury is one of the places from which there is evidence of pre-Conquest guilds. They were not necessarily trading associations but groups who joined together for mutual help. The general character of such guilds is well illustrated by the regulations surviving for the Thegns' Guild at Cambridge, which have been preserved in a gospel book from Ely Abbey.

> Here in this writing is the declaration of the enactment which this fellowship has determined in the thegns' guild in Cambridge. First, that each was to give to the others an oath of true loyalty, in regard to religious and secular affairs, on the relics; and all the Fellowship was ever to aid him who had most right. If any guild-brother die, all the guildship is to bring him to where he desired, and he who does not come for that purpose is to pay a sester of honey; and the guild-ship is to provide half the provisions for the funeral feast in honour of the deceased. . . . (*EHD*, 136)

The mutual help included the prosecution of feuds as though the guild brothers were indeed kinsmen. Other regulations for a guild at Bedwyn reveal a concern to help each other in such matters as rebuilding houses after fire. These guilds were social as well as religious associations and in some there is an emphasis on the brewing of ale; at Abbotsbury 'he who undertakes a brewing and does not do it satisfactorily is to be liable to his entrance-fee, and there is to be no remission'. Equally disruptive were insults and accusations of lying or cheating, and provision is made for the amendment of such offences.

The royal character of towns, and the effectiveness of royal control over them, is shown most clearly by the coinage which was, in the reign of Edward the Confessor, produced at over 70 mints. Not all boroughs had a mint at that time but the largest ones did and some, including Bruton in Somerset and Torksey in Lincolnshire, had had mints earlier in the century. On the other hand, there are only two exceptions, Bury St Edmunds and Launceston, to the rule that all mints known to have produced coin in the reigns of both Edward and William were Domesday boroughs. Bury may not technically have been a borough in 1086 although the abbey had encouraged the development of an urban variety of occupations including bakers, ale-brewers, washerwomen and shoemakers, and on the eve of the Conquest that abbot was granted a moneyer by the king as freely 'as I have my own anywhere in any of my boroughs'. Launceston is described as a market in the Cornish Domesday, rendering 20 shillings, but by the middle of the twelfth century it was a free borough.

There was in eleventh-century England only one coinage, the king's, and one denomination of coin, the silver penny, which was struck on dies that were issued to the moneyers by the king. There are slight differences between individual dies but at any one time the same design or type was used in all mints. Coins had on their obverse a stylized portrait of the king, generally in profile, with his name, and on the reverse a simple and easily recognized pattern around which the name of the mint and moneyer is given. The differences between the royal portraits and the designs on the reverse make it possible to recognize different types easily and they are now known by such names as Pointed Helmet, Small Cross, Long Cross or Expanding Cross. The design of the coins was changed at frequent intervals – in the reign of Edward the Confessor every two or three years – and there are some references in Domesday Book to what happened when the money was changed. At Shrewsbury the king was said to have three moneyers who 'after they had purchased their dies, as other moneyers of the kingdom did, on the fifteenth day paid to the king 20 shillings each, and this was done on any change of the coinage', and the account of Worcester shows that the moneyers of that mint paid the same amount for dies at London.

In recent years the study of the surviving coins has transformed our knowledge of the working of this pre-Conquest coinage (Lyon, 1976). It has, for example, been possible to show that when the type changed most of the old coins quickly went out of circulation, although some were hoarded in stores of wealth. More surprising has been the discovery that these changes of the coinage were sometimes accompanied by changes in the weight of a penny and consequently of the pound, which consisted of 240 pence. There were apparently some attempts to standardise the weight but this was only done successfully after the Conquest, when the standard of 22.5 grains in a pennyweight was firmly settled and distinguished as 'sterling' (Grierson, 1961b).

By reducing the weight of the pound and consequently producing more coins from a given weight of silver, the agents of pre-Conquest kings could more easily make payments, for example to mercenaries, as long as the coins were accepted in markets and elsewhere at face value. The king's own revenues were of course also affected, and to compensate for this some payments to the king had to be made at a special rate of 20 pence for every 16 due, a premium greater than any of the observed reductions in the weight of the penny (Harvey, 1967). There were also some significant increases in the pennyweight, most notably in 1051 when it was raised from 17 to 25 grains (1.1 to 1.7 grams), a change that appears to have coincided with the disbanding in that year of the Scandinavian fleet which had been employed by English kings since 1012 (Lyon, 1971). Once the king no longer had to pay large sums to these seamen he could afford to raise the weight of the pound and so increase the value of the many revenues that were collected by weight rather than at the face value of the coins. This unparalleled weight increase in 1051 was also unusual in that it occurred within the currency of one type of coin, that known as Expanding Cross, which consequently exists in two forms, heavy and light, the effect being to raise the average weight of the type to about 22 grains, which was close to the standard that had been maintained, with slight fluctuations, before the reign of Cnut. In 1018 Cnut made the largest of all the payments to Scandinavian warriors: the *Chronicle* reports that it was 72,000 pounds, and it was then that the pennyweight was reduced to about 17 grains and kept at that level until 1051.

The surviving coins show that with relatively small variations the standard set at any one time was maintained very effectively in all the mints of the kingdom, in most types the weight of over half the coins being within 10 per cent of the apparent standard. According to a law of Edgar the standard was based on that prevailing at Winchester and London, and there is a reference in Cnut's reign to a payment of silver by the standard of the *husting*, the London court (III Edg 8; S, 1465). All markets and mints would, of course, have had to keep a current standard, and Æthelred ruled that all those who had charge of towns should keep weights marked 'according to the weight at which my money is received', a phrase that itself implies that royal revenues were an important consideration when the standard was changed. The ways in which English kings controlled their currency are not yet fully understood, but that control was certainly effective and is remarkable testimony to their authority and to the efficiency of their government, as is the fact that transactions were normally made in coin which was accepted at its face value, without premiums or demands for payment by weight.

The study of the pre-Conquest coinage has to be based on the coins themselves, for the documentary references, although illuminating, give no indication of the complexity of the system or the effectiveness of royal control over it. As the coins in circulation in England were reminted from time to time, it is necessary to study those which were withdrawn from circulation by being lost or exported and which have been discovered either as loose finds, often made during excavations, or, more numerously, in hoards. The main evidence comes from the period 990 to 1051 because it was then that large numbers of coins were removed from England to Scandinavia as tribute or pay. The total number of English coins found in Scandinavia is not known but is certainly well over 50,000, and this body of material makes it possible to investigate the English coinage much more systematically in the first half of the eleventh century than in the second, when we depend almost entirely on hoards found in England. Consequently we know far more about the coinage of Æthelred or Cnut than of William the Conqueror, and the discovery of one large hoard (like that found at Beaworth in Hampshire in 1833 containing over 6000 coins, mostly of the last type issued by William, known as *Paxs*) can transform our knowledge of one issue.

When large numbers of coins survive it is possible to gain some idea of the relative productivity and, therefore, of the relative importance, of different mints. A recent analysis of some 36,000 coins of the period 973–1066 has shown that 24 per cent came from London, 10 per cent from York, 9 per cent from Lincoln, and 7 per cent from Winchester (Petersson, 1969). Unfortunately in that analysis the other mints have been grouped regionally so that it is possible to say only that 15 mints in south-eastern England produced 9 per cent of the coins while the 26 mints of Wessex and the South-west produced 11 per cent. These overall percentages conceal great variations; Lincoln ranged from 4 per cent or less at the end of the tenth century to as much as 16 per cent in the first type of Edward the Confessor and in his reign the percentage of coins produced in London was once as high as 37 but was normally less than 20. Despite the size of the sample on which the analysis was based, there is a possibility that it is not completely representative, for less than 6400 coins came from English collections while over 32,000 came from Scandinavian finds, and the coins exported to Scandinavia may not correctly represent the coinage current in England at the time. Nevertheless these proportions are a useful tentative guide to the relative importance of the major mints and they also show how productivity could vary. An alternative basis for comparing the relative importance of mints is provided by estimates of the number of moneyers operating from time to time. When a large number of coins survives it is possible to determine the number of moneyers with some certainty, but when we only have a few there is more room for error. We can, for example, be confident that mid-eleventh-century Warwick was a two-moneyer mint, but of the 8 types of coin issued by William the Conqueror, only 5 are known for Warwick, and for 3 of these only one moneyer is known in each type. When we come to William's last type – *Paxs* – well known, thanks to the Beaworth hoard, we have no fewer than 28 Warwick coins which were struck by three moneyers, not because it had by then become a three-moneyer mint, but because one of the normal complement of two was replaced in the period during which that type was being issued. It is therefore possible to discover the number of moneyers working at every mint both in the first half of the century and at the end of William's reign, and these figures have been used as an index of the activity of mints. The result may, however, be misleading because one moneyer may have been more productive than another. At Lincoln at least sixteen moneyers were responsible for the 93 known coins of the first type issued for Edward the Confessor at that mint, but while some moneyers are represented by only one coin, 23 were struck by one man, Godric (Mossop, 1970). Numismatists can help by identifying the dies used to produce the coins and the number of dies gives a much better indication of a mint's activity than the number of moneyers. Only one large mint, Lincoln, has been systematically analysed in this way, but the coins recovered in the Beaworth hoard make it possible to gain some idea of the number of dies used in each mint to produce the last type of coin issued for William I. The coins of this type show that, although Cambridge and Steyning were then both one-moneyer mints, Cambridge is represented by 1 surviving reverse die, while Steyning has 5. The contrast is equally marked in such two-moneyer mints as Hertford, Stafford and Tamworth, all with 2 dies, and Chichester with 10, and Lincoln, Wallingford and Warwick with 9 dies each. The largest mints were Canterbury (39 dies), London (49 dies) and Winchester (50 dies), and all had eight moneyers.

These figures are taken from the British Museum Catalogue and, although a systematic study may yield more material (at Lincoln, for example, three additional reverse dies have been identified), they do provide a reasonable basis for comparison between mints twenty years after the Conquest. Knowing the number of dies does not, of course, mean that we know how many coins were struck with them, for each die may have been little or much used, but as there are good reasons for thinking that 15,000 coins, or £60, was the maximum that could be struck with one reverse die, a die-analysis based on a large enough sample can make it possible to estimate the total capacity of a mint. If, as seems likely, we know all the reverse-dies used at Lincoln to strike the *Paxs* coinage of William I, their number, 12, suggests that no more than £700 of that type could have been produced at Lincoln, a total that may be compared with a possible maximum of about £3000 for Winchester or £60 for Cambridge. The total number of reverse dies for that coinage recorded in the British Museum Catalogue is 537, indicating a probable maximum of the order of £30,000.

The recent study of the eleventh-century coinage has transformed our knowledge of the monetary system of the English kings and has also provided some basis for estimating the relative importance of mints and, therefore, of the communities they served, but the main source of information for eleventh-century towns is Domesday Book, in which towns were included in an attempt to 'discover what dues the king ought to have in twelve months from the shire', and they are normally described at the beginning of each county section along with the dues owed from the shire itself. The work was not completed and the blank folios at the beginning of the descriptions of Middlesex and Hampshire, left for the descriptions of London and Winchester, were never used. The main interest of the compilers was in the revenues and services due from each town, and although additional information was sometimes given about the mint, tolls, specific payments, or even the penalties for various offences, such detail was not strictly necessary and it was possible to describe some towns very briefly indeed. Rochester is dealt with in two lines –

> The city of Rochester in the time of King Edward was worth 100 shillings. When the bishop received it, a like sum. It is now worth £20, and yet he who holds it pays £40 –

and the account of Bedford gives little more than its assessment for military service (and by implication for the geld) and its value. Elsewhere, particular attention is paid to the tenements from which the king had lost his customary dues, with no attempt to enumerate the others. At Gloucester, for example, only the 53 tenements which for various reasons no longer paid customary dues are noted, and there is no hint that it was a large and flourishing town which had, early in the twelfth century, no fewer than 631 burgesses and 10 churches. The description of some towns can be supplemented from Domesday's account of those rural estates which included urban tenements among their assets, but there is no reason to assume that all these tenements were carefully noted. In the final version of Domesday Book there was some selection of the material that had been collected in the enquiry and the rents from urban tenements are likely to have been among details that were often omitted. In Warwick 113 borough-tenements are noted as belonging to estates in the shire, but only 26 are separately mentioned in Domesday's account of those estates; if Domesday had not specifically mentioned these holdings in its account of the borough, our information about eleventh-century Warwick would be misleadingly incomplete. Even when Domesday apparently gives full details, as at Guildford where 175 men were said to be living on 75 *haws*, there is inevitably much uncertainty about the number of inhabitants for we do not know the size of urban households nor can we have any information about the people who lived in a town or its suburbs but were omitted from Domesday because they contributed neither customary dues nor geld. The population figures that can be deduced from Domesday Book are therefore incomplete, but they do show that some towns were, for the period, very large indeed, and they justify the assertion that at least one-tenth of the population lived in towns.

2 *Origins*

Many English towns are on the sites of Roman ones but, with the possible exception of London, they were institutionally new creations. Some were continuously occupied, and in many places the remains of Roman buildings and walls provided the physical framework within which the later English towns grew, but the urban organization of the Roman towns did not survive long enough to provide the institutional framework for English urban development.

When the imperial government abandoned responsibility for the defence of Britain, the towns of the province, with their recently strengthened defences, continued as centres of government controlled, as we suppose, by urban oligarchs or native princes, some of whom employed German warriors whose graves have been discovered in and near several Roman towns, including Winchester, York, Norwich, Leicester and Dorchester-on-Thames. There are certainly abundant signs of continued activity well into the fifth century in many Roman towns that have been investigated – for example: Silchester, Wroxeter, *Verulamium*, Canterbury and Winchester – but by the middle of the sixth century all signs of continued corporate existence in these and other Roman towns had disappeared. At Winchester, for example, Roman property boundaries were by then being disregarded by the people who still occupied the site, demonstrating a breakdown in the communal authority, and the streets of the medieval city, which there as elsewhere naturally passed through the walls where the gates had been, did not follow the line of the Roman streets within the walls. Only in London does the continuity of Roman streets in the form of Cheapside and Eastcheap encourage belief in the possibility that organized urban life continued with sufficient vigour to maintain such customary rights of way.

The word used by the English for Roman towns was *ceaster*, from Latin *castra* meaning a camp, and it has produced such modern names as Chester, Caistor-by-Norwich and Exeter. It was also used for Roman fortifications. There were exceptions, including Canterbury, 'the *burh* (or fortification) of the men of Kent', and Lincoln, which was known by its Roman name, *Lindum colonia*, and is *Lindocolina* in Bede, but there are numerous examples of the normal usage ranging from *civitas* capitals like *Venta Belgarum* which became *Uuintancaestir*,

Winchester, to small towns like Ancaster, first named in the twelfth century, *Anecastre*, or such forts as Doncaster and Horncastle, both of which are named in Domesday Book, *Donecastre* and *Hornecastre*. Some of the apparent exceptions were called *ceaster* in some texts, thus London is called *Lunden ceaster* in the ninth-century translation of Bede, and Bath, like York, was sometimes called a *ceaster*. Some Roman towns, notably Silchester and Wroxeter, did not survive or recover as towns, and many forts, like Bewcastle and Ribchester, remained places of slight importance; but the use of *ceaster* is generally a good indication that the English thought the place originally had Roman fortifications, and they were generally right. The English names were often a development of the Romano-British ones but there were exceptions: Dorchester-on-Thames, *Dorcic*, was apparently *Tamesis* in Roman times, and Leicester, *Ratae Coritanorum*, was given an English name, *Ligera ceaster*.

Like the Franks in Gaul, some English kings had palaces within former Roman cities. The king of Kent, for example, had a palace in Canterbury when Augustine arrived in 597, and there was certainly a royal hall in London in the seventh century, possibly in the former military fort at Cripplegate (Biddle and Hudson, 1973, p. 20). It has been plausibly suggested that a West Saxon royal palace was established in the Roman forum of Winchester, and there is no doubt that the *principia*, the headquarters building, in York was occupied long after the Roman withdrawal, and it may possibly have been a royal residence. Kings, of course, also had rural palaces, like Yeavering, abandoned after Edwin's reign, and Bamburgh. The distinction between Roman and non-Roman centres of power was in general carefully observed by Bede, who called the former *civitates*, and used a variety of words, *urbs*, *villa*, *vicus* and even *locus*, for the latter. The episcopal subscriptions to the council at *Clofesho* in 803 (B, 312) reserve the word *civitas* for Roman towns: Lichfield, Hereford, Sherborne, Elmham and Selsey are simple *ecclesiae*. Some sees, like Dorchester-on-Thames and Worcester, were established in relatively unimportant Roman centres but they all, Roman and non-Roman alike, became the nuclei of communities which had some urban features. Episcopal churches, like royal palaces, naturally attracted craftsmen and servants, who formed communities which often resembled towns, and so too did monasteries. Bury St Edmunds is a good if late example of this kind of development, but many monasteries must have resembled 'holy cities' soon after their foundation in the seventh and eighth centuries.

Religious communities were particularly important centres for local exchange because of the crowds that were attracted to them on major festivals. Local exchanges outside the framework of urban markets are well attested in the Roman Empire, and after the collapse of Roman authority in Britain some of these must have continued to function. Some were based on Celtic festivals and after the conversion to Christianity they were associated with particular saints and held in the vicinity of their shrines. Buying and selling could, however, take place at any time. Edward the Elder attempted to limit transactions to special markets, *ports*, under royal control, but when Athelstan repeated this regulation it was with the qualification that it applied only to the purchase of goods worth more than 20 pence. The Domesday markets show that transactions were not confined to royal *ports* or *burhs*. Our sources unfortunately have little to say about these fairs or non-urban markets. Whatever their earlier history most were not under any effective form of royal control by the eleventh century and yielded relatively small sums to their 'owners'. The Domesday account of them is certainly incomplete. It omits, for example, the yearly market at Stow in Lincolnshire for which there is good independent evidence.

Merchants who came from other kingdoms were, like Christian pilgrims, strangers in need of protection. They could of course band together for mutual support, but they could do little if the hostility of the natives was aroused; it is small wonder that the Frisians fled from York in the eighth century when one of their number killed a Northumbrian noble. Traders could be protected by various people, as is shown by a late seventh-century Kentish law (Hlothhere and Eadric, 15) dealing with the responsibilities of those who gave shelter for three nights to a 'stranger, a trader or any other man who has come across the frontier', but it was best provided by kings who could extend their peace to cover such men. As late as the eleventh century the penalty for breaking the peace given by the king himself was far higher than if it had been given by one of his agents. The king's direct interest in men 'who came across frontiers' is made clear in another late seventh-century law, from Wessex, in which it is declared that the king should receive a large part of the wergeld of any stranger (Ine, 23). Several early English law-codes deal with the regulation of strangers, sometimes described as traders: they must keep to the road and take care to proclaim their presence should they leave it, on pain of being treated as thieves; they must make their transactions before witnesses or the king's reeve, a precaution against theft that was greatly elaborated in the tenth century; and in the laws of Alfred it was ordained that traders should bring before the king's reeve the men they intended to take with them when travelling through the country (Wi, 28; Ine, 20; Alf, 34). This responsibility of the king's agent for merchants provides the background to Æthelweard's account of the first Viking attack on Wessex; when Beaduheard, the king's *exactor*, heard that three ships had arrived he quickly rode 'to the port, thinking they were merchants rather than enemies, and commanding them imperiously he ordered them to be sent to the royal vill, but he and his companions were straightaway killed by them'. The Norwegian called Ottar who visited Alfred a century later was probably himself a merchant; the fact that he gave the king a gift of walrus tusks and acknowledged him as his lord was natural conduct, reflecting the mutual advantages of such a relationship.

Foreign merchants could travel inland, with permission, but it must normally have been more economical, and possibly safer, to do business in coastal markets which could be reached direct. One English word for such a market was *wīc*, deriving from Latin *vicus*, a word that was used in the first and second centuries to describe the smallest units of self-administration in the Roman provinces but which by the fourth and fifth centuries appears to have been used for small towns. This was certainly one of the senses in which the Germanic invaders borrowed this word into their languages. It was later used for places with specialized functions such as dairy or cattle farming, evidenced by such names as Butterwick and Chiswick, or salt-production at Droitwich, Nantwich, Middlewich and Northwich. It was also used at a very early date for important harbours and markets; London, which Bede described as a market or *emporium* for the many peoples who came to it by land and sea, is called *Lundenwic* in a seventh-century Kentish law code regulating the witnessing of transactions there (Hlothhere and Eadric, 16); York was another, as its English name, *Eoforwic*, shows. Ipswich is first mentioned in the late tenth century, but archaeological evidence shows that it was a flourishing centre of activity three hundred years before. In Kent there were at least two *wīc*, Sandwich, first mentioned in connection with a Viking attack in 851, and Fordwich, where the monastery of Reculver was granted the freedom of toll on a ship in the mid-eighth century (S, 29). The *wīc* that has been most thoroughly investigated so far is *Hamwic* or *Hamwih*, the predecessor of Southampton, established by the end of the seventh century at the confluence of the rivers Test and Itchen, close by the Roman fort of *Clausentum* (Holdsworth, 1976). *Hamwih* is first mentioned as a market in 721 and excavation has demonstrated the existence of gravelled streets apparently laid out on a regular pattern, with some running down to the shore and others at right angles to them. The site is large, material has been found over an area of some 60 acres, and the finds, which include almost 200 coins, show that occupation began before the end of the seventh century, as is implied by the written evidence. It was abandoned in the early years of the eleventh century in favour of *Hamtun* immediately to the west, by then distinguished as Southampton, a site that appears to have been developed in the early tenth century, possibly for reasons of defence as part of the West Saxon programme of fortifications against the Viking raiders. One factor that may well have played an important part in the shift was the increasing use in the eleventh century of larger ships with a deeper draught for which the new harbour on the Test was more convenient than the old wharves on the Itchen. *Hamwih* has yielded evidence of a wide range of handicrafts; apart from pottery and cloth which were probably produced in most large settlements, the discovery of iron slag, lead waste and bronze crucibles shows that it was an active centre for metal-working and no doubt many of the pins, buckles and strap ends that have been found there were produced locally. Large quantities of bone and antler have been found, waste and offcuts as well as complete objects such as combs, of which many different kinds occur, and pins. Keys, whether or not they were made in *Hamwih*, show that its inhabitants had locked containers, boxes and chests and perhaps even rooms, of which virtually all other traces have disappeared. The main importance of *Hamwih* was, however, as a market, and there is abundant evidence of imports from far afield, conspicuously including pottery, glass and lava querns from the Rhineland. Contacts within Britain are revealed by whetstones, querns, lamps and spindle whorls of non-local stone, including a few pieces which probably come from the midlands. It was the presence of merchants from different parts of England as well as overseas that presumably created the demand for the local craftsmen who made the combs, pins, belts, strap-ends that survive and who doubtless also made clothing and wooden objects that have left little or no trace.

English coastal markets like *Hamwih* were in close contact with similar trading places across the Channel, including Quentovic, and, most important of all, Dorestad on a branch of the lower Rhine. Dorestad flourished in the eighth and early ninth centuries and its size, about eight times that of *Hamwih*, reflects the importance of the traffic that passed through it between western Europe and the north. Scandinavia and the Baltic were the main source for some commodities, such as furs, walrus ivory and amber, that were highly prized in the west but were hard, if not impossible, to obtain elsewhere. Dorestad also had the advantage of being well placed on the route by which such Rhenish produce as wine, pottery and metal-work (especially fine swords) reached the sea on its way to England or the Baltic.

In return for their protection, kings benefited from tolls that were levied at these coastal markets. A small group of charters dated between 733 and 764, mostly issued by Mercian kings, granted to several religious houses freedom of toll on one or more ships at London, Fordwich, Sarre or an unnamed port (S, 29; 86–8; 91; 98; 143; 1612; 1788). So for example Æthelbald of Mercia granted in 734 to the bishop of Rochester

> the entrance, that is the toll of one ship, whether one of his own or of any other man, hitherto belonging to me or my predecessors by royal right in the port of London, (S, 88; *EHD*, 66)

and Rochester apparently considered it worth having this grant confirmed a century later by Berhtwulf, king of Mercia. These texts show that tolls were a royal prerogative and imply that the places at which they were collected were under royal control or protection. Kings had other rights in such places, including the privilege of pre-emption; as Domesday Book reports, the king's reeve had first choice of any marten-pelts that arrived at Chester.

The only other place for which there is evidence of royal toll before Domesday Book was Droitwich. By the end of the ninth century the rulers of Mercia were taking tolls on waggon and horse loads of salt at *Saltwic*, as it was then described, and there is some charter evidence, of uncertain authenticity, for similar tolls there two centuries earlier (S, 83; 97; 1824). Unfortunately there is no such early evidence for the Cheshire brine springs or Wiches, but Domesday Book describes an elaborate tariff of tolls on waggons, horse and man loads at Nantwich and these were clearly well established long before the Conquest. The use of the term *wic* for inland brine springs is significant. In Merovingian Gaul tolls were certainly a continuation of Roman imperial tolls, and the same may have been true of tolls in Britain (Sawyer, 1977, p. 148). The brine springs at Droitwich and in Cheshire were exploited in Roman times, and probably long before, as were some of the main coastal markets, notably London and Dover (p. 87). The use of the Latin word *vicus*, in its English form *wīc*, for these places suggests that royal rights to toll at such places had their origins in the Roman period.

Kings protected these places by extending their peace to cover visiting merchants. Breach of the king's peace always attracted the heaviest penalties; at York, for example, according to Domesday Book, if peace given by the hand or seal of the king were broken, the penalty payable to the king was 96 pounds, twice as much as for breach of peace given by the earl. Sometimes breach of the king's peace was punished collectively; Edgar's devastation of Thanet is believed to be a response to attacks on York merchants (*EHD*, 4, *s.a.*, 974). The effectiveness of this royal protection is best shown by the fact that some of these coastal markets were originally undefended. Some had Roman fortifications, whether or not they were maintained in a defensible state, but *Hamwih* was not protected in this way. This suggests that royal authority was normally respected internally. It was, however, no protection against the Vikings, seaborne raiders who had no respect for the authority of English kings and who discovered in these places rich opportunities for plunder or the extortion of tribute. In 829 a Frankish missionary, Anskar, on his way to the Swedish market of Birka in the company of a group of merchants from Dorestad, was attacked by pirates, and five years later this form of piracy reached Dorestad itself, which was attacked in 834 and in the four following years. These Danish or Baltic Vikings were originally drawn into western Europe by the prospect of plundering merchants and markets but they soon discovered that churches and monasteries were rich alternative sources of loot and tribute. Even after this discovery, the markets were not neglected. In response to these attacks some Roman walls appear to have been restored or strenghtened, and in the eleventh century the defences of eleven towns had a Roman basis: Canterbury, Chester, Chichester, Colchester, Exeter, Gloucester, Lincoln, London, Rochester, Winchester and York. Many others were first fortified by Alfred and his children, Edward and Æthelflæd, as a deliberate and effective defence against Viking invaders.

We are fortunate to have a very remarkable text from the early tenth century listing 30 West Saxon *burhs*. It is known as the

Burghal Hidage and gives for each *burh* the number of hides allocated for the maintenance and manning of its defences. Lewes and Malmesbury each had 1200 hides, while Wallingford and Winchester had twice that number. In contrast some were much smaller; Lyng had 100 hides, Lydford 140 and Southampton 150. The significance of these hidages is explained as follows:

> For the maintenance and defence of an acre's breadth of wall 16 hides are required. If every hide is represented by one man, then every pole of wall can be manned by 4 men. Then for the maintenance of 20 poles of wall 80 hides are required, and for a furlong 160 hides are required by the same reckoning as I have stated above. For 2 furlongs 320 hides are required; for 3 furlongs 480 hides. Then for 4 furlongs 640 hides are required. . . . If the circuit is greater, the additional amount can easily be deduced from this account, for 160 men are always required for 1 furlong, then every pole is manned by 4 men. (Hill, 1969)

According to this, Winchester, with 2400 hides, should have had defences 3300 yards long, which is remarkably close to the actual length of the Roman walls, 3280 yards. Similarly, the ramparts of Wareham are 2180 yards long, a figure that corresponds closely to the length deducible from the text, 2200 yards. Not all these fortified centres were towns, some were no more than forts and one, Shaftsey, was an island in the Thames.

The *Burghal Hidage* shows that there was a close connection between the size of a *burh* and the number of hides needed to man it, and it is possible that the total assessment recorded for some Domesday shires may have been determined by the size of the *burhs* that were separately listed in Domesday Book along with the renders due from the shire. Thus Berkshire, with a Domesday assessment of 2473 hides* has only one *burh* separately listed, Wallingford, which, according to the *Burghal Hidage*, needed 2400 hides to man it. In Hampshire only one *burh* is separately listed, Southampton, but a blank space was left in Domesday for Winchester. According to the *Burghal Hidage* these two *burhs* needed a total of 2550 hides, while the total Domesday assessment for Hampshire was 2588 hides. In Dorset the only *burhs* listed in both the *Burghal Hidage* and Domesday Book are Wareham and Shaftes-

* The 'Domesday' assessments used here are those given by Maitland (1897, p. 400). The totals in Darby (1977, p. 336) are based on the modern, not the Domesday, shires.

bury; according to the *Burghal Hidage* they needed 2300 hides, while the Domesday assessment of the county is 2277 hides. In most shires the figures do not work out so neatly because either the *Burghal Hidage* does not include them or some *burhs* had been enlarged in the century and a half that separated the *Burghal Hidage* from Domesday Book; that might, for example, explain why Oxfordshire was assessed in Domesday at 2412 hides, while in the *Burghal Hidage* Oxford needed only 1400 hides. Another, and possibly more important, reason for the difference between the assessment of a shire in Domesday and the hides needed to maintain its *burh* was the tendency in the middle years of the eleventh century to reassess part or all of a shire. The difference that might result from such reassessments can be seen in a list of shires known as the *County Hidage* which gives an assessment for thirteen of them. There are several versions. Kemble (1849, i. 493–4) printed one from a mid-thirteenth-century copy (B. L., Cotton Claudius B vii fo. 204^v) but the version used here comes from a manuscript of approximately the same date, Jesus College, Oxford, MS 29, fos 194^v–5 (Morris, 1872, pp. 145–6). It is appended to a list of bishoprics that was compiled *c.* 1100, but the list of shires appears to be somewhat earlier than Domesday Book. It is instructive to follow Maitland's example (1897, p. 456) and compare the figures in this list with the shire assessments of Domesday Book.

	County Hidage (Jesus College)	Domesday Book
Wiltshire	4800	4050
Bedfordshire	1200	1193
Cambridgeshire	2500	1233
Huntingdonshire	850	747
Northamptonshire	3200	1356
Gloucestershire	3400	2388
Worcestershire	1200	1189
Herefordshire	1200	1324
Warwickshire	1200	1338
Oxfordshire	2400	2412
Shropshire	2400	1245
Cheshire	1200	512
Staffordshire	500	505

If, as seems likely, the entry for Huntingdonshire in the *County Hidage, viij hundred hida and half hundred* is a misunderstanding of an

Old English formula for 750, *eahtotha healf hund*, the agreement between these figures was even closer than appears from this list. There
is nothing surprising about the disagreement over Northamptonshire
for there is abundant evidence to show that the assessment of that shire
was massively reduced in the middle of the eleventh century (Hart,
1970). The assessments of Shropshire and Cambridgeshire appear to
have been halved and that of Cheshire had been even more drastically
reduced. The assessment of Cheshire in the *County Hidage* is consistent
with the division of that shire into twelve hundreds. According to the
Domesday account of Chester, 'For the repair of the city wall the reeve
used to call up one man from each hide of the county' (DB, i. 262b),
and if the formula stated in the appendix to the *Burghal Hidage* applied
there, 1200 hides would be enough to maintain 1650 yards of wall,
which is close to the length of the land walls of Chester, estimated by
David Hill at about 1710 yards. This not only encourages confidence in
the figures given in the *County Hidage*, it also provides another example
of a shire assessment related to the size of its *burh* and illustrates how
assessments could be changed.

There were, of course, *burhs* outside Wessex. One version of the
Burghal Hidage adds the Mercian *burhs* of Buckingham, Worcester and
Warwick, and we are fortunate to have a charter issued in the last
years of the ninth century by Æthelred, ruler of Mercia, and his wife
after they had fortified Worcester. In it they granted to the church of
Worcester 'half of all the rights which belong to their lordship,
whether in the market or in the street, both within the fortification and
outside' but they reserved to themselves the waggon shilling and load
penny 'which are to go to the king's hand as it always did at *Saltwic*
[that is Droitwich] but otherwise the land-rent, the fine for fighting,
theft or dishonest trading, and contributions to the borough-wall and
all fines for offences which admit of compensation are to belong half to
the lord of the church, for the sake of God and St Peter, exactly as it
has been laid down as regards the market place and streets' (S, 223;
EHD, 99). James Tait (1936, p. 20) and Sir Frank Stenton (1971, p.
529) believed that this market had recently been established within the
newly constructed fortifications and that Worcester illustrates the
growth of local markets under the protection of defences constructed
and maintained by royal authority. It is, however, more probable that
an occasional market for local exchanges, possibly meeting weekly, already existed in the vicinity of the cathedral church and that this charter

is evidence not for the creation of a market but for the extension of authority over it by rulers who had formerly enjoyed similar rights elsewhere, notably at Droitwich.

Several of the places listed in the *Burghal Hidage* are similarly likely to have been the sites of well-established local markets. Some were never more than forts and were abandoned soon after the Viking threat receded, but others housed substantial communities which flourished during the tenth century and were later described as important and populous towns in Domesday Book. Towns also flourished in the Danelaw and three, York, Lincoln and Norwich, are among the largest described in Domesday; they were already prosperous when the West Saxons gained control of them during the first half of the tenth century. There are indications that the street plan of Lincoln was at least partly laid out while it was under Scandinavian rule, and it was Viking kings in York who, in about 895, began to produce a silver coinage in that city. The early history of Norwich is obscure but it was already an important mint in the early tenth century and appears to have been a major centre while under Scandinavian control, as it certainly was in the mid-eleventh century (Campbell, 1975b). The trade on which these towns depended for their prosperity may in part have been stimulated by the Vikings themselves. Many of the Scandinavians who settled in England brought their share of the plunder and tribute gathered in years of campaigning. Some of their loot has survived in treasure hoards, notably the large one found at Cuerdale, near Preston, which contained over 7000 coins, 1000 of them from Frankish mints. The York coinage minted by the Vikings was modelled on Frankish types and the silver it contained probably came from Frankia. The presence of relatively wealthy Viking colonists must have encouraged the development of local markets and crafts. Archaeological investigations are showing that in all these places craftsmen were producing goods, sometimes decorated in distinctive Scandinavian styles, to meet the demands of these local landowners. Similar developments have also been recognized in such English towns as Winchester and Southampton.

In the tenth century English kings attempted to limit trade to the markets that they controlled. This was partly to hamper traffic in stolen goods and to help the detection of theft, but it also enhanced royal prestige and increased royal resources; in Domesday Book, as we have seen, the *burhs* figure prominently among the royal assets. One other consequence of this extension of royal control over local markets was a change in meaning of the word *port*. It derived from the Latin word *portus* which meant a harbour and is used in that sense in some place-names such as Portsmouth and Portchester. By the tenth century it was being used for inland markets, and Oxford's town meadow is called Port Meadow. Lords other than the king followed his example, or at least they did so after the Norman Conquest. One of the complaints made to the Domesday commissioners in Lincolnshire was that at Barton-on-Humber and at South Ferriby Norman lords were taking toll on bread, fish, hides and many other commodities for which nothing had been given before the Conquest; at Grimsby there was a similar complaint. It was at this time that new markets were being established or moved: for example, in Cornwall the Sunday market that had been held at St Germans before the Conquest was moved by the count of Mortain to be held at his castle.

The earlier extension of royal authority over local markets did not affect Northumbria where, on the eve of the Conquest, there was only one town and one mint, albeit very large, at York. Elsewhere in the north exchanges must have taken place in the traditional manner, at markets. None is mentioned in Domesday Book but we may suspect that many of the northern markets which appear in later texts, especially in charters granting or confirming them, were already old in the eleventh century.

The commodities of trade are only mentioned incidentally. A letter of Charlemagne to Offa shows that the English then exported cloaks, and an early eleventh-century list of tolls at Arras lists English cheeses. At the same time an Italian text about customs arrangements shows that a highly prized English export was hunting-dogs. There are also references throughout the whole period, from the seventh century to the eleventh, to a trade in slaves. Archaeological evidence has previously tended to be limited to such durable goods as pottery and metal-work but modern techniques are making it possible to detect, preserve and study other materials, including cloth, and we may hope in the future to learn a great deal more about the goods that passed through markets, both inland and coastal.

In the seventh and eighth centuries the main traffic appears to have been in luxury goods of high value and slight bulk. In the market places to which long-distance traders came, from Dorestad or the Baltic, there was naturally some demand for basic goods, if only to feed the merchants and their servants. They must sometimes have needed tools and stores for their return journey, and the discoveries at *Hamwih* show some of the miscellaneous crafts that developed in such places. By the eleventh century, trade in bulkier and less valuable commodities was increasingly significant and an account of the tolls levied at London in the reign of Æthelred included timber, cloth, fish, *crapiscis* (probably whales), wine, hens, eggs, cheese and butter (IV Atr 2). Special mention is made of men from Rouen, Flanders, Pontheiu, Normandy, and *Francia*, as well as from Liège, Nivelles and Huy, the last probably bringing their speciality, metal-work. The subjects of the German emperor were allowed the same privileges as the English and were allowed to buy wool and to provision their ships with up to three live pigs. They had no right to pre-emption and paid their toll in the form of cloth, pepper, gloves and vinegar. This text shows that London's links were with ports across the Channel and the North Sea, and that much of its trade was in bulk goods of an ordinary, not luxury, kind. There is some evidence of trade between England and Italy at this time, but the quantities were tiny compared with the traffic with northern Europe.

Trade does not need coined money. In the earlier seventh century coins were not produced in Britain and although some were imported from Frankia their distribution was restricted and they served other purposes than commerce. The first English coins were produced in the mid-seventh century at a number of places in the south-east. They were originally of gold, but before the end of that century they were made almost exclusively of silver. These silver coins were called pennies by contemporaries but they were dumpy objects, very different from the thin and regular pennies produced later in the eighth century, and they are normally called *sceattas* to distinguish them. Mints were first indicated on the coins in the reign of Athelstan when there were 26, but by the end of Edgar's reign there were 60 and more were established under Æthelred. This vast increase in the number of mints is remarkable testimony to the success of English kings in extending their authority, but the growing volume of coin also reflects an increasing demand for it for purposes of trade. Money was certainly needed to pay royal dues and taxes, and Domesday Book shows that many rents were paid in cash and that money was widely used. For peasants to have money they had to earn it by their labour or produce, and there must, therefore, have been active markets in which the goods they, or their lords, produced could be sold. The fact that Æthelred had to gather money by taxation in order to pay tribute to the Vikings shows that it was dispersed through society; he did not control any major source of supply. As already suggested the Vikings may themselves have imported some treasure to England, they certainly redistributed it, but the main increase in the amount of money in circulation occurred in the last quarter of the tenth century. In the 960s a very large silver mine was discovered at Rammelsberg in the Harz mountains of Germany, and thereafter German coin was distributed very widely throughout the Baltic and the east as Germans bought furs and other exotic products of those regions. The Germans also encouraged the growth of the Flemish cloth industry, and possibly the English as well, but as coinages were well controlled in England and Flanders any German silver that was imported had to be converted into legal tender. The location of the main English mints and the largest towns is consistent with the hypothesis that the main economic activity lay in the east, and that the silver came from abroad (Sawyer, 1965). This is no more than a hypothesis, but the English certainly had some means of replenishing their supply of silver to make good the massive withdrawals by the Vikings under Æthelred, and later by the Norman conquerors. Native sources can hardly have maintained the amount in circulation, and the most productive mints are in any case not close to the main possible sources, none of which was abundant enough to produce the large sums needed. Domesday Book shows that the most valuable areas were those that were later important as sheep-producing areas, and the fact that the demesne flocks of sheep recorded in Domesday Book are of much the same size as, or larger than, the demesne flocks on the same estates in the twelfth and thirteenth centuries suggests that the sheep population in the eleventh century was as large as it was later when wool exports are known to have been substantial. The fact that most sheep bones found by archaeologists are from animals which are about six-years old also suggests that they were kept for their wool, not their meat. Wool was of course not the only basis of England's wealth. Much else was exported, but the best explanation of England's relative wealth in the eleventh century appears to be a credit trade-balance, which was widely dispersed throughout the countryside and in its turn stimulated the economic activity that is implied by the flourishing markets and their craftsmen. And as the trade flourished, kings prospered, both from the exploitation of their own estates, and from the taxation drawn from the estates of others.

VII

The church and society

Religions naturally reflect and reinforce the societies in which they de-
velop, and early English Christianity was no exception. The institutions of the church mirrored those of the world. Bishops ruled dioceses
that were based on kingdoms and, when men acquired private rights
over land, their estates became parishes. The language and literature of
the church was easily understood by laymen. Christians talked about
lords and kinsmen, and presented God as the King of Kings. Many of
the stories in the Old Testament were very much like the stories men
told about seventh-century kings and it was in the churches of England
that memories of the pagan past were treasured in poems like *Beowulf*
or visually in such strange achievements as the carvings on the Franks
Casket. There was no great divide between the church and the world.
Some leading churchmen, like Bede and Boniface, were committed to
the church as children, but many others were converted after a secular
career. Benedict Biscop and Guthlac both renounced the world when
they were 25 and Hild was 33 when she did the same. After conversion
even the most austere could not entirely escape the world. Guthlac had
many visitors to his Fenland retreat and St Cuthbert travelled widely in
Northumbria and was consulted on dynastic as well as religious matters.

The church also participated fully in that process of gift-exchange
that was basic in Dark Age society. The gifts of churchmen were often
spiritual, but not always. When Æthelberht II, king of Kent, sent greet-
ings to Archbishop Boniface he also sent 'a few little gifts: a silver-gilt
chalice weighing three and a half pounds and two woollen cloaks'. They
were not sent

with the purpose or expectation of receiving any earthly profit or return; but rather on bended knees begging you what is far more necessary, that in these evil days of manifold and unexpected troubles and in this world so filled with scandals you will deign to aid us with the frequent support of your prayers. (Boniface, 75)

He did, however, add one further request, for a pair of falcons of a kind that were difficult to obtain in Kent. Boniface himself frequently sent gifts of spices or towels and when he rebuked King Æthelbald of Mercia he took care to send 'as a token of true affection and devoted friendship; a hawk and two falcons, two shields and two lances', which he described as 'a trifling gift' (55). Churches were also endowed with land in the expectation of a return. As many charters explain, donors looked for some reward from God, in the next world if not in this.

The penitential system by which churchmen tried to reform the world was also well adapted to contemporary circumstances. It prescribed an elaborate tariff of penances, graded according to the seriousness of the offence, that was in effect the spiritual equivalent of the tariffs of compensations familiar in secular law. Some of the elements in Christian teaching that did not easily fit current custom tended to be ignored. The frequent complaints about concubines, adultery and illegitimacy show that the Christian ideas on marriage were slow to make headway against older habits, and the teaching on forgiveness was also hard to accept, as King Sigeberht discovered (p. 95). Germanic society certainly had ways of converting enmities into friendships but it was only done with difficulty. Christian rulers could of course always justify their hostility towards others as the fulfilment of God's will. Eddius says of Ecgfrith that he was

strong like David in crushing his enemies yet lowly in the sight of God, breaking the necks of the tumultuous tribes and their warlike kings, emboldened as he was by the help of God, in all things always gave thanks to God. . . . So, unwavering in spirit and true-hearted, on the advice of his counsellors trusting God, like Barak and Deborah, . . . with a band of men no greater than theirs he attacked a proud enemy and by the help of God overthrew them with his tiny force. (c. 20)

Bishops took their place in the company attending kings and together with secular nobles advised in peace and war. It was with the advice and

counsel of bishops and other wise men that kings made laws and it was
often said to be with their help that hostilities were ended and treaties
of peace concluded (p. 107). The households of many bishops closely
resembled those of the secular nobility, from whose ranks most, if not
all of them, were recruited. Many bishops rode fine horses, and had
large retinues, and when Wilfrid, on his death-bed, divided up his
treasure of gold, silver and precious stones, he was behaving just like
the great secular lord he might have been. Bishops, priests and other
clergy were all assigned their places in the hierarchical system of compensations by which society was regulated. Their oaths were highly
valued and in seventh-century Kent the word of a bishop, like that of a
king, was incontrovertible even if unsupported by an oath. Æthelberht's laws begin with a statement of the compensations due for theft
of the property of churches and churchmen:

> The property of God and the Church with a twelve-fold compensa-
> tion; a bishop's property with an eleven-fold compensation; a
> priest's property with a nine-fold compensation,

and the peace of the church was protected by a two-fold compensation
which made it like the king's.

In the early missionary days of the church in England a crucially
important role was played by austere and holy men. When they died
their power did not vanish but continued in their mortal remains;
relics were repositories of great supernatural power. Austerity, however, was not a virtue in a shrine, and some were lavishly adorned, as
Guthlac's was by Æthelbald. These shrines were often served by
clerks or monks who formed communities that were much like other
monastic communities that were founded in very large numbers after
about 650. This enthusiasm for monasticism is only explicable on the
assumption that these foundations served the spiritual needs of society
in a most acceptable way. They certainly fitted well into the contemporary pattern of society with its groups of kinsmen. A monastery was
a new sort of kinship group, with the abbot as father and lord, surrounded by his spiritual brothers, some of whom were also natural kinsmen. The leadership of such communities was often hereditary. One
remarkable example is the house established on Spurn Point by Wilgils
which 'by the gift of his sanctity' passed by legitimate succession and
was at the end of the eighth century held by Alcuin, the friend and

adviser of Charlemagne, who wrote a *Life* of Wilgils' son, the missionary Willibrord (*EHD*, 157).

Such communities did not have to be very austere to serve their religious purposes; austerity might be a sign of power in a holy man, it was less appropriate for a saint or for the community that gathered round his shrine. Bede had a very clear idea of what a monastery should be and deplored the 'innumerable places allowed the name of monasteries by a most foolish manner of speaking but having nothing at all of a monastic way of life' (*EHD*, 170). His main complaints about these sham monasteries seem to have been that they were ruled by laymen and that their members had wives and children. They might call themselves monks, promise obedience, receive the tonsure and 'perform with assiduous attention what should be done within the precincts of monasteries', but they nevertheless had 'nothing at all of a monastic way of life'. Laxity and licence could also afflict regularly constituted monasteries. Bede saw the destruction of Coldingham by fire as a divine judgement and reported, with evident approval, the condemnation and prophecy that came from one of its devout inmates, called Adomnán and therefore presumably an Irishman.

> The cells that were built for praying and for reading have become haunts of feasting, drinking, gossip and other delights; even the virgins who are dedicated to God put aside all respect for their profession and, whenever they have leisure, spend their time weaving elaborate garments with which to adorn themselves as if they were brides, so imperilling their virginity, or else make friends with strange men. So it is only right that a heavy vengeance from heaven should be prepared for this place and for its inhabitants in the form of raging fire. (*HE*, iv. 25)

Austere standards must have been difficult to maintain in houses to which kings retired, as Æthelbald did to Bardney, or that were ruled by the sisters, daughters, widows or even wives of kings. In England, as elsewhere in western Europe, a favoured form of monastic community was double, consisting of a house for women as well as one for men. Most if not all of these double monasteries were royal foundations and were ruled by abbesses, themselves members of royal families. One of the most famous was at Whitby, founded by Hild, a close relative of King Edwin. As Bede explains, she established a Rule and members of the community were taught

to observe strictly the virtues of justice, devotion, and chastity and
other virtues too, but above all things to continue in peace and
charity. After the example of the primitive church, no one was rich,
no one was in need, for they had all things in common and none had
any private property. (*HE*, iv. 23)

Bede is careful not to say that the community was austere, and excavations have shown that he was right, for many signs of opulence have
been found: large quantities of imported pottery, exotic metal-work
and many coins in marked contrast to the austerities of Jarrow (Cramp,
1976). This church was the burial-place of several members of the
Northumbrian royal family: King Oswiu, his wife and daughter, and
also of Edwin.

The burial-places of kings and their close relatives give some indication of where they thought the greatest spiritual power was to be
found. Some abdicated to die in Rome, the great cult centre of the
western church, but others had to be content with resting-places at
home. These were not always cathedral churches but monasteries,
often double ones; Æthelred was buried at Bardney, where St Oswald's
relics were, Æthelbald at Repton, and although some West Saxon
kings were buried at Winchester Alfred's brothers were buried at
Sherborne or Wimborne and, according to Florence of Worcester,
Athelstan was buried at Malmesbury and Edmund at Glastonbury.

Following Bede we naturally tend to think of the eighth-century
church primarily in terms of bishops and dioceses, while recognizing
the great importance of a few monasteries like Jarrow, Whitby and
Canterbury. An alternative and revealing guide to the thoughts of
other English churchmen is provided by a text known as *The List of
Saints' Resting Places* that survives in two eleventh-century manuscripts. It lists over 50 places, shown in figure 10 (p. 239), in which
saints were buried. As David Rollason (1978) has shown, it was based
on a ninth-century compilation probably made in Mercia or Northumbria that gave the resting-places of 31 saints. As may be seen from the
map, where the original entries are distinguished, none was in Wessex.
The list was revised in the tenth century and enlarged by the addition
of many more saints in Wessex and elsewhere. Taken together with
what is known about the preferred burial-places of English kings and
bishops, this list provides a significantly different view of Christian

Figure 10   *The List of Saints' Resting Places*
Based on Rollason (1978).

Saints' Resting Places
▲ Original list (9th. century)
● Additions

England from that emphasized by Bede in the conclusion of the *Ecclesiastical History* where he lists all the English bishoprics.

Most, if not all, these shrines were served by some form of religious community, and there were many other communities as well. Many were called minsters, an English word deriving from Latin *monasterium*, a name that implies some communal basis. Some impression of the scale of some early religious houses may be gained from the magnificent remains of the seventh-century church at Brixworth in Northamptonshire. The only historical evidence for this church is a statement by a twelfth-century historian of Peterborough Abbey, Hugh Candidus, that a colony of monks was sent to Brixworth from Peterborough, then called *Medeshamstede*, in the seventh century (Mellows, 1949, p. 15). Brixworth underlines the incompleteness of our knowledge of the early church and serves as a warning against assuming that places that are not mentioned in early texts were of little account. Bede and later monastic reformers may well have been right to deny that many of these churches were true monasteries, but they did play an important, if obscure, role in English religious life and continued to do so even after the Norman Conquest. They were not necessarily great centres of learning and scholarship. Some important monasteries exhibited very low standards of Latinity. In the early ninth century Canterbury produced some charters that are so confused that their meaning is unclear and a century later someone in the community of St Cuthbert composed a form for blessing milk and honey that makes liturgical nonsense, for it incorporates the greater part of the form for blessing an altar cross. It is not surprising that in the ninth century there was a tendency to record complicated transactions in English rather than Latin and that liturgical manuscripts, including such beautiful books as the Lindisfarne Gospels, were in the tenth century furnished with interlinear translations. A form of service could, however, be effective without being comprehended and no doubt must have sounded most impressive to observers who were even less learned than the clergy.

Religious communities of all kinds were particularly vulnerable to Viking attacks. Even the poorest were potential sources of slaves. In the face of such danger flight was a sensible precaution and some communities, especially those on exposed sites like St Mary's at Lyminge or St Cuthbert's on Lindisfarne, sought shelter: St Mary's in Canterbury and St Cuthbert's at Norham on the Tweed. In 875, when

Halfdan began to raid the north from a base on the Tyne, the community of St Cuthbert moved again to Carlisle and then wandered for seven years before finding a new resting-place at Chester-le-Street. That migration is well known because it was carefully recorded. The more abundant records of continental churches make it possible to trace many similar migrations in the Carolingian empire and it is likely that there were more in England. Such moves may indeed be the cause of otherwise unexplained translations of relics. St Cuthbert's was not the only northern community to survive Viking attacks. On their travels, St Cuthbert's relics stayed for a while in a monastery at Crayke, about 12 miles north of York, which may have been a double monastery for its 'abbot' had a woman's name (*EHD*, p. 93), and a community of some kind appears also to have survived at Norham in the early tenth century.

We are relatively well informed about St Cuthbert's because that community was richly endowed and well protected either by St Cuthbert himself or by kings and others who recognized his power. Its traditions were carefully recorded in the twelfth century by members of the reformed community that was then responsible for the cult. Some other communities were less well served and disappeared, either because they were physically destroyed or because they were secularized to such an extent that they no longer maintained any pretence of a religious function. Despite widespread secularization, and some destruction, many communities did survive to provide a basis for later monasteries whose members did not always regard their uncouth predecessors with much favour. The histories of several monasteries that were founded in the twelfth century, Kirkstall is a good example, mention the previous presence on their sites of hermits. Some may indeed have been hermits, that form of religious expression was increasingly popular in the late eleventh century, but it is also possible that some were members of old-fashioned religious communities that had survived the upheavals of the Norman Conquest and before.

The main general upheaval that occurred before the Norman Conquest was, of course, due to the Vikings who undoubtedly disrupted the church. Apart from driving some communities into exile, permanent or temporary, their attacks caused interruptions in some episcopal successions. Those of East Anglia, Leicester and Lindsey were all interrupted in the years after 869. Their attacks may also have been responsible for the disappearance of some religious houses, but violence was not the only, or main, cause. Some communities collapsed because Vikings, or others, seized their estates. St Cuthbert's lost estates to Ragnald and his followers, but they had earlier suffered at the hands of English rulers. Another, and perhaps more important, cause for the disappearance of religious communities was the replacement of the local aristocrats, on whom they had depended, by Scandinavians who did not share the religious enthusiasms of the men they displaced.

The Scandinavians were, in time, converted to Christianity. Paganism was briefly reinforced in early tenth-century Northumbria by the arrival of Ragnald and other descendants of Ivarr who put such emblems as a raven or Thor's hammer on the coins of York, but by the middle of the tenth century Christianity had been restored in the Danelaw, and all England was under some form of episcopal rule.

After the disruption of the Viking raids and conquests, there was growing enthusiasm for a reform of monasticism in which the Benedictine Rule, suitably elaborated and modified, was accepted as the basis for true monastic observance. On the continent this movement owed much to the encouragement of Carolingian rulers, especially Louis the Pious, and it was at a council held under his auspices at Aachen in 817 that the programme of reform was fully elaborated. The reforming ideas did not spread as rapidly as the idealists hoped but they did reach England, where there was also resistance. According to Asser, Alfred's attempt to introduce this reformed monasticism was frustrated either by the Viking attacks or, as he thought more likely, by the wealth of the English. It was in fact not until the middle years of the tenth century that these new standards of monastic observance had much influence in England and that was mainly due to the support given them by King Edmund and, even more, by King Edgar. These rulers came to believe that the spiritual support of monks living according to the Benedictine Rule was particularly valuable and with their encouragement several old communities, including the cathedrals of Winchester and Worcester, were reformed, and new ones founded, generally on sites of ancient sanctity like Crowland, Ely and Peterborough. In return for this royal patronage the monks not only offered up prayers for the king and his family, they also acknowledged his lordship and these houses therefore became key centres of royal influence, a role of particular importance in areas that had no long tradition of loyalty to West Saxon kings.

Earlier English kings had looked for, and obtained, similar support from unreformed religious communities. Many charters survive to record the continuing flow of benefactions to some of these houses and Athelstan clearly recognized the importance of such communities, especially in distant parts of his newly united kingdom. He went out of his way to patronize and encourage Northumbrian cults, especially that of St Cuthbert. His Scottish campaign of 934 gave him an opportunity to visit and make gifts to the shrines of Beverley and Ripon, but it was to St Cuthbert that he made the most magnificent gifts. He gave several books including Bede's metrical and prose *Life* of the saint, which survives at Corpus Christi College, Cambridge, and some vestments, including an early tenth-century stole and maniple that were placed in the shrine and are still preserved at Durham (Battiscombe, 1956).

There are some signs that West Saxon interest in Northumbrian cults, especially Cuthbert's, began before Athelstan's reign, perhaps even in the ninth century. Asser reports that Alfred made gifts to Northumbrian as well as to Mercian monasteries but there is more positive evidence. St Cuthbert was included, along with Guthlac, in the Litany in a service book, known as Leofric A, that was compiled in southern England, possibly Glastonbury, shortly before or after 900 (Hohler, 1975). The relics collected in Edward the Elder's great foundation of New Minster at Winchester show a similar interest in Northumbrian saints, for the list includes Acca of Hexham and Wilfrid as well as Cuthbert who was accorded special respect by being placed third (between St Peter and St Stephen) (Birch, 1892, pp. 147–8). The presence of Guthlac in the Leofric Litany shows an interest in Mercian as well as Northumbrian saints that was more dramatically displayed in 909 when Æthelred of Mercia and his wife Æthelflæd removed the relics of St Oswald from Bardney and rehoused them at Gloucester. This West Saxon and Mercian interest in the saints of those parts of England that had come under Danish rule or influence was a natural response to the Viking conquests. St Cuthbert was the most important Bernician saint and the encouragement of his cult was the religious counterpart of West Saxon attempts to gain some influence over the Lords of Bamburgh, north of Scandinavian York. The contemporary interest in Oswald and Guthlac suggests that Edward the Elder and his sister used the same technique in dealing with the southern Danelaw. The *List of Saints' Resting Places* was revised in the tenth century, and the entry about Oswald was expanded to explain that 'his head is with

St Cuthbert, his right arm is at Bamburgh and the rest of his body is in the New Minster at Gloucester'. The fact that, after entries concerning St Alban and St Columba, the *List* begins with Northumbrian and Mercian shrines may mean that it was itself a by-product of this interest in the saints of Viking England. It is, therefore, not surprising that after the crushing defeat of the Scandinavians at Tettenhall in 910 a new Viking ruler in York, Ragnald, should have been the enemy of St Cuthbert – he seized the saints' estates – just as he was also the enemy of Ealdred who, according to the tenth-century *Historia de Sancto Cuthberto* (c. 22), was loved by King Edward just as his father, Eadwulf of Bamburgh, had been loved by King Alfred.

Some of the estates that churches lost were gifts made soon after the conversion. Æthelberht's laws show that the church in Kent already had some property in his day, and later in the seventh century monasteries were particularly successful in attracting endowments from both kings and nobles. The church also acquired rights to a variety of renders. The earliest to be mentioned by a specific name was church-scot which, according to Ine's laws, had to be paid 'from the haulm and the hearth where one resides at mid-winter' (c. 61) and was later due at Martinmass (11 November). Other payments included soul-scot, a burial fee, plough-alms paid after Easter, and Romescot, a contribution to Peter's Pence due on St Peter's day (1 August), a tribute paid to the papacy at least as early as the ninth century. Above all there were tithes, which may originally have been voluntary but had become obligatory by the tenth century and probably much earlier. These renders appear initially to have been made to churches that were founded in or near royal *tūn*. When a bishop travelled round his diocese he would naturally stay on the royal estates, whether or not he was accompanying the king. Both Paulinus and Aidán did this and Bede mentions that on one such estate Aidán had a church (*HE*, iii. 17). By the end of the century it is likely that there were few royal *tūn* without an associated church. They were in effect the first parish churches. It was from them that bishops did their work of preaching and baptizing, and they were initially served by members of the bishop's *familia* or household, and later by communities of clerks or chaplains. The renders paid to these churches were the spiritual equivalent of the secular dues owed to the king at his *tūn*. It is reasonable to assume that as the secular obligations were granted away so too were the spiritual dues. When a monastery, whether founded by a king or nobleman, was given the privilege of perpetual inheritance and freedom from the normal obligations to the royal *tūn*, it must commonly have acquired rights to at least part of the ecclesiastical tribute at the same time. In the ninth and later centuries laymen acquired similar privileges for secular purposes and were able to divert at least some of the ecclesiastical dues to churches on their own estates. According to Edgar's laws such churches were entitled to a larger proportion of the tithe if they had graveyards (II Edg 2), and in such circumstances they presumably also received soul-scot. Church-scot continued to be paid to the ancient churches that had always had it, what were called the Old Minsters, and these minsters also retained a right to the greater part of the tithes.

This system can be studied best in eleventh-century Kent thanks to some detailed records preserved at Christ Church, Canterbury, and other Kentish houses (Barlow, 1963, pp. 180–2). These show what dues were owed to the archbishop from 13 Old Minsters. Before they were reorganized by the Norman archbishop Lanfranc, these dues included payments of honey or mead, sheep, loaves and specific money payments for wine and for chrism, the baptismal oil. There were also larger payments that probably represent church-scot. The 'mother churches' gathered these dues from their own dependent churches, Milton, for example, had twelve. The archbishop of Canterbury and his associate the bishop of Rochester were probably more successful in retaining control of these minster churches than some other bishops. Elsewhere some became independent monasteries, or were acquired by such monasteries, as happened, after the Conquest, in Kent where Milton, with all its churches, was granted by William I to St Augustine's Abbey.

Records of this kind have not survived for other bishoprics, but a writ of Edward the Confessor shows how the archbishop of York was considered to be the protector of Beverley minster:

My will is that the minster and its property belonging thereto shall be free as any other minster is in all things: and whatever bishop shall be over it that it be subject to him, and that he be its protector and guardian under me, so that no one but he shall take anything from it and so that he shall not permit to be alienated any of the things that lawfully pertain thereto, in so far as he wishes to be secure from God and St John and all the saints in whose honour the holy foundation is consecrated. And my will is that minster life and assembly shall always be maintained there as long as any man shall live. (S, 1067)

Bishops were not always successful in retaining their rights. Some monasteries gained exemption from episcopal control, and several minsters were especially privileged and in the twelfth century were recognized as royal free chapels with well-defined immunities over districts that had once been 'shires' (Denton, 1970)

The texts that make it possible to study the Kentish minsters and their dependent churches also reveal the existence of over 400 churches in that county, twice the number recorded in Domesday Book (p. 136). Kent was not unusual in having so many churches. In counties where Domesday Book appears to list most if not all churches, the numbers are comparable. It records 427 in Suffolk and 249 in Norfolk. In other counties, as the Kentish evidence makes clear, Domesday does not attempt to record all the churches and in some, like Buckinghamshire and Bedfordshire, in each of which it only notes four, it is obviously an inadequate guide. The documentary and archaeological evidence suggests that by the middle of the eleventh century there were few English settlements far removed from a church, and by then almost all the later parish churches of England existed, although some had not yet acquired parochial status.

Some of the churches were very old indeed. There are several early references to nobles building churches on their estates and it would be wrong to assume that because most of the pre-Conquest churches were built in the tenth or eleventh centuries there were no earlier churches on their sites. At one, Kirkdale in Yorkshire, there is an inscription showing that it was rebuilt in the decade before the Conquest. Pre-Conquest stone carvings, some as early as the eighth century, have been discovered in the fabric of many English churches, or nearby. For example, a recent survey in the Tees valley has listed about 300 fragments of stone carvings from 37 places, in only six of which is there any architectural evidence of a pre-Conquest church (Morris, 1976). Relatively important religious centres are implied in some places by the discovery of large numbers of pieces, at both Gainford and Sockburn there were over thirty. Some of these carvings appear to have been architectural and imply the existence of a stone church, but many others were grave markers or grave slabs and are evidence of early graveyards. Another indication that a graveyard is very early is provided by

Figure 11 English dioceses *c.* 1050

The diocesan boundaries are taken from Ordnance Survey, *Map of Monastic Britain,* and Barlow (1963, p. 161). The sees are of all periods.

the discovery of graves of a very early type with personal possessions. These have been found in many parts of England, at Mentmore in Buckinghamshire, Soham in Cambridgeshire and at Sysonby in Leicestershire, for example. Some churches, especially in East Anglia, even contain pagan cremations and it is not uncommon for a churchyard to be an extension or development of a pagan cemetery. This happens at Sancton in Yorkshire, Black Bourton in Oxfordshire and Breedon in Leicestershire (Morris, 1978). All this evidence implies the existence of Christian graveyards and possibly of churches in many places long before they can have become parochial centres. A church could not become a parish church until the estate on which it stood was granted a privileged status by a charter, or book, and became what was called book-land. Book-land could be detached for some ecclesiastical purposes from the ancient parish of the royal minster. The close connection between parish and book-land explains why parochial boundaries are often the same as the bounds of estates as described in pre-Conquest charters, or books. The agreement is not always complete, many adjustments have been made to both estate and parish boundaries since the eleventh century, but it is very common for them to follow the same line for part of their circuit and there are several places where the parish boundary recorded in nineteenth-century Tithe Awards agrees exactly with the bounds of tenth- or eleventh-century charters.

Over 300 English churches have clear traces of pre-Conquest fabric. The great cathedral and monastic churches have all been rebuilt, perhaps many times, and their early architectural history has to be deduced from excavations. These can yield remarkable results, Winchester being an outstanding example, but too often the excavations are fragmentary or have been badly recorded. It is some compensation that so many small and unpretentious churches have survived in whole or part. These are obviously of great architectural and liturgical interest, but they also serve as an effective reminder of the close involvement of the church with English life at all levels. Everywhere men paid their church dues and tithes, more or less willingly, and helped to build and rebuild the churches that were for centuries the largest and most dramatic buildings that most men ever saw. Children beat the parish bounds at Rogation tide so that they would never be forgotten. The rhythm of the year was marked as it always has been by festivals, but these slowly became Christian and old beliefs and customs survived in a new guise. Our sources inevitably draw attention to the great cathedrals and monasteries, and to the ideas and actions of great men, but the slow transforming work of the church in the countryside and in the towns was no less important. The churches that survive, in all parts of the country, and the collections of memorial stones that are even more numerous, show how widespread and permanent that influence was long before the Normans came.

VIII

The consequences of
the Norman Conquest

One important result of the Norman Conquest of England was the creation of many close links between England and Normandy, but that does not mean that the English were isolated from the continent before 1066. Edward the Confessor, who spent his youth in Normandy as an exile, had a great admiration for the Normans which he showed in a preference for Norman advisers and by modelling his new church at Westminster on the recently constructed abbey of Jumièges. After 1046 there were never fewer than three foreign bishops holding English sees, and for the last five years of Edward's reign the bishop of London was a Norman and four other sees had bishops from Lorraine. English churchmen attended some of the reforming councils in France and Italy, and the requirement that each new archbishop had to collect his pallium from the pope ensured that these leaders could not escape some contact with the papal reform movement. Ealdred was, indeed, forced to surrender his bishopric of Worcester before he could obtain papal recognition of his elevation to the see of York. The English were, therefore, not unaware of the new ideas and standards that were beginning to gain support in the western church. Economically the contacts between England and the continent were even closer. Already by the early eleventh century London was one of the greatest cities in Europe and had trading links with many parts of the continent from Rouen to Germany, and there were other thriving English towns whose prosperity depended in large measure on the export of wool for the growing industry of Flanders. The merchants from Rouen, Huy, Nivelles and Liège as well as those from Flanders and Germany who are specifically mentioned in London toll regulations early in the century (p. 232) may possibly have introduced new ideas; they certainly brought much treasure, and this was a powerful agent in the transformation of both rural and urban England, a process that continued throughout the century and was probably not much affected by the Conquest.

The Normans nevertheless greatly strengthened England's connections with the continent for they did not abandon or neglect their interests in Normandy even though many found rich opportunities in England. William himself remained duke after he became king and was buried in his own church of St Stephen's at Caen. What is more, there are indications that William wished to leave England and Normandy as an undivided inheritance (Le Patourel, 1971) and the split between duchy and kingdom that did in fact follow his death proved to be only temporary. Many of William's leading barons, such as William de Warenne, Roger de Beaumont and Roger de Montgomery, followed his example and retained extensive estates in Normandy (Le Patourel, 1966). Men like these must have regarded their English estates as little more than a source of revenue and, if necessary, of men. There were, of course, many with little or no land on the continent who soon settled down in the new country, but it is interesting to discover that the Lacys, who acquired great estates in the north and west of England, did not dispose of their small family property in Normandy (Wightman, 1966). The tendency of the conquerors to treat England and Normandy as a unit was underlined by their attitude to the church; for the first generation they established very few religious houses in England and continued to regard their family foundations in Normandy with special favour, endowing them richly with English estates and churches (Matthew, 1962). It was left to a later generation, in the twelfth century, to found monasteries in England on any scale. For many of the Norman conquerors of England, including those who settled, Normandy was long regarded in a special sense as home.

The Conquest, which created such complex links between England and Normandy, was not a simple operation begun in 1066 and completed by the final collapse of English resistance in about 1072. It was, in fact, a stage in the expansion of Norman power, an expansion that began before 1066 and continued in the twelfth century with conquests elsewhere in the British Isles. The great need of the duke was for resources with which to sustain the loyalty of the warriors on whom his power ultimately depended and it is not surprising that such a successful ruler as William should have had a reputation for great greed. England was attractive not only because the royal succession was disputed, and William's claim a good one, but because it was a prosperous country with a good silver coinage and a system of taxation that had been developed earlier in the century to pay a mercenary army. The relatively abundant supply of money meant not only that the king could tax the country but that he and his followers could hope to take their rents in cash; they did not need to settle to gain their profit from England. The conquerors also hoped for booty and in 1067, after his coronation, William ostentatiously paraded his newly won wealth throughout the duchy. His churches in Caen profited from both booty and rents, and their construction owed much to the wealth of England (Musset, 1966).

The need for enlarged resources did not disappear immediately England was conquered. The demand for land and revenue was continuous, and there was continuing pressure to extend the frontiers and to expropriate those Englishmen who had managed to retain any of their estates. William's sons, in their turn, needed to reward their own supporters when they succeeded to the kingdom and this was sometimes done even at the expense of Normans as, for example, when the Montgomery family was overthrown, and their estates confiscated, in 1102. There was also a Norman expansion independent of the duke, a movement that led, earlier in the century, to Italy and Sicily and, after the conquest of England, to Scotland and Ireland. The Normans were not, of course, the only greedy and violently acquisitive men in western society in the eleventh century, but they do show a special vitality which may be partly explained by the fact that the duchy was itself created by a migration of adventurers, over whom ducal authority was not fully asserted until the time of William himself.

The Normans conquered England by force and even after William had been accepted as king and crowned on Christmas Day 1066 there was opposition from both Danish claimants and English rebels, the most serious threat being in Northumbria, which William had good cause to fear would be used as a base for a new Danish attempt at conquest. Northumbrian resistance was finally crushed by a ruthless and systematic devastation in the winter of 1069–70 after which the 'perfidious people of that province' were finally reduced to submission.

The Conquest, and the subsequent campaigns, were accomplished with the help of mercenary troops who were paid off and sent home as soon as possible, although a large force of mercenaries was again recruited in 1085 when William feared another Danish invasion. Under normal conditions, William's control of England depended on a relatively small number of his followers and their knights. The main centres of power were the castles, at first simple structures of earth and wood erected in such key towns as Exeter, Lincoln, Shrewsbury and York, under the control of royal agents. In the frontier areas the needs of aggression and defence made well-protected castles, private as well as royal, necessary, but in the great part of England William is unlikely to have encouraged or even allowed the construction of very elaborate strongholds unless they were under the control of his trusted agents (Colvin, 1963; Yver, 1955).

It has been argued that William, who undoubtedly thought of himself as Edward's heir, originally intended to rule as an English king, using English agents and that he had no wish to dispossess Englishmen other than those who had opposed him in the Hastings campaign. This seems unlikely. His followers certainly expected rewards and one of the main inducements to join the invading army must have been the prospect of sharing the landed as well as the silver wealth of England. Even in the early days, in 1067, while William was parading his new riches and long-haired hostages in Normandy, a violent looting operation was in progress. In the event, revolts occurred which provided opportunities for forfeiture, but some of the English seem to have lost their land without opposing the Conqueror. The beneficiaries of these forfeitures were the Normans and others on whom William himself depended, in Normandy as well as in his new kingdom.

It is impossible to determine how many foreigners settled in England as a result of the Conquest. Some wild estimates, like Creasy's of more than 200,000, can be dismissed with confidence and could be altogether ignored were it not for their acceptance in at least one discussion of the linguistic effect of the Conquest (Prins, 1952, p. 22). In fact the number of foreigners who were granted land in William's reign seems to have been less than 2000 and the total immigration is unlikely to have exceeded 10,000. The native population at that time was certainly more than 1,000,000 and may have been, despite the disastrous consequences of the campaigns of the Conquest, as much as 1,500,000.

Whatever fate William intended for the English aristocracy, he undoubtedly preserved the machinery of English government. The system of shires and hundreds or wapentakes was continued unchanged, and William, like Edward before him, declared his wishes to his agents and the men of the shires by means of sealed writs. The only modification in the sophisticated and carefully controlled English coinage was the successful standardization of the weight of the pound, and therefore of the penny, the standard being known as 'sterling', and the pre-Conquest tax of *heregeld* was reactivated. Perhaps the greatest monument to the excellence of the machinery of English royal government and the extent of the Normans' debt to it is Domesday Book. This was commissioned by William at Christmas 1085 and completed in a year; a remarkable achievement that depended as much on the English administrative apparatus as on the drive and efficiency with which the Normans manipulated it.

There were few legal innovations. William promised the Londoners that they should be 'worthy of all the laws they had been worthy of in the days of king Edward'. The courts were the same and their procedure was not changed much, the only substantial innovation being trial by combat, a procedure hitherto unknown in England. As Lady Stenton has remarked, in her study of English justice after the Conquest, 'a striking fact about the procedural development of the early twelfth century is its dependence on the Anglo-Saxon past' (Stenton, 1965a, p. 6). Some changes of detail were, of course, inevitable after such a violent seizure of power and the displacement of the English élite, but the continuity is more significant than the change. It has been well summed up by Frank Barlow: 'On the whole it seems that William's monarchy was Edward's run at full power' (1965, p. 124).

The machinery of English government was therefore preserved but the personnel, especially in positions of great responsibility, was changed. After 1072 few important posts were held by Englishmen. After that English sheriffs are rare, and by then only two of the bishops were Englishmen. Some natives did continue in royal service and a study of the place-names in the Domesday manuscripts suggests that one or more Englishmen were involved in the final stages of that enquiry (Sawyer, 1956). The officials who were apparently least affected by the Conquest were the moneyers and well into the twelfth century most of these appear from their names to have been natives (Dolley, 1966b).

The replacement of the main royal agents by foreigners meant that English was no longer the language of government. It is not surprising that the sealed writs by which royal grants were notified to the shire court, and which before the Conquest had always been in English, were after 1070 in Latin; by then few of the addressees could have understood an English writ. It is likely that many of them did not understand Latin either, but the churchmen did, the bishops and clerks who provided the literate personnel of Anglo-Norman government, and it was their activity that ensured that Latin was the language of twelfth-century English government. The language spoken by most of the invaders was, of course, Norman French. William abandoned his attempt to learn English but in the second generation many, like Henry I, had been brought up in England and knew at least some English. Even as late as the end of the twelfth century there were some distinguished men, like William Longchamp, bishop of Ely, chancellor and later justiciar, who had the disadvantage of knowing no English, but Richard fitz Nigel's account of the situation a century after the Conquest is probably correct for the majority of the free landholders of any stance: 'Nowadays, when English and Normans live close together and marry and give in marriage to each other, the nations are so mixed that it can scarcely be decided (I mean in the case of freemen) who is of English birth and who of Norman' (*Dialogus*, p. 53).

It is well known that French, or more strictly Anglo-Norman, the language of this Anglo-Norman aristocracy, deeply influenced the English language, but it should perhaps be emphasized that this influence belongs more to the thirteenth and fourteenth centuries than to the twelfth. Unfortunately there are very few texts that can be assigned with confidence to the twelfth century, but the Peterborough Chronicle is certainly one of them. The last section of this work, written after 1154, shows developments in orthography, grammar and syntax that are in part due to French influence and there is also a small number of French loan words limited 'to words associated with government or with the ruling classes' (Clark, 1970, p. lxix). There are also loans from Norse and, most numerous of all, from Latin. This text was, of course, written for a monastery, a bilingual or trilingual community of Anglo-Normans, in which French (and Latin) influence is not unexpected. What is perhaps surprising is how slight that French influence was even a century after the Conquest. At that time French, or Anglo-Norman, had probably affected the speech of the majority, that is the unfree, even less, but in the nature of things the language of the illiterate is hard to study.

It seems likely that, however bilingual the Anglo-Norman aristocracy may have been, there were problems of communication with the mass of the people. Few leading churchmen had the advantage of Samson, abbot of Bury St Edmunds, in being able to preach in his native Norfolk dialect. By the end of the century the demand for preaching that could be understood by the English who knew no French or Latin led to the production of collections of homilies and other religious writings in English, and French influence is more clearly marked in these than in the Peterborough Chronicle. The progress of that influence can be well illustrated by a comparison of the two versions of Layamon's *Brut* separated by about a generation in the first half of the thirteenth century (Serjeantson, 1935, pp. 117–20). The real flood of French loan words into English began in the thirteenth century, after the loss of Normandy, and was due in large measure to the general admiration then felt for French civilization. French literature provided models for many European literatures, German and Icelandic as well as English, French church architecture was widely acknowledged to be the ideal, and Paris housed the greatest university of Christian Europe. French influenced other European languages besides English, including Italian and, if less permanently, German. The reason French influence was particularly strong in England was the fact that the English aristocracy was French-speaking. That was certainly a consequence of the Norman Conquest, but for more than a century after that conquest the language of the conquerors had very little effect on that of the conquered.

The gulf between the Anglo-Norman aristocracy and the English majority is to some extent obscured by the revolution in personal nomenclature that followed the Conquest. The names used by the conquerors very quickly gained popularity and long before the end of the twelfth century the majority of people for whom we have evidence had names that were virtually unknown in England before 1066. The total number of these post-Conquest innovations is large but a very small number soon became conspicuously popular and were very frequently used. These popular names tended to be those that were favoured by the royal family and their closest connections, and a study of twelfth-century Essex documents has revealed that the most popular names were William, Robert, Richard, Ralph, Roger, Hugo, Walter and, among the less popular, John. In a collection of deeds from the following century 250 individuals are named, 160 of whom shared six names, the most popular then being William and John (Reaney, 1958, pp. xix–xx). This transformation of personal nomenclature happened first in London, where already by the end of the twelfth century English names were rare and those that do occur seem often to have been the names of immigrants from the provinces where habits were more conservative (Ekwall, 1947, p. 90).

The effect of the Norman Conquest on the personal nomenclature of England has been compared with that of the ninth-century Scandinavian conquests, but there are significant differences. The Scandinavians not only introduced a large number of names, they also had an active tradition of name formation with the result that by the eleventh century many Scandinavian names, including some formed in England, were current in the Danelaw (Fellows Jensen, 1968). There was, however, no concentration on a few popular names, and the continuing vitality of name formation is in marked contrast with the stable stock of names introduced by the Normans. Another significant difference is that, whereas the Scandinavian names were grafted on to, and became part of, an Anglo-Scandinavian personal nomenclature which included many English names, after the Norman Conquest English names were replaced by continental ones; there was very little that was English about the Anglo-Norman stock of names. There are about as many cases of parents with Scandinavian names giving their children English names as of the reverse process, but very few English names were given by parents with French ones; the change was almost always in the other direction (Fellows Jensen, 1968, pp. lxii–lxiv; Ekwall, 1947, pp. 91–8). It would therefore be unsafe to assume that a French name after the middle of the twelfth century implies French ancestry. The onomastic revolution after the Norman Conquest cannot be used as a measure of the scale of French immigration, or of the scale and intensity of other forms of French influence.

The first people to be affected were naturally the aristocracy, the landholders and prominent burgesses. Already before the end of the eleventh century notable Englishmen were giving French names to their children and according to Ekwall this was common in London by 1100 (Ekwall, 1947, p. 98). The name-giving habits of the peasants changed more slowly and are less well documented. Even in the thirteenth and fourteenth centuries Old English and Scandinavian names continued in use in some parts of England, and it may well be that many names have escaped our records, for later surnames and field names show the survival of some pre-Conquest names that are otherwise unrecorded (Voitl, 1963; Reaney, 1953; von Feilitzen, 1945). It is probable that the records of the twelfth and thirteenth century do not fully reveal the scale of the survival of English names among the unremembered poor and that even in this respect the gulf between the Anglo-Norman aristocracy and the mass of the peasantry was larger than it appears to have been.

As well as the displacement of the English from positions of power and influence as agents of the king, there was a wholesale replacement or subordination of English landowners. In 1086 Englishmen held slightly more than a twentieth of the total landed wealth of England as tenants in chief of the king, and only two held extensive estates, Thurkill of Warwick and Coleswein of Lincoln, and neither was large by the standards of the Norman invaders. Indeed, one of the most striking features of the distribution of land at the end of William the Conqueror's reign is the way in which a very small group held a very large proportion of the available land. In Domesday Book 20 of William's followers held between them well over half the land that had been distributed to laymen, which itself amounted to about half the total land described (Corbett, 1926, pp. 507–11). This was a remarkable change from the situation in 1065 when there were a few great lay estates, notably those belonging to the earls, but when most of England was held by relatively small landowners. Many of these men forfeited their estates by opposing William in 1066 or in later revolts, and some went into exile in Scotland, Denmark or even farther afield to Byzantium where the English formed a distinctive element in the Varangian Guard (Stenton, 1970, pp. 325–44). Some estates were seized violently in the confusion of the Conquest, but William's aim seems to have been 'that every child should be his father's heir', and many transfers were at least cloaked with legitimacy. Some such ordered transfer is implied by the cases in Domesday Book of individual Normans holding all the estates of one or more Englishmen, their *antecessores*. After William's death the Normans continued to extend their conquests, and they also continued to displace the English survivors, the most notable case being Hugh de Beaumont's acquisition of Thurkill's estates. Thurkill's heirs survived in the twelfth century as subtenants of a small part of his former estate and many other English families are later found in a similar situation, as subtenants on part of their former property. It was at this level that the English élite survived. These men had little wealth, power or influence at court but they must have played a significant part in the life of the local community, both in the village and perhaps the shire, and must have been important agents of the continuity from pre-Conquest to Anglo-Norman England, and it seems likely that it was in this group that intermarriage was most frequent and bilingualism most common.

The Normans were quick to seize the opportunities that English towns offered them. Men came from Rouen and Caen to London, and at Norwich, Nottingham and elsewhere French boroughs grew up alongside the English ones. But even in London, where this foreign immigration was apparently greatest, the English survived both as the majority of the population and also as a significant element in the urban élite. As late as 1130 most of the aldermen of London were English and at the same date about half the people named in a list of St Paul's tenants had English names and were probably of English descent. The French element among the canons of St Paul's was greater but in 1115 three or four of them had English names as against eight or nine with French ones (Ekwall, 1947, pp. 100–17).

One of the most remarkable testimonies to the vigour of the Normans is their architectural achievement. Already before the conquest of England they were constructing large buildings that excited the admiration of contemporaries. After the Conquest they rebuilt the major English churches with such enthusiasm that our knowledge of Anglo-Saxon architecture has to be based on the smaller churches that escaped their attentions. In contrast, the superiority of English painting and drawing over the Norman is and was then recognized (Wormald, 1944). Already before the Conquest Norman manuscript illumination owed much to English models and the Bayeux Tapestry is of English design as well as workmanship (Alexander, 1970; Stenton, 1965b). The English delight in linear design gave their architectural sculpture a flat aspect and after the Conquest the Normans, who employed English sculptors in some of their most important buildings such as Ely and Durham, seem to have been so influenced by the English tradition that the promise of early eleventh-century Norman sculpture was not fulfilled, and even in Normandy there was a tendency to treat 'sculpture as surface enrichment' (Zarnecki, 1966).

There are very interesting differences between the general effect achieved in the romanesque churches of England and Normandy. Later rebuilding has not left much of the first Norman churches in England but enough has survived, e.g., at Blyth, Winchester and Lastingham, to show that they were very similar in form and decoration to the contemporary churches of Normandy. The Normans were, however, soon greatly influenced by the English enthusiasm for 'surface enrichment'. The beak-head ornament, so familiar in and largely confined to village churches, was certainly an English contribution and it may be that the chevron ornament, which is such a distinctive feature of twelfth-century Anglo-Norman architecture, also had an English origin; it was certainly first used at Durham (Borg, 1967). The result of this blending of English decorative tradition with Norman architectural skills was the development of an Anglo-Norman style which, in its tendency to elaborate geometric decoration, is very different from the austere elegance of eleventh-century Norman architecture. Durham, which is commonly regarded as one of the finest of all Norman churches in England, is in fact very different from the Norman churches of Normandy and should be recognized as one of the earliest and best examples of a distinctive Anglo-Norman tradition.

The Normans, who seem to have appreciated and even admired English painting, drawing, sculpture and decoration, could not understand Old English and consequently the native vernacular tradition was soon undermined. The literature of the twelfth century was in Latin and Anglo-Norman, but some of its subject-matter was English. In the twelfth century there was an almost antiquarian interest in the English past which led to such works as William of Malmesbury's *Gesta Regum* and *Gesta Pontificum* as well as Gaimar's *Estorie des Engleis*, and Latin versions of the Old English laws were produced. There was also some copying of other English texts and Neil Ker has catalogued 27 manuscripts containing Old English written about 1100 or later, and these include the two main collections of laws, the Peterborough version of the *Chronicle* and several collections of homilies. He has also demonstrated from additions, notes and glosses that older manuscripts 'were valued and commonly consulted until at earliest the end of the twelfth century' (Ker, 1957, p. xlviii).

The Norman Conquest has been described as a cultural disaster but that is to do less than justice either to the Norman contribution to English architecture or to the willingness of the conquerors to accept what the English had to offer. The Anglo-Norman culture of the twelfth century owed as much to England as it did to Normandy.

The Normans were a remarkably adaptable people and William and his sons ruled England in much the same way as English kings had done, using and improving the machinery of English royal government. The Norman aristocracy did not fit quite as neatly into the shoes of their English *antecessores*, not because they were determined to impose an alien system or were unwilling to accept what they found, but because the scale of their landholding made more elaborate subtenancies necessary, and their continuing demand for money and men led to important developments in the way obligations were assessed. The Normans did not attempt to reproduce in England the society with which they were familiar in Normandy, although their background and their continuing continental interests ensured that English society would never be the same again. Many of the distinctive features of Anglo-Norman England were, therefore, neither survivals from pre-Conquest England nor Norman importations but were in fact created in England after the Conquest. In the current controversy about the evolution of Anglo-Norman feudalism, no one now maintains that it was 'brought fully fledged from France' (Prestwich, 1963; Harvey, 1970). The evolutionary character of the Norman Conquest has recently been further underlined by the suggestion that the motte, for long taken as a symbol of Norman innovation in the art of war, was itself developed in England during the campaigns of the Conquest (Davison, 1967). It was in their willingness to experiment, to use what they found to hand, as in the art of government, and to devise new solutions and change old habits, as in the arts of war and building, that the Norman conquerors showed their extraordinary adaptability and resourcefulness. The result, in the twelfth century, was a society that was neither Norman nor English but was, in a very real sense, Anglo-Norman.

Bibliographical note

The main purpose of this bibliographical note is to draw attention to some recent publications, many of which also serve as guides to earlier literature. Sir Frank Stenton (1971, pp. 688–730) and Professor Dorothy Whitelock (*EHD*, a second edition is due to appear in 1978) have provided very full and critical bibliographical surveys, which may be supplemented for the eleventh century by Douglas and Greenaway (1953) and Altschul (1969). Annual lists of current publications are provided, without comment, in *ASE*.

Sources

The best general guides are *EHD* and Douglas and Greenaway (1953), and, for the early period, Dumville (1977a). Manuscripts containing Old English are listed and fully described by Ker (1957), supplement (1976). The earliest manuscripts are all listed with full bibliographies in *CLA*, vol. 2 of which, devoted to British Libraries, is now in a second edition (1972). Bishop (1971) is an important study of tenth- and eleventh-century manuscripts. Current work is listed in *Scriptorium*.

Plummer's edition of the Parker and Peterborough versions of the *Chronicle* has been reissued with a note on the commencement of the year and a revised bibliography by Dorothy Whitelock in 1952. There are two main translations. Garmonsway's is a direct rendering of the texts in Plummer, with the same pagination, and Whitelock *et al.* (1961) is particularly valuable in showing how versions differ and in providing corrected dates. Both have excellent bibliographies, as does Parkes (1976). Most other chronicles are listed and discussed in *EHD* and Douglas and Greenaway (1953). Recent publications include Hunter Blair (1964), Offler (1970) and Baker (1975) on the *Historia Regum* attributed to Simeon of Durham. Davies (1977) has drawn attention to the potential value of the earliest entries in some late chronicles. For Welsh annals Hughes (1973) is important. While awaiting his new edition of the *Historia Brittonum* it is necessary to refer to Dumville (1975, 1977c). Irish sources are discussed by Hughes (1972) and for the earliest Irish annals see Smyth (1972).

The text of Gildas' *De excidio Britanniea*, published by Mommsen and with a parallel translation by Williams, needs revision, see Davies (1939), Winterbottom (1976) and Dumville (1977a, pp. 183–4). On his language see Kerlouégan (1968) and Winterbottom (1977) and on his historical importance Miller (1975a). Its date is discussed by Miller (1975c). For Bede's *Historia Ecclesiastica* Plummer's edition is indispensable including, among other things, a superb index and a chronological analysis that is followed here, subject to the corrections proposed by Harrison (1976). Colgrave and Mynors include readings from the Leningrad manuscript and print a parallel translation. The most illuminating modern discussions of Bede are Campbell (1966) and Hunter Blair (1970a). Bonner (1976) covers many aspects of Bede's life and work, and Hunter Blair (1970b) is an attractive introduction to his other writings. The reliability of Asser's *Life of Alfred*, ed. Stevenson (1904), has been demonstrated by Whitelock (1968).

Bolton (1967) is the first part of a general survey of the Latin literature of the period, and for the vernacular literature the papers in Stanley (1966) may be supplemented by Gatch (1976). Recent studies of particular writers include Winterbottom (1977) on Aldhelm and Hunter Blair (1976) on Alcuin. Letters and letter collections are described and discussed in *EHD*, pp. 571–9, and saints' *Lives* in *EHD*, pp. 568–71 and Woolf (1966). Adomnán's *Life of Columba* has been edited and translated by the Andersons, and other Irish lives are discussed by Hughes (1972, pp. 217–47). The *List of Saints' Resting Places* has been discussed by Rollason (1978); Battiscombe (1956) contains detailed studies of the shrine of one saint, Cuthbert, and his relics. Hohler (1975) is a vigorous demonstration of the importance of liturgical texts. For coronation *Ordines* see Nelson (1977; 1978).

The main edition of English laws is Liebermann (1903–16). Attenborough (1922) and Robertson (1925) are more accessible and provide parallel translations, Downer (1972) has edited, translated and discussed the *Laws of Henry I*. For the background to the laws see now Wormald (1977b). The importance, and relevance, of Irish laws has been demonstrated by Binchy (1943), and for a recent discussion see Hughes (1972). The value of genealogies and king-lists has long been recognized. Some texts have recently been published by Dumville (1976) and the problems that have to be faced in using them are helpfully discussed by Dumville (1977b). For episcopal lists see Page (1965; 1966).

Recent research on charters has been reviewed by Brooks (1972). All pre-Conquest English charters are listed in Sawyer (1968), with references to manuscripts and discussions. The publication of a new edition by the British Academy has begun with Campbell (1973a) on Rochester and Sawyer (1978a) on Burton. Some new manuscripts have been discovered, notably the original of S 1031, now printed by Barlow (1970, pp. 333–5). The most recent addition to the county lists published by Finberg and Hart is Hart (1975). Gelling (1976) is a major contribution to the study of charter boundaries. For Welsh charters see Davies (1973a). The study of Domesday Book was put on a sound footing by Galbraith (1961). Important recent contributions are Harvey (1971; 1975). The *Domesday Geography* has been completed; its conclusions are summarized in Darby (1977), who also provides a key to the whole enterprise.

It is particularly difficult to keep abreast of archaeological discoveries and the surveys in Wilson (1976) already need revision. Current work is listed in *Med. Arch.* It is also necessary to consult the relevant issues of *British Archaeological Reports* and the *Research Reports* of the Council for British Archaeology. The publication of Sutton Hoo has begun (Bruce-Mitford, 1976). The standard work on churches is Taylor and Taylor (1965) and a third volume has been announced. The remarkable recent developments in numismatic studies have been reviewed by Lyon (1976), and the material is being made more accessible thanks to the *Sylloge* of coins being published by the British Academy. Particular attention may be drawn to Blunt (1974), Blunt, Lyon and Stewart (1963), Dolley and Skaare (1961), Dolley and Blunt (1961), Dolley (1966a), Grierson (1961a) and Metcalf (1974). The English Place-Name Society continues to publish county surveys. Recent work in place-name studies has been reviewed by Cameron (1976) and by Fellows Jensen (1973; 1978). Baugh (1957) is a good general book on linguistic history.

Secondary works

The standard work on Roman Britain is Frere (1967). The best general guide to current work is provided by *Britannia*. Many books and articles have been devoted to the end of Roman rule in Britain and to the obscure period that followed. They are discussed by Dumville (1977a). Recent developments in the study of early English settlements are commented on, with particular reference to Hampshire, by Biddle (1976c). Of the many general books on English history before the Norman Conquest particular attention may be drawn to *EHD* with its detailed references to, and many translations of, the sources. The best book on the conversion is Mayr-Harting (1972), supplemented by Campbell (1971; 1973b), articles of major importance. Attention should also be drawn to John (1970) and to Sims-Williams (1975; 1976), and to the papers in Kirby (1974). Important contributions to the discussion of the monastic reformation of the tenth century are reprinted in John (1960; 1966). The papers in Parsons (1975) cover most aspects of that topic. For the non-monastic church in the eleventh century the standard work is Barlow (1963).

Bullough (1965) is a most valuable discussion of recent work on early English society, including Aston's demonstration (1958) of the antiquity of the manor. Charles-Edwards (1972) uses Irish evidence to illuminate early developments in England and Charles-Edwards (1976a) has a more general interest than its title may suggest. The range of current work on settlement is well represented by the papers in Sawyer (1976), and Fellows Jensen (1975) reviews the evidence for Viking settlements in particular.

The development of royal government in and after the tenth century is described, and put in its continental context, by Campbell (1975b) and Whitelock (1959) is also important. Work done on towns since Tait (1936) has been conveniently summarized by Reynolds (1977). For early urban developments see Biddle (1974; 1976a), and on particular towns the articles and maps in Lobel (1969), and in Lobel and Johns (1975). For Winchester see Biddle (1976b).

There are several good surveys of the Norman Conquest. Douglas (1964) is the fullest with an excellent bibliography, Barlow (1965) and Loyn (1967) are good introductions and Brown (1969) is an excellent statement of what may be called a conservative view. The Conquest has been put in its continental background by Le Patourel (1976). The prolonged debate on feudalism has been reviewed by Prestwich (1963), and see now Brown (1973). Military institutions are fully discussed by Hollister (1962; 1965) and the economic aspects very thoroughly treated by Lennard (1959).

The best introduction to the Celtic parts of the British Isles is pro-

vided by Binchy's revised edition of Dillon and Chadwick (1972). For
Scotland Duncan (1975) is a major work of synthesis, with a good
bibliography. For Wales Lloyd (1939) may be supplemented by Jones
(1972), and for the early period Davies (1978). For Ireland Hughes
(1966), Mac Niocaill (1972) and Ó Corráin (1972) are good general
introductions, and for Irish society Binchy (1970b) is of fundamental
importance.

Bibliography

A guide to journal abbrevations are on p. x.

Abt – Laws of Æthelberht, ed Liebermann i. 3–8; trans. Attenborough 1922, pp. 4–17; cf. *EHD* 29.

ADDYMAN, P. V. and LEIGH, D. (1973), 'The Anglo-Saxon village at Chalton, Hampshire: Second interim report', *Med. Arch.* 17, pp. 1–25.

ADOMNÁN, *Life of Columba*, ed A. O. and M. O. Anderson, Edinburgh, 1961.

AETHELWEARD, *The Chronicle of Æthelweard*, ed A. Campbell, London, 1962.

ALCOCK, L. (1971), *Arthur's Britain: History and archaeology A.D. 367–634*.

ALDHELM, *Opera*, ed R. Ehwald, in *MGH AA* 15, 1919.

ALEXANDER, J. J. G. (1970), *Norman Illumination at Mont St Michel, 966–1100*, London.

Alf – Laws of Alfred, ed Liebermann i. 16–89; trans. Attenborough 1922, pp. 62–93; cf. *EHD* 33.

ALTSCHUL, M. (1969), *Anglo-Norman England*, Cambridge.

ANDERSON, M. O. (1973), *Kings and Kingship in Early Scotland*, Edinburgh.

APPLEBAUM, S. (1972), 'Roman Britain', in H. P. R. Finberg (ed.), *The Agrarian History of England and Wales*, I, ii Cambridge, 1972, pp. 5–267.

APPLEBAUM, S. (1975), 'Some observations on the economy of the Roman villa at Bignor, Sussex', *Britannia* 6, pp. 118–32.

Armeis Prydein. The Prophecy of Britain, ed Sir Ifor Williams, English version by Rachel Bromwich, Dublin, 1972.

As – Laws of Athelstan, ed Liebermann i. 146–83; trans. Attenborough 1922, pp. 122–69; cf. *EHD* 35–7.

ASSER, *Life of King Alfred*, ed W. H. Stevenson 1904, reissued with additions by Dorothy Whitelock, Oxford, 1959.

ASTON, T. H. (1958), 'The Origins of the Manor in England', *TRHS*, 5th ser., 8, pp. 59–83.

Atr – Laws of Æthelred, ed Liebermann i. 216–70; trans. Robertson 1925, pp. 5231–3; cf. *EHD* 42–6.

ATTENBOROUGH, F. L. (1922), *The Laws of the Earliest English Kings*, London.

BAKER, D. (1975), 'Scissors and paste: Corpus Christi, Cambridge, MS. 139 again', *St. Church Hist.* 11, pp. 83–123.

BANNERMAN, J. (1974), *Studies in the History of Dalriada*, Edinburgh.
BARING, F. (1896), 'Domesday Book and the Burton Cartulary', in D.C. Douglas and G. W. Greenaway, *English Historical Documents, ii, 1042–1189*, London, 1953, pp. 98–102.
BARLEY, M. W. and HANSON, R. P. C. (eds) (1968), *Christianity in Britain, 300–700*, Leicester.
BARLOW, F. (1963), *The English Church 1000–1066: A constitutional history*, London.
BARLOW, F. (1965), *William I and the Norman Conquest*, London.
BARLOW, F. (1970), *Edward the Confessor*, London.
BARROW, G. W. S. (1969), 'Northern English society in the early Middle Ages', *Northern Hist.* 4, pp. 1–28.
BARROW, G. W. S. (1973), *The Kingdom of the Scots; Government, Church and Society from the Eleventh to the Fourteenth Century*, London.
BARTLEY, D. D., CHAMBERS, C. and HART–JONES, B. (1976), 'The vegetational history of parts of South and East Durham', *New Phytologist* 77, pp. 437–68.
BARTRUM, P. C. (1970), 'Rhieinwg and Rheinwg', *BBCS* 24, pp. 23–7.
BATTISCOMBE, C. F. (1956), *The Relics of St. Cuthbert*, Oxford.
BAUGH, A. C. (1957), *A History of the English Language*, 2nd edn, London.
BEDE, *Historia Ecclesiastica Gentis Anglorum*, ed C. Plummer, *Venerabilis Baedae Opera Historica*, 2 vols, Oxford, 1896; trans. B. Colgrave and R. A. B. Mynors, *Bede's Ecclesiastical History of the English People*, Oxford, 1969.
BEDE *VC* – Bede, *Prose Life of St Cuthbert*, ed and trans. B. Colgrave, 1960, pp. 142–307.
BEOWULF – *Beowulf and the Fight at Finnsburg*, ed F. Klaeber, 3rd edn, Boston, 1941; trans. G. N. Garmonsway and J. Simpson *Beowulf and its Analogues*, London, 1968, pp. 3–83.
BIDDLE, M. (1974), 'The development of the Anglo-Saxon town', *Topografia Urbana e Vita Cittadina nell'alto medioevo in Occidente* (Settimane di studio del Centro Italiano di Studi sull'alto medioevo, 21; Spoleto), pp. 203–30.
BIDDLE, M. (1976a), 'Towns' in D. M. Wilson (ed.), *The Archaeology of Anglo-Saxon England*, London, 1976, pp. 99–150.
BIDDLE, M. (1976b), *Winchester in the Early Middle Ages*, Oxford.
BIDDLE, M. (1976c), 'Hampshire and the origins of Wessex', *Problems in Economic and Social Archaeology*, ed G. de G. Sieveking *et al.*, London, pp. 323–42.
BIDDLE, M. and HILL, D. (1971), 'Late Saxon planned towns' *Antiquaries J.* 51, pp. 70–85.
BIDDLE, M. and HUDSON, D. M. (1973), *The Future of London's Past: A survey of the archaeological implications of planning and development in the nation's capital*, Worcester.

BIELER, L. (1963), *The Irish Penitentials*, Dublin.

BINCHY, D. A. (1943), 'The linguistic and historical value of the Irish law tracts', *PBA* 29, pp. 195–227.

BINCHY, D. A. (1970a), *Celtic and Anglo-Saxon Kingship*, Oxford.

BINCHY, D. A. (1970b), *Críth Gablach*, Dublin.

BIRCH, W. de G. (1885–99), *Cartularium Saxonicum*, 3 vols and index, London.

BIRCH, W. de G. (1892), *Liber Vitae: Register and martyrology of New Minster and Hyde Abbey*, London.

BISHOP, T. A. M. (1971), *English Caroline Minuscule*, Oxford.

BLUNT, C. E. (1974), 'The coinage of Athelstan, King of England 924–39', *Brit. Numismatic J.* 42, pp. 35–160.

BLUNT, C. E., LYON, C. S. S. and STEWART, B. H. I. H. (1963), 'The coinage of Southern England, 796–840', *Brit. Numismatic J.* 32, pp. 1–74.

BOLTON, W. F. (1967), *A History of Anglo-Latin Literature 597–1066*, Princeton.

BONIFACE, *The Letters of Saint Boniface*, trans. E. Emerton, New York, 1940.

BONNER, G. (ed.) (1976), *Famulus Christi: Essays in commemoration of the thirteenth centenary of the birth of the Venerable Bede*, London.

BONNEY, D. J. (1969), 'Two tenth-century Wiltshire Charters concerning land at Avon and at Collingbourne', *Wilts. Arch. Mag.* 64, pp. 56–64.

BONNEY, D. J. (1972), 'Early boundaries in Wessex', *Archaeology and the Landscape*, ed P. J. Fowler, London, 1972, pp. 168–86.

BONNEY, D. J. (1976), 'Early boundaries and estates in Southern England' in P. H. Sawyer (ed.), *Medieval Settlement: Continuity and change*, London, 1976, pp. 72–82.

BORG, A. (1967), 'The development of chevron ornament', *J. Brit. Arch. Assoc.* 30, pp. 122–40.

BROMWICH, R. (1961), *Trioedd Ynys Prydein: The Welsh Triads*, Cardiff.

BROOKS, N. (1971), 'The development of military obligations in eighth- and ninth-century England', in P. Clemoes and K. Hughes (eds), *England before the Conquest: Studies presented to Dorothy Whitelock*, Cambridge, 1971, pp. 69–84.

BROOKS, N. (1972), 'Anglo-Saxon charters: The work of the last twenty years', *ASE* 3, pp. 211–31.

BROWN, R. A. (1969), *The Normans and the Norman Conquest*, London.

BROWN, R. A. (1973), *Origins of English Feudalism*, London.

BROWN, T. J. (1972), 'Northumbria and the Book of Kells', *ASE* 1, pp. 219–46.

BRUCE-MITFORD, R. (1972), *The Sutton Hoo Ship-Burial: A handbook*, 2nd edn, London.

BRUCE-MITFORD, R. (1976), *The Sutton Hoo Ship-Burial I: Excavations, background, the ship, dating and inventory*, London.

BULLOUGH, D. A. (1965), 'Anglo-Saxon institutions and early English society', *Annali della Fondazione italiana per la storia amministrativa* 2, pp. 647–59.

BYRNE, F. J. (1973), *Irish Kings and High-Kings*, London.

CAM, H. M. (1932), 'Manerium cum hundredo: The hundred and the hundredal manor', *EHR* 47, pp. 353–76; reprinted in H. M. Cam, *Liberties and Communities in Medieval England*, Cambridge, 1944, pp. 64–90.

CAM, H. M. (1933), 'Early groups of hundreds' in *Historical Essays in Honour of James Tait*, ed, J. G. Edwards *et al.* Manchester, pp. 13–25; reprinted in H. M. Cam, *Liberties and Communities in Medieval England*, Cambridge, 1944, pp. 91–106.

CAM, H. M. (1944), *Liberties and Communities in Medieval England*, Cambridge.

CAMERON, K. (1968), 'Eccles in English place-names', in M. W. Barley and R. P. C. Hanson (eds), *Christianity in Britain, 300–700*, Leicester, 1968, pp. 87–92.

CAMERON, K. (1976), 'The significance of English place-names', *PBA* 62, pp. 135–55.

CAMPBELL, A. (1973a), *The Charters of Rochester*, British Academy.

CAMPBELL, J. (1966), 'Bede', in T. A. Dorey (ed.), *Latin Historians*, London, 1966, pp. 159–90.

CAMPBELL, J. (1971), 'The first century of Christianity in England', *Ampleforth J.* 76, pp. 12–29.

CAMPBELL, J. (1973b), 'Observations on the conversion of England', *Ampleforth J.* 78, pp. 12–26.

CAMPBELL, J. (1975a), 'Norwich', in M. D. Lobel and W. H. Johns (eds), *The Atlas of Historic Towns*, 2, London, 1975.

CAMPBELL, J. (1975b), 'Observations on English government from the tenth to the twelfth century', *TRHS*, 5th ser., 25, pp. 39–54.

CASEY, J. and REECE, R. (eds) (1974), *Coins and the Archaeologist*, London.

CHADWICK, H. M. (1905), *Studies in Anglo-Saxon Institutions*, Cambridge.

CHADWICK, H. M. (1907), *The Origin of the English Nation*, Cambridge.

CHADWICK, N. K. (1955), *Poetry and Letters in Early Christian Gaul*, London.

CHADWICK, N. K. (ed.) (1964), *Celt and Saxon*, Cambridge.

CHARLES-EDWARDS, T. M. (1972), 'Kinship, status and the origins of the hide', *PP.* 56, pp. 3–33.

CHARLES-EDWARDS, T. M. (1974), 'Native political organization in Roman Britain and the origin of MW *brenhin*', in M. Mayrhofer *et al.* (eds), *Antiquitates Indogermanicae ... Gedenkschrift für Hermann Guntert*, Innsbruck, 1974, pp. 35–45.

CHARLES-EDWARDS, T. M. (1976a), 'The distinction between land and moveable wealth in Anglo-Saxon England', in P. H. Sawyer (ed.), *Medieval Settlement: Continuity and change*, London, 1976, pp. 180–7.

CHARLES-EDWARDS, T. M. (1976b), 'The social background to Irish *Peregrinatio*', *Celtica* 11, pp. 43–59.

Chronicle, ed C. Plummer, *Two of the Saxon Chronicles Parallel*, Oxford, 1899; trans. by G. N. Garmonsway, *The Anglo-Saxon Chronicle*, 2nd edn, London, 1960; and by D. Whitelock *et al.*, *The Anglo-Saxon Chronicle: A revised translation*, London, 1961.

CLARK, C. (1970), *The Peterborough Chronicle 1070–1154*, Oxford.

CLEMOES, P. and HUGHES, K. (eds) (1971), *England Before the Conquest: Studies presented to Dorothy Whitelock*, Cambridge.

Cn – Laws of Cnut, ed Liebermann i. 273–371; trans. Robertson 1925, pp. 140–219; cf. *EHD* 47–50.

COLVIN, H. M. (1963), 'The Norman Kings, 1066–1154', in H. M. Colvin (ed.), *The History of the King's Works*, 1, London, 1963, pp. 19–50.

CONSTANTIUS, *Life of St Germanus of Auxerre*, ed with French trans. by R. Borius (Sources Chrétiennes, 112), Paris.

CORBETT, W. J. (1926), 'The development of the duchy of Normandy and the Norman Conquest of England', *Camb. Med. Hist.* 5, pp. 481–520.

COX, B. (1973), 'The significance of the distribution of English place-names in *-hām* in the Midlands and East Anglia', *J. Eng. P-N Soc.* 5, pp. 15–73.

COX, B. (1976), 'The place-names of the earliest English records', *J. Eng. P-N Soc.* 8, pp. 12–66.

CRAMP, R. (1976), 'Monkwearmouth and Jarrow: The archaeological evidence', in G. Bonner (ed.), *Famulus Christi: Essays in commemoration of the thirteenth centenary of the birth of the Venerable Bede*, London, 1976, pp. 5–18.

DARBY, H. C. (1977), *Domesday England*, Cambridge.

DARBY, H. C. and CAMPBELL, E. M. J. (eds) (1962), *The Domesday Geography of South-East England*, Cambridge.

DAVIES, W. (1973a), 'Liber Landavensis: Its construction and credibility', *EHR* 88, pp. 335–51.

DAVIES, W. (1973b), 'Middle Anglia and the Middle Angles', *Midland Hist.* 2, pp. 18–20.

DAVIES, W. (1977), 'Annals and the origin of Mercia', in A. Dornier (ed.) *Mercian Studies*, Leicester, 1977, pp. 17–29.

DAVIES, W. (1978), 'Land and power in early medieval Wales', *PP*.

DAVIES, W. and VIERCK, H. (1974), 'The contexts of *Tribal Hidage*: Social aggregates and settlement patterns', *Frühmittelalterliche Studien* 8, pp. 223–93.

DAVIES, W. H. (1939), 'Gildas: Some textual notes and corrections', *Pap. Brit. Sch. Rome* 15, pp. 42–8.

DAVISON, B. K. (1967), 'The origins of the castle in England', *Arch. J.* 114, pp. 202–11.

DENTON, J. H. (1970), *English Royal Free Chapels 1100–1300*, Manchester.

Dialogus – *Dialogus de Scaccario*, ed C. J. Johnson, London, 1950.

DILLON, M. and CHADWICK, N. K. (1972), *The Celtic Realms*, 2nd edn revd by D. A. Binchy, Dublin.

DODGSON, J. M. (1966), 'The significance of the distribution of the English place-name in -ingas, -inga- in south-east England', Med. Arch. 10, pp. 1–29.

DODGSON, J. M. (1973), 'Place-names from hām distinguished from hamm names in relation to the settlement of Kent, Surrey and Sussex', ASE 2, pp. 1–50.

DOLLEY, R. H. M. (ed.) (1961), Anglo-Saxon Coins, London.

DOLLEY, R. H. M. (1966a), The Hiberno-Norse Coins in the British Museum, London.

DOLLEY, R. H. M. (1966b), The Norman Conquest and the English Coinage, London.

DOLLEY, R. H. M. (1973), 'The Eadgar Millenary – a note on the Bath mint', Seaby's Coin and Medal Bulletin, May 1973, pp. 156–9.

DOLLEY, R. H. M. (1976), 'The coins', in D. M. Wilson (ed.), The Archaeology of Anglo-Saxon England, London, 1976, pp. 349–72.

DOLLEY, R. H. M. and BLUNT, C. E. (1961), 'The chronology of the coins of Ælfred the Great', in R. H. M. Dolley (ed.), Anglo-Saxon Coins, London, 1961, pp. 77–95.

DOLLEY, R. H. M. and SKAARE, K. (1961), 'The coinage of Æthelwulf, king of the West Saxons', in R. H. M. Dolley (ed.), Anglo-Saxon Coins, London, 1961, pp. 63–76.

DORNIER, A. (ed.) (1977), Mercian Studies, Leicester.

DOUGLAS, D. C. (1964), William the Conqueror, London.

DOUGLAS, D. C. and GREENAWAY, G. W. (1953), English Historical Documents, ii, 1042–1189, London.

DOWNER, L. J. (ed.) (1972), Leges Henrici Primi, Oxford.

DUMVILLE, D. N. (1975), '"Nennius" and the Historia Brittonum', Studia Celtica 10–11, pp. 78–95.

DUMVILLE, D. N. (1976), 'The Anglian collection of royal genealogies and regnal lists', ASE 5, pp. 23–50.

DUMVILLE, D. N. (1977a), 'Sub-Roman Britain: History and legend', History, n.s. 62, pp. 173–92.

DUMVILLE, D. N. (1977b), 'Kingship, genealogies and regnal lists', in P. H. Sawyer and I. N. Wood (eds), Early Medieval Kingship, Leeds, 1977, pp. 72–104.

DUMVILLE, D. N. (1977c), 'On the north British section of the Historia Brittonum', Welsh Hist. Rev. 8, pp. 345–54.

DUMVILLE, D. N. (1978), 'The Ætheling: A study in Anglo-Saxon constitutional history', ASE 7.

DUNCAN, A. A. M. (1975), Scotland: The making of the kingdom, Edinburgh.

EDDIUS – The Life of Bishop Wilfrid by Eddius Stephanus, ed B. Colgrave, Cambridge, 1927.

Edg – Laws of Edgar, ed Liebermann i. 192–215; trans. Robertson 1925, pp. 16–39; cf. EHD 39–41.

Edm – Laws of Edmund, ed Liebermann i. 184–91; trans. Robertson 1925, pp. 6–15; cf. *EHD* 38.

Edw – Laws of Edward the Elder, ed Liebermann i. 138–45; trans. Attenborough 1922, pp. 114–21.

EKWALL, E. (1947), *Early London Personal Names*, Lund.

EKWALL, E. (1960), *The Concise Oxford Dictionary of English Place-Names*, Oxford.

Episc. – *Episcopus*, ed Liebermann, i. pp. 477–9.

FAULL, M. L. (1974), 'Roman and Anglian settlement patterns in Yorkshire', *Northern Hist.* 9, pp. 1–25.

FAULL, M. L. (1977), 'British survival in Anglo-Saxon Northumbria', in L. Laing (ed.), *Studies in Celtic Survival*, Oxford, pp. 1–55.

FELIX, *Life of Guthlac*, ed B. Colgrave, Cambridge, 1956.

FELLOWS JENSEN, G. (1968), *Scandinavian Personal Names in Lincolnshire and Yorkshire*, Copenhagen.

FELLOWS JENSEN, G. (1972), *Scandinavian Settlement names in Yorkshire*, Copenhagen.

FELLOWS JENSEN, G. (1973), 'Place-name research and northern history: A survey', *Northern Hist.* 8, pp. 1–23.

FELLOWS JENSEN, G. (1974), 'English place-names such as Doddington and Donnington', *Sydsvenska Ortnamnssällskapets Årsskrift*, pp. 26–65.

FELLOWS JENSEN, G. (1975), 'The Vikings in England: A review', *ASE* 4, pp. 181–206.

FELLOWS JENSEN, G. (1978), 'Place-names and settlement in the North Riding of Yorkshire', *Northern Hist.* 14.

FINBERG, H. P. R. (ed.) (1972a), *The Agrarian History of England and Wales*, I, ii, Cambridge.

FINBERG, H. P. R. (1972b), 'Anglo-Saxon England to 1042', in H. P. R. Finberg (ed.) *The Agrarian History of England and Wales*, I, ii, Cambridge, 1972, pp. 385–525.

FORD, W. J. (1976), 'Some settlement patterns in the central region of the Warwickshire Avon', in P. H. Sawyer (ed.), *Medieval Settlement: Continuity and change*, London, 1976, pp. 274–94.

FOX, C. (1955), *Offa's Dyke*, Oxford.

FRERE, S. S. (1967), *Britannia*, London.

GALBRAITH, V. H. (1961), *The Making of Domesday Book*, Oxford.

GATCH, M. M. (1976), 'Beginnings continued: A decade of studies of Old English prose', *ASE* 5, pp. 225–43.

GELLING, M. (1960), 'The element *hamm* in English place-names: A topographical investigation', *Namn och Bygd* 48, pp. 140–62.

GELLING, M. (1961), 'Place-names and Anglo-Saxon paganism', *Univ. Birm. Hist. J.* 8, pp. 7–25.

GELLING, M. (1967a), 'English place-names derived from the compound *wīchām*', *Med. Arch.* 11, pp. 87–104.

GELLING, M. (1967b), 'The charter bounds of Æscesbyrig and Ashbury', *Berks. Arch. J.* 63, pp. 5–13.

GELLING, M. (1973), 'Further thoughts on pagan place-names' in F. Sandgren (ed.), *Otium et Negotium: Studies presented to Olof von Feilitzen*, Stockholm, pp. 109–28.

GELLING, M. (1976), *The Place-Names of Berkshire, part III*, English Place-Name Society, Cambridge.

GELLING, M. (1977), 'Latin loan words in Old English place-names', *ASE* 6, pp. 1–13.

GILDAS, *De excidio et Conquestu Britanniae*, ed T. Mommsen, *MGH AA* 13, pp. 1–85; ed and trans. H. Williams, *Gildas*, 2 vols, London, 1899–1901.

GLANVILLE, *The Treatise on the Laws and Customs of the Realm of England commonly called Glanville*, ed G. D. G. Hall, London, 1965.

Gododdin – The Gododdin: The oldest Scottish poem, trans. K. Jackson, Edinburgh, 1969.

GRIERSON, P. (1959), 'Commerce in the Dark Ages: A critique of the evidence', *TRHS*, 5th ser., 9, pp. 123–40.

GRIERSON, P. (1961a), 'La fonction sociale de la monnaie en Angleterre aux viie–viiie siècles', *Moneta e Scambi nell'alto medioevo* (Settimane di studio del Centro Italiano di studi sull'alto medioevo, 8; Spoleto), pp. 341–62.

GRIERSON, P. (1961b), 'Sterling', in R. H. M. Dolley (ed.), *Anglo-Saxon Coins*, London, 1961, pp. 266–83.

GRIERSON, P. (1977), *The Origins of Money*, London.

HAMP, E. P. (1975), 'Social gradience in British spoken Latin', *Britannia* 5, pp. 150–62.

HARMER, F. E. (1950), '*Chipping* and *Market*: A lexicographical investigation', in Sir Cyril Fox and B. Dickins (eds), *Early Cultures of North-West Europe*, Cambridge, 1950, pp. 335–57.

HARRISON, K. (1976), *The Framework of Anglo-Saxon History to A.D. 900*, Cambridge.

HART, C. R. (1970), *The Hidation of Northamptonshire*, Leicester.

HART, C. R. (1971), 'The tribal hidage', *TRHS*, 5th ser., 21, pp. 133–57.

HART, C. R. (1973), 'Athelstan "half king" and his family', *ASE* 2, pp. 115–44.

HART, C. R. (1975), *The Early Charters of Northern England and the North Midlands*, Leicester.

HARVEY, S. (1967), 'Royal revenue and Domesday terminology' *Econ. Hist. Rev.* 2nd ser. 20, pp. 221–8.

HARVEY, S. (1970), 'The knight and the knight's fee in England', *PP* 49, pp. 3–43.

HARVEY, S. (1971), 'Domesday Book and its predecessors' *EHR* 86, pp. 753–73.

HARVEY, S. (1975), 'Domesday Book and Anglo-Norman governance', *TRHS*, 5th ser., 25, pp. 175–93.

HAWKES, S. C. (1969), 'Early Anglo-Saxon Kent', *Arch. J.* 126, pp. 186–92.

HAWKES, S. C. (1974), 'Some recent finds of late Roman buckles', *Britannia* 5, pp. 36–93.

HAWKES, S. C. and DUNNING, G. C. (1961), 'Soldiers and settlers in Britain, fourth to fifth century: With a catalogue of animal-ornamented buckles and related belt-fittings', *Med. Arch.* 5, pp. 1–70.

HILL, D. (1969), 'The burghal hidage: The establishment of a text', *Med. Arch.* 13, pp. 84–92.

HILL, D. (1974), 'Offa's and Wat's Dykes – Some exploratory work on the frontier between Celt and Saxon', in T. Rowley (ed.), *Anglo-Saxon Settlement and Landscape*, Oxford, 1974, pp. 102–7.

Historia Brittonum, ed T. Mommsen, *MGH AA* 13, pp. 111–222; trans. A. W. Wade-Evans, *Nennius's 'History of the Britons'*, London, 1938.

Historia de Sancto Cuthberto, in T. Arnold (ed.), *Symeonis Monachi Opera Omnia*, 1, Rolls Series, 1892, pp. 196–214.

HLOTHHERE and EADRIC, Laws of, ed Liebermann i. 9–11; with trans. Attenborough 1922, pp. 18–23; *EHD* 30.

HOHLER, C. E. (1975), 'Some service books of the later Saxon church', in D. Parsons (ed.), *Tenth-Century Studies*, Chichester, 1975, pp. 60–83.

HOLDSWORTH, P. (1976), 'Saxon Southampton: A new review', *Med. Arch.* 20, pp. 26–61.

HOLLISTER, C. W. (1962), *Anglo-Saxon Military Institutions on the Eve of the Norman Conquest*, Oxford.

HOLLISTER, C. W. (1965), *The Military Organization of Norman England*, Oxford.

HOSKINS, W. G. (1963), *Provincial England*, London.

HUGGINS, R. M. (1975), 'The significance of the place-name *wealdhām*', *Med. Arch.* 19, pp. 198–201.

HUGHES, K. (1966), *The Church in Early Irish Society*, London.

HUGHES, K. (1972), *Early Christian Ireland: Introduction to the sources*, London.

HUGHES, K. (1973), 'The Welsh Latin Chronicles: *Annales Cambriae* and related texts', *PBA* 59, pp. 233–58.

HUNTER BLAIR, P. (1950), 'The *Moore Memoranda* on Northumbrian history', in Sir Cyril Fox and B. Dickins (eds), *The Early Cultures of North-West Europe*, Cambridge, 1950, pp. 243–57.

HUNTER BLAIR, P. (1964), 'Some observations on the *Historia Regum* attributed to Symeon of Durham', in N. K. Chadwick (ed.), *Celt and Saxon*, London, 1964, pp. 63–118.

HUNTER BLAIR, P. (1970a), 'The historical writings of Bede', *La Storiografia Altomedioevale* (Settimane di studio del Centro Italiano di studi sull'alto medioevo 17; Spoleto), pp. 197–221.

HUNTER BLAIR, P. (1970b), *The Age of Bede*, London.

HUNTER BLAIR, P. (1971), 'The letters of Pope Boniface V and the mission of Paulinus to Northumbria', in P. Clemoes and K. Hughes (eds), *England before the Conquest: Studies presented to Dorothy Whitelock*, Cambridge, 1971, pp. 5–13.

HUNTER BLAIR, P. (1976), 'From Bede to Alcuin', in G. Bonner (ed.), *Famulus Christi: Essays in commemoration of the thirteenth centenary of the birth of the Venerable Bede*, London, 1976, pp. 239–60.

INE– Laws of Ine, ed. Liebermann i. 89–123; with trans. Attenborough 1922, pp. 36–61; *EHD* 32.

JACKSON, K. (1953), *Language and History in Early Britain*, Edinburgh.

JACKSON, K. (1963), 'Angles and Britons in Northumbria and Cumbria', in O'Donnell, 1963, pp. 60–84.

JACKSON, K. (1964), 'On the Northern British Section in Nennius', in N. K. Chadwick (ed.), *Celt and Saxon*, Cambridge, 1964, pp. 20–62.

JOHN, E. (1960), *Land Tenure in Early England*, Leicester.

JOHN, E. (1966), *Orbis Britanniae*, Leicester.

JOHN, E. (1970), 'The social and political problems of the early English church', in J. Thirsk (ed.), *Land, Church and People: Essays to H. P. R. Finberg*, London, 1970, pp. 39–63.

JOHNSON, S. (1975), 'Vici in Lowland Britain', in W. Rodwell and T. Rowley (eds), *The 'Small Towns' of Roman Britain*, Oxford, pp. 75–83.

JOLLIFFE, J. E. A. (1926), 'Northumbrian Institutions', *EHR* 41, pp. 1–42.

JOLLIFFE, J. E. A. (1933), *Pre-Feudal England: The Jutes*, Oxford.

JONAS, *Life of St Columbanus*, ed B. Krusch, *MGH Scriptores rerum merovingicarum* 4 (1902); partial trans. W. C. McDermott, *Monks, Bishops and Pagans*, Philadelphia, 1949, pp. 75–113.

JONES, G. R. J. (1972), 'Post-Roman Wales', in H. P. R. Finberg (ed.), *The Agrarian History of England and Wales*, I, ii, Cambridge, 1972, pp. 283–382.

JONES, G. R. J. (1975), 'Early territorial organization in Gwynedd and Elmet', *N. Hist.* 10, pp. 3–27.

JONES, G. R. J. (1976), 'Multiple estates and early settlement', in P. H. Sawyer (ed.), *Medieval Settlement: Continuity and change*, London, 1976, pp. 15–40.

KELLEHER, J. V. (1968), 'The pre-Norman Irish genealogies', *Irish Hist. St.* 16, pp. 138–53.

KEMBLE, J. M. (1849), *The Saxons in England*, 2 vols, London.

KENT, J. P. C. (1961), 'From Roman Britain to Saxon England', in R. H. M. Dolley (ed.), *Anglo-Saxon Coins*, London, 1961, pp. 1–22.

KER, N. R. (1957), *A Catalogue of Manuscripts Containing Anglo-Saxon*, Oxford.

KER, N. R. (1976), 'A supplement to *Catalogue of Manuscripts containing Anglo-Saxon*', *ASE* 5, pp. 121–32.

KERLOUÉGAN, F. (1968), 'Le Latin du *De Excidio Britanniae* de Gildas', in

M. W. Barley and R. P. C. Hanson (eds), *Christianity in Britain, 300–700*, Leicester, 1968, pp. 151–76.

KIRBY, D. P. (1963), 'Bede and Northumbrian chronology', *EHR* 78, pp. 514–27.

KIRBY, D. P. (ed.) (1974), *Saint Wilfrid at Hexham*, Newcastle upon Tyne.

LEGG, J. W. (1901), *English Coronation Records*, London.

LENNARD, R. V. (1959), *Rural England 1086–1135*, Oxford.

LE PATOUREL, J. (1966), *Norman Barons*, London.

LE PATOUREL, J. (1971), 'The Norman Succession, 996–1135', *EHR* 86, pp. 225–50.

LE PATOUREL, J. (1976), *The Norman Empire*, Oxford.

LEVISON, W. (1946), *England and the Continent in the Eighth Century*, Oxford.

Liber Vitae Ecclesiae Dunelmensis, intr. by A. H. Thompson, Surtees Soc., 136, 1923.

LIEBERMANN, F. (1903–16), *Die Gesetze der Angelsachsen*, 3 vols, Halle.

Life of Ceolfrith, ed C. Plummer, *Venerabilis Baedae Opera Historica*, Oxford, 1896, i. pp. 388–404; *EHD*, 155.

Life of Cuthbert, ed and trans. B. Colgrave, *Two lives of St Cuthbert*, Cambridge, 1940, pp. 60–139.

Life of Oswald, ed J. Raine, *The Historians of the Church of York*, 1, Rolls Series, 1879, pp. 399–475.

LLOYD, Sir J. E. (1939), *A History of Wales*, 2 vols, 3rd edn, London.

LOBEL, M. D. (ed.) (1969), *The Atlas of Historic Towns*, 1, London.

LOBEL, M. D. and JOHNS, W. H. (eds) (1975), *The Atlas of Historic Towns*, 2, London.

LOSCO-BRADLEY, S. (1974), 'The Anglo-Saxon settlement at Catholme, Barton-under-Needwood, Staffordshire. Interim Report: 1973–4', *Trent Valley Arch. Res. Com. Rep.* no. 8, pp. 3–34.

LOWE, E. A. (1931–71), *Codices Latini Antiquiores*, Oxford.

LOYN, H. R. (1953), 'The term *ealdorman* in the translations prepared at the time of King Alfred', *EHR* 68, pp. 513–25.

LOYN, H. R. (1955), 'Gesiths and thegns in Anglo-Saxon England from the seventh to the tenth century', *EHR* 70, pp. 529–49.

LOYN, H. R. (1961), 'Boroughs and mints, A.D. 900–1066', in R. H. M. Dolley (ed.), *Anglo-Saxon Coins*, London, 1961, pp. 122–35.

LOYN, H. R. (1962), *Anglo-Saxon England and the Norman Conquest*, London.

LOYN, H. R. (1967), *The Norman Conquest*, 2nd edn, London.

LOYN, H. R. (1971), 'Towns in late Anglo-Saxon England: The evidence and some possible lines of enquiry', in P. Clemoes and K. Hughes (eds), *England before the Conquest: Studies presented to Dorothy Whitelock*, Cambridge, 1971, pp. 115–28.

LOYN, H. R. (1974a), 'Kinship in Anglo-Saxon England', *ASE* 3, pp. 197–209.

LOYN, H. R. (1974b), 'The hundred in England in the tenth and early eleventh centuries', in H. Hearder and H. R. Loyn (eds), *British Government and Administration: Studies presented to S. B. Chrimes*, Cardiff, 1974, pp. 1–15.

LOYN, H. R. (1977), *The Vikings in Wales*, London.

LYON, C. S. S. (1971), 'Variations in currency in late Anglo-Saxon England', in R. A. G. Carson (ed.), *Mints, Dies and Currency: Essays in memory of Albert Baldwin*, London, 1971, pp. 101–20.

LYON, C. S. S. (1976), 'Some problems in interpreting Anglo-Saxon coinage', *ASE* 5, pp. 173–224.

LYON, C. S. S. and STEWART, B. H. I. H. (1961), 'The Northumbrian Viking coinage in the Cuerdale hoard', in R. H. M. Dolley (ed.), *Anglo-Saxon Coins*, London, 1961, pp. 96–121.

MACALISTER, R. A. S. (1949), *Corpus Inscriptionum Insularum Celticarum* 2, Dublin.

MacNEILL, M. (1962), *The Festival of Lughnasa*, Oxford.

MAC NIOCAILL, G. (1972), *Ireland before the Vikings*, Dublin.

MAITLAND, F. W. (1897), *Domesday Book and Beyond*, Cambridge.

MANN, J. C. (1961), 'The administration of Roman Britain', *Ant.*, 35, pp. 316–20.

MANN, J. C. (1971), 'Spoken Latin in Britain as evidenced in the inscriptions', *Britannia* 2, pp. 218–24.

MATTHEW, D. (1962), *The Norman Monasteries and their English Possessions*, London.

MAUSS, M. (1969), *The Gift: Forms and functions of exchange in archaic societies*, trans. I. Cunnison (repr.), London.

MAYR-HARTING, H. (1972), *The Coming of Christianity to Anglo-Saxon England*, London.

MEANEY, A. (1964), *A Gazetteer of Early Anglo-Saxon Burial Sites*, London.

MELLOWS, W. T. (1949), *The Chronicle of Hugh Candidus*, London.

METCALF, D. M. (1974), 'Monetary expansion and recession: Interpreting the distribution patterns of seventh- and eighth-century coins', in J. Casey and R. Reece (eds), *Coins and the Archaeologist*, Oxford, 1974, pp. 206–23.

METCALF, D. M. (1977), 'Monetary affairs in Mercia in the time of Æthelbald', in A. Dornier (ed.), *Mercian Studies*, Leicester, 1977, pp. 87–106.

MILLER, M. (1975a), 'Bede's use of Gildas', *EHR* 90, pp. 241–61.

MILLER, M. (1975b), 'Historicity and the pedigrees of the Northcountrymen', *BBCS* 26, pp. 255–80.

MILLER, M. (1975c), 'Relative and absolute publication dates of Gildas's *De Excidio* in medieval scholarship', *BBCS* 26, pp. 169–74.

MILLER, M. (1975d), 'Stilicho's Pictish War', *Britannia* 6, pp. 141–5.

MILLER, M. (1978a), 'Eanfrith's Pictish son', *Northern Hist.* 14.

MILLER, M. (1978b), 'The last British entry in the "Gallic Chronicles"', *Britannia* 9.

MILLER, M. (1979), 'Dates of Deira', *ASE* 8.

MITCHELL, S. K. (1951), *Taxation in Medieval England*, New Haven.

MORRIS, C. D. (1976), 'Pre-conquest sculpture of the Tees Valley', *Med. Arch.* 20, pp. 140–6.

MORRIS, C. D. (1977), 'Northumbria and the Viking settlement: The evidence for landholding', *Arch. Aeliana* 5th ser. 5, pp. 81–103.

MORRIS, J. (1974), Review of J. N. L. Myres and B. Green, *The Anglo-Saxon Cemeteries of Caistor-by-Norwich and Markshall, Norfolk,* 1973, *Med. Arch.* 18, pp. 225–32.

MORRIS, R. (1872), *An Old English Miscellany*, Early English Texts Society, old ser. 49, London.

MORRIS, R. (1978), *The Church in British Archaeology*, Council for British Archaeology.

MORRIS, W. A. (1910), *Frankpledge System*, Harvard Historical Studies 14, Harvard.

MOSSOP, H. R. (1970), *The Lincoln Mint c. 890–1279*, ed V. Smart, Newcastle upon Tyne.

MUSSET, L. (1966), 'Les Conditions financières d'une réussite architecturale: les grandes églises romanes de Normandie', in *Mélanges René Crozet*, Poitiers, pp. 303–13.

MYRES, J. N. L. (1935), 'The Teutonic settlement of northern England', *History* 20, pp. 250–62.

MYRES, J. N. L. (1960), 'Pelagius and the end of Roman rule in Britain', *J. Rom. St.* 50, pp. 21–36.

MYRES, J. N. L. (1969), *Anglo-Saxon Pottery and the Settlement of England*, Oxford.

MYRES, J. N. L. (1970), 'The Angles, the Saxons and the Jutes', *PBA* 56, pp. 145–74.

MYRES, J. N. L. and GREEN, B. (1973), *The Anglo-Saxon Cemeteries of Caistor-by-Norwich and Markshall, Norfolk*, Oxford.

NASH-WILLIAMS, V. E. (1950), *The Early Christian Monuments of Wales*, Cardiff.

NELSON, J. L. (1977), 'Inauguration rituals', in P. H. Sawyer and I. N. Wood (eds), *Early Medieval Kingship*, Leeds, 1977, pp. 50–71.

NELSON, J. L. (1978), 'The earliest royal *Ordo*: Some historical and liturgical aspects', in M. Wilks and B. Tierney (eds), *Festschrift for Walter Ullman*, Cambridge, 1978.

Ó CORRÁIN, D. (1972), *Ireland Before the Normans*, Dublin.

O'DONNELL (1963), *Angles and Britons* (O'Donnell Lectures), Cardiff.

O'DONOVAN, M. A. (1972, 1973), 'An interim revision of episcopal dates for the province of Canterbury, 850–950', I, *ASE* 1, pp. 23–44; II, *ASE* 2, pp. 91–113.

OFFLER, H. S. (1970), 'Hexham and the *Historia Regum*', *Trans. Archit. Arch. Soc. Durham and Northumberland*, n.s. 2, pp. 51–62.

OLSEN, O. and SCHMIDT, H. (1977), *Fyrkat I: Borgen og bebyggelsen*, Copenhagen.

OZANNE, A. (1962), 'The Peak dwellers', *Med. Arch.* 6–7, pp. 15–52.

PAGE, R. I. (1965, 1966), 'Anglo-Saxon episcopal lists', I and II, *Nottingham Med. St.* 9, pp. 78–95; III, ibid., 10, pp. 2–24.

PARKES, M. B. (1976), 'The Palaeography of the Parker Manuscript of the *Chronicle*, Laws and Sedulius, and historiography at Winchester in the late ninth and tenth centuries', *ASE* 5, pp. 149–71.

PARSONS, D. (ed.) (1975), *Tenth-Centuries Studies*, Chichester.

PERCIVAL, J. (1976), *The Roman Villa*, London.

PETERSSON, H. B. A. (1969), *Anglo-Saxon Currency, King Edgar's Reform to the Norman Conquest*, Lund.

PHYTHIAN-ADAMS, C. (1977a), 'Jolly cities: Goodly towns: The current search for England's urban roots', *Urban Hist. Yearbook*, pp. 30–9.

PHYTHIAN-ADAMS, C. (1977b), 'Rutland reconsidered', in A. Dornier (ed.), *Mercian Studies*, Leicester, 1977, pp. 63–84.

PRESTWICH, J. O. (1963), 'Anglo-Norman feudalism and the problem of continuity', *PP* 26, pp. 39–57.

PRESTWICH, J. O. (1968), 'King Æthelhere and the battle of the Winwaed', *EHR* 83, pp. 89–95.

PRINS, A. A. (1952), *French Influence in English Phrasing*, Leiden.

PROCOPIUS, ed and trans. H. B. Dewing, 7 vols, London, 1914–40.

RAHTZ, P. (1976), 'Buildings and rural settlements', in D. M. Wilson (ed.), *The Archaeology of Anglo-Saxon England*, London, 1976, pp. 29–98, 405–52.

RAHTZ, P. (1977), 'The archaeology of West Mercian towns', in A. Dornier (ed.), *Mercian Studies*, Leicester, 1977, pp. 107–29.

REANEY, P. H. (1953), 'Notes on the survival of Old English personal names in Middle English', *Studier i modern Språkvetenskap* 18, pp. 84–112.

REANEY, P. H. (1958), *A Dictionary of British Surnames*, London.

REES, W. (1963), 'Survivals of ancient Celtic custom in medieval England', in O'Donnell, 1963, pp. 148–68.

REYNOLDS, S. (1977), *An introduction to the History of English Medieval Towns*, Oxford.

RICHARDS, M. (1960), 'The Irish settlements in south-west Wales', *J. Roy. Soc. Ant. Ireland* 90, pp. 133–62.

RIVET, A. L. F. (1964), *Town and Country in Roman Britain*, 2nd edn, London.

ROBERTSON, A. J. (1925), *The Laws of the Kings of England from Edmund to Henry I*, Cambridge.

ROBERTSON, A. J. (1956), *Anglo-Saxon Charters*, Cambridge.

ROBERTSON, A. S. (1974), 'Romano-British coin hoards; their numismatic, archaeological and historical significance', in J. Casey and R. Reece (eds), *Coins and the Archaeologist*, Oxford, 1974, pp. 12–36.

ROBERTSON, E. W. (1872), *Historical Essays*, Edinburgh.

RODWELL, W. J. and RODWELL, K. (1977), *Historic Churches – A wasting asset*, Council for British Archaeology, *Research Report* 19, London.

ROELEVELD, W. (1974), *The Holocene Evolution of the Groningen Marine-Clay District, supplement, Berichten van de Rijksdienst voor het Oudheidkundig Bodemonderzoek* 24.

ROESDAHL, E. (1977), *Fyrkat II: Oldsagerne og gravpladsen*, Copenhagen.

ROLLASON, D. (1978), 'List of Saints' resting places in Anglo-Saxon England', *ASE* 7.

ROSS, A. S. C. (1940), *The Terfinnas and Beormas of Ohthere*, Leeds School of English Texts and Monographs 7, Leeds.

ROUND, J. H. (1899), 'The settlement of the south- and east-Saxons', in *The Commune of London and Other Studies*, London, pp. 1–27.

ROWLEY, T. (ed.) (1974), *Anglo-Saxon Settlement and Landscape*, Oxford.

RUTHERFORD, A. (1976), 'Giudi revisited', *BBCS* 26, pp. 440–4.

SAWYER, P. H. (1956), 'The place-names of the Domesday manuscripts', *Bul. John Rylands Lib.* 38, pp. 483–506.

SAWYER, P. H. (1965), 'The wealth of England in the eleventh century', *TRHS* 5th ser. 15, pp. 145–64.

SAWYER, P. H. (1968), *Anglo-Saxon Charters: An annotated list and bibliography*, London.

SAWYER, P. H. (1971), *The Age of the Vikings*, 2nd ed, London.

SAWYER, P. H. (1975a), 'The Charters of Burton Abbey and the unification of England', *Northern Hist.* 10, pp. 28–39.

SAWYER, P. H. (1975b), 'Charters of the reform movement: The Worcester archive', in D. Parsons (ed.), *Tenth-Century Studies*, Chichester, 1975, pp. 84–93.

SAWYER, P. H. (ed.) (1976), *Medieval Settlement: Continuity and change*, London.

SAWYER, P. H. (1977), 'Kings and merchants' in P. H. Sawyer and I. N. Wood (eds), *Early Medieval Kingship*, Leeds, pp. 139–58.

SAWYER, P. H. (1978a), *The Charters of Burton Abbey*, British Academy, London.

SAWYER, P. H. (1978b), 'Some sources for the history of Viking Northumbria', in R. D. Hall (ed.), *Viking Age York and its Context*, Council for British Archaeology, *Research Report* 27, London.

SAWYER, P. H. and WOOD, I. N. (eds) (1977), *Early Medieval Kingship*, Leeds.

SERJEANTSON, M. S. (1935), *A History of Foreign Words in English*, London.

SIMS-WILLIAMS, P. (1975), 'Continental influence at Bath monastery in the seventh century', *ASE* 4, pp. 1–10.

SIMS-WILLIAMS, P. (1976), 'Cuthswith, seventh-century abbess of Inkberrow, near Worcester, and the Würzburg manuscript of Jerome on Ecclesiastes', *ASE* 5, pp. 1–21.

SISAM, K. (1953a), *Studies in the History of Old English Literature*, Oxford.

SISAM, K. (1953b), 'Anglo-Saxon royal genealogies', *PBA* 39, pp. 287–48.

SMITH, A. H. (1956a), *English Place-Name Elements*, English Place-Name Society 26, Cambridge.

SMITH, A. H. (1956b), 'Place-names and the Anglo-Saxon settlement', *PBA* 42, pp. 67–88.

SMYTH, A. P. (1972), 'The earliest Irish annals: Their first contemporary entries and the earliest centres of recording', *Proc. Roy. Irish Ac.* 72, Section C, pp. 1–48.

SMYTH, A. P. (1975), *Scandinavian York and Dublin* I, Dublin.

SMYTH, A. P. (1977), *Scandinavian Kings in the British Isles, 850–880*, Oxford.

SMYTH, A. P. (1978), *Scandinavian York and Dublin* II, Dublin.

STANLEY, E. G. (ed.) (1966), *Continuations and Beginnings: Studies in Old English literature*, London.

STENTON, D. M. (1965a), *English Justice between the Norman Conquest and the Great Charter, 1066–1215*, London.

STENTON, F. M. (1910), *Types of Manorial Structure in the Northern Danelaw*, Oxford.

STENTON, F. M. (1913), *The Early History of the Abbey of Abingdon*, Reading.

STENTON, F. M. (1965b), *The Bayeux Tapestry*, 2nd edn, London.

STENTON, F. M. (1970), *Preparatory to 'Anglo-Saxon England', Being the Collected Papers of Frank Merry Stenton*, Oxford.

STENTON, F. M. (1971), *Anglo-Saxon England*, 3rd edn, Oxford.

STEVENS, C. E. (1937), 'Gildas and the civitates of Britain', *EHR* 52, pp. 193–201.

STEVENS, C. E. (1940), 'The British Sections of the "Notitia Dignitatum"', *Arch. J.* 97, pp. 125–54.

STEVENS, C. E. (1957), 'Marcus, Gratian, Constantine', *Athenaeum* (Pavia) 35, pp. 316–47.

STEWART-BROWN, R. (1936), *The Serjeants of the Peace in Medieval England and Wales*, Manchester.

SWANTON, M. (1964), 'An Anglian cemetery at Londesborough in East Yorkshire', *Yorks. Arch. J.* 41, pp. 262–86.

TAIT, J. (1936), *The Medieval English Borough*, Manchester.

TAYLOR, H. M. and TAYLOR, J. (1965), *Anglo-Saxon Architecture*, 2 vols, Cambridge.

THOMAS, A. C. (1968), 'The evidence from north Britain', in M. W. Barley and R. P. C. Hanson (eds), *Christianity in Britain, 300–700*, Leicester, 1968, pp. 93–122.

THOMAS, A. C. (1971), *The Early Christian Archaeology of North Britain*, Oxford.

THOMAS, A. C. (1972), 'The Irish settlements in post-Roman western Britain: A survey of the evidence', *J. Roy. Inst. Cornwall* VI (4), pp. 251–74.

THOMPSON, E. A. (1977), 'Britain, A.D. 406–410' *Britannia* 8, pp. 303–18.

TOMLIN, R. (1974), 'The date of the "Barbarian Conspiracy"', *Britannia* 5, pp. 303–9.

TOYNBEE, J. M. C. (1968), 'Pagan motifs and practices in Christian art and ritual in Roman Britain', in M. W. Barley and R. P. C. Hanson (eds), *Christianity in Britain, 300–700*, Leicester, 1968, pp. 177–92.

TURVILLE-PETRE, J. E. (1957), 'Hengest and Horsa', *Saga-Book of the Viking Society* 14, pp. 273–90.

VOITL, H. (1963), 'Die englische Personennamenkunde, 2, Die Entwicklung nach der Normannischen Eroberung', *Archiv für das Studien der neueren Sprachen und Literaturen*, 200, pp. 108–18.

VON FEILITZEN, O. (1937), *The Pre-Conquest Personal Names of Domesday Book*, Uppsala.

VON FEILITZEN, O. (1945), 'Some unrecorded Old and Middle English personal names', *Namn och Bygd* 33, pp. 69–98.

WADE-MARTINS, P. (1975), 'The origins of rural settlement in East Anglia', in P. J. Fowler (ed.), *Recent Work in Rural Archaeology*, Bradford on Avon, pp. 137–57.

WALKER, H. E. (1956), 'Bede and the Gewissae – The political evolution of the heptarchy and its nomenclature', *Camb. Hist. J.* 12, pp. 174–86.

WALLACE-HADRILL, J. M. (1971), *Early Germanic Kingship in England and on the Continent*, Oxford.

WALLACH, L. (1951), 'Charlemagne's *De litteris colendis* and Alcuin', *Speculum* 26, pp. 288–305.

WALMSLEY, J. F. R. (1968), 'The *Censarii* of Burton Abbey and the Domesday population', *N. Staffs. J. Field St.* 8, pp. 73–80.

WARD, G. (1936), 'The Wilmington Charter of A.D. 700', *Arch. Cant.* 48, pp. 11–28.

WATSON, W. J. (1926), *The History of the Celtic Place-names of Scotland*, Edinburgh.

WELCH, M. G. (1971), 'Late Romans and Saxons in Sussex', *Britannia* 2, pp. 232–7.

WEST, S. E. (1969), 'The Anglo-Saxon village of West Stow', *Med. Arch.* 13, pp. 1–20.

WEST, S. E. with PLOUVIEZ, J. (1976), 'The Roman site at Icklingham', *E. Anglian Arch., Rep. No. 3, Suffolk*, pp. 63–125.

WHITELOCK, D. (1951), *The Audience of Beowulf*, Oxford.

WHITELOCK, D. (1955), *English Historical Documents c. 500–1042*, London.

WHITELOCK, D. (1959), 'The dealings of the kings of England with Northumbria in the tenth and eleventh centuries', in P. Clemoes (ed.), *The Anglo-Saxons: Studies presented to Bruce Dickens*, London, 1959, pp. 70–88.

WHITELOCK, D. *et al.* (1961), *The Anglo-Saxon Chronicle: A revised translation*, London.

WHITELOCK, D. (1968), *The Genuine Asser*, Reading.

Wi – Laws of Wihtred, ed Liebermann: pp. 12–14; with trans. Attenborough (1922), pp. 24–31: *EHD* 31.

WIGHTMAN, W. E. (1966), *The Lacy Family in England and Normandy 1066–1194*, Oxford.

WILLIAM OF MALMESBURY, *Gesta Regum Anglorum*, ed W. Stubbs, 2 vols, Rolls Series, 1887–9.

WILLIAMS, I. (1972), *The Beginnings of Welsh Poetry*, ed Rachel Bromwich, Cardiff.

WILSON, D. M. (ed.) (1976), *The Archaeology of Anglo-Saxon England*, London.

WINTERBOTTOM, M. (1976), 'Notes on the text of Gildas', *J. Theol. St.* n.s. 27, pp. 132–40.

WINTERBOTTOM, M. (1977), 'Aldhelm's prose style and its origins', *ASE* 6, pp. 39–76.

WOOD, I. N. (1977), 'Kings, kingdoms and consent', in P. H. Sawyer and I. N. Wood (eds), *Early Medieval Kingship*, Leeds, 1977, pp. 6–29.

WOOLF, R. (1966), 'Saints' Lives', in E. G. Stanley (ed.), *Continuations and Beginnings: Studies in Old English Literature*, London, 1966, pp. 37–66.

WOOLF, R. (1976), 'The ideal of men dying with their lord in the *Germania* and in *The Battle of Maldon*', *ASE* 5, pp. 63–81.

WORMALD, C. P. (1976), 'Bede and Benedict Biscop', in G. Bonner (ed.), *Famulus Christi: Essays in commemoration of the thirteenth centenary of the birth of the Venerable Bede*, London, 1976, pp. 141–69.

WORMALD, C. P. (1977a), 'The uses of literacy in Anglo-Saxon England and its neighbours', *TRHS*, 5th ser., 27, pp. 95–114.

WORMALD, C. P. (1977b), '*Lex Scripta* and *Verbum Regis*: Legislation and Germanic kingship, from Euric to Cnut', in P. H. Sawyer and I. N. Wood (eds), *Early Medieval Kingship*, Leeds, 1977, pp. 105–38.

WORMALD, F. (1944), 'The survival of Anglo-Saxon illumination after the Norman Conquest', *PBA* 30, pp. 127–45.

YVER, J. (1955), 'Les châteaux forts en Normandie jusqu'au milieu de XIIᵉ siècle', *Bulletin de la Société des antiquaires de Normandie* 53, pp. 28–115, 604–9.

ZARNECKI, G. (1966), '1066 and architectural sculpture', *PBA* 52, pp. 87–104.

Index